MONGOLIAN NOMADIC SOCIETY

NORDIC INSTITUTE OF ASIAN STUDIES
Recent Monographs

67. ISLAM AND POLITICS IN AFGHANISTAN
    Asta Olesen
68. EXEMPLARY CENTRE, ADMINISTRATIVE PERIPHERY
    Hans Antlöv
69. FISHING VILLAGES IN TOKUGAWA JAPAN
    Arne Kalland
70. THE HONG MERCHANTS OF CANTON
    Weng Eang Cheong
71. ASIAN ENTREPRENEURIAL MINORITIES
    Christine Dobbin
72. ORGANISING WOMEN'S PROTEST
    Eldrid Mageli
73. THE ORAL TRADITION OF YANGZHOU STORYTELLING
    Vibeke Børdahl
74. ACCEPTING POPULATION CONTROL
    Cecilia Nathansen Milwertz
75. MANAGING MARITAL DISPUTES IN MALAYSIA
    Sharifah Zaleha Syed Hassan and Sven Cederroth
76. SUBUD AND THE JAVANESE MYSTICAL TRADITION
    Antoon Geels
77. FOLK TALES FROM KAMMU – VI: A STORY-TELLER'S LAST TALES
    Kristina Lindell, Jan-Öjvind Swahn and Damrong Tayanin
78. KINSHIP, HONOUR AND MONEY IN RURAL PAKISTAN
    Alain Lefebvre
79. THAILAND AND THE SOUTHEAST ASIAN NETWORKS OF THE VIETNAMESE REVOLUTION, 1885–1954
    Christopher E. Goscha
80. INDIAN ART WORLDS IN CONTENTION
    Helle Bundgaard
81. CONSTRUCTING THE COLONIAL ENCOUNTER
    Niels Brimnes
82. RELIGIOUS VIOLENCE IN CONTEMPORARY JAPAN
    Ian Reader
83. MONGOLIAN NOMADIC SOCIETY
    Bat-Ochir Bold
84. INDIGENOUS PEOPLES AND ETHNIC MINORITIES OF PAKISTAN
    Shaheen Sardar Ali and Javaid Rehman
85. LEE KUAN YEW: THE BELIEFS BEHIND THE MAN
    Michael D. Barr

MONGOLIAN NOMADIC SOCIETY

A Reconstruction of the 'Medieval' History of Mongolia

Bat-Ochir Bold

Routledge
Taylor & Francis Group

LONDON AND NEW YORK

Nordic Institute of Asian Studies
Monograph Series No. 83

First published 2001 by Curzon Press

Published 2013 by Routledge
2 Park Square, Milton Park, Abingdon, Oxon OX14 4RN
711 Third Avenue, New York, NY, 10017, USA

Routledge is an imprint of the Taylor & Francis Group, an informa business

First issued in paperback 2016

Copyright © 2001 Bat-Ochir Bold
All illustrations and maps are copyright of the author and may not be reproduced without his express permission.

All rights reserved. No part of this publication may be reproduced, stored in a retrieval system, or transmitted, in any form or by any means, electronic, mechanical, photocopying, recording, scanning or otherwise, without the prior permission in writing of the publisher, or as expressly permitted by law, or under the terms agreed with the appropriate reprographics rights organisation.

British Library Catalogue in Publication Data

Bold, Bat-Ochir
 Mongolian nomadic society : a reconstruction of the
 'medieval' history of Mongolia. - (NIAS monographs ; no. 83)
 1.Nomads - Mongolia - History 2.Mongolia - History
 I.Title
 951.7

ISBN 13: 9780700711581 (hbk)
ISBN13: 9781138976399 (pbk)

Typeset by the Nordic Institute for Asian Studies

To my parents
Prof. L. Bat-Ochir and Kh. Cendjav

Contents

Preface ix
Note on Transliteration x
Introduction *xv*
1 Starting-point for viewing the history of the Mongols   1
2 Economic conditions and their development   25
3 Socio-political organisation in the development of Mongolia   79
4 Social strata of Mongolian nomadic society   109
5 The effect of Lamaism on traditional Mongolian nomadic society   130
6 The dynamics of the development of Mongolian nomadic society   146
Concluding remarks   161
Notes   165
List of People, Places and Terms   174
References   179
Index   199

Maps

1 The Mongol empire in the 13th century *xi*
2 Mongolia about 1800 *xii*
3 The Mongols in Asia today *xiii*

Figures

1 Emergence of nomadic livestock keeping in East, South and Central Mongolia 31
2 Development phases of mobile livestock keeping in West Mongolia 32
3 Approximate migration patterns of Mongolian nomadic livestock keepers in the twelfth to nineteenth centuries 55
4 (a) Administrative structure of Khalkha Mongolia before the Manchurian period and (b) the Manchurian-Chinese administration system during the 19th century 106, 108
5 (a) Changes in temperature, (b) frequency of winter thunderstorms in intervals of 30 years (f_{30}), and (c) changes in frequency of dust falls in intervals of 30 years (f_{30}) 152
6 Correlation between number of years and (a) direct migration records in intervals of 30 years (f_{30}), (b) frequency of war (f_{30}) and (c) changes in administrative borders between Han and nomad powers along the longitude 110° E 153
7 Model of the social system of the nomads of Central Asia 156

Tables

1 An animal count in the Secen Khan *Aimag* from the year 1841 40
2 Quantitative relation between animal types 40
3 Total quantity of livestock in about 1220 41
4 Comparison of land usage in Mongolian nomadic economy with land usage in the European pre-industrial economy 49
5 Transformation of the most important administrative terms in the course of Mongolian history 98

Preface

This work is the result of many years of research which I began while studying the philosophy of history at the University of Ulaanbaatar. I was able to continue this research as a DAAD grant awardee at the Humboldt University in Berlin from 1990, and complete it within the framework of post-doctoral studies via the HEP (*Hochschulerneuerungsprogramm* – University Renewal Programme) at the Free University in Berlin. Throughout these years I learnt a good deal in my professional life. In particular, the fall of the Berlin Wall in the transition period 1989–90, the consequent collapse of socialism, and the radical change in its ideologised way of thinking opened up new perspectives for me personally. When, as an eyewitness from the faraway country of the nomads, I experienced how people knocked the Berlin Wall down with all their strength and resources, I was convinced that the same could be done in the future to Mongolian historiography, which has been petrified and cemented by decades of communist ideology.

I would like to take this opportunity to express my thanks to my German friends and colleagues for their immeasurable help and encouragement in my research work in general, and for their guidance and cooperation. I would also like to thank my colleagues at NIAS for their encouragement in the continuation of my research in Scandinavia, especially Leena Höskuldsson and Gerald Jackson for their friendly and professional help in this work's publication. I thank also my friend John Duggan for his help with preparation of this work in English. And finally, my heartfelt thanks go to my wife – for without her unique support and tolerance this work would never have been completed.

Bat-Ochir Bold
Reykjavik 2000

A Note on Transliteration

There is no satisfactory solution to the problem of transliteration when one is dealing with words from many languages and scripts. In this work I attempt to transliterate Mongolian, Tibetan, Manchurian, Chinese and Arabic words, names and titles according to the popular transliteration system of the respective languages. I have preferred to transcribe most Mongolian terms in accordance with modern Mongolian. But for some well-known Mongolian names (e.g. Genghis Khaan) I have used the spelling conventionally followed by European Orientalists today. Chinese names and terms are transcribed using the pinyin transliteration system. Terms appearing in citations and in book titles, however, are preserved as they appear in the original work. For this reason some terms may appear in various transliteration forms.

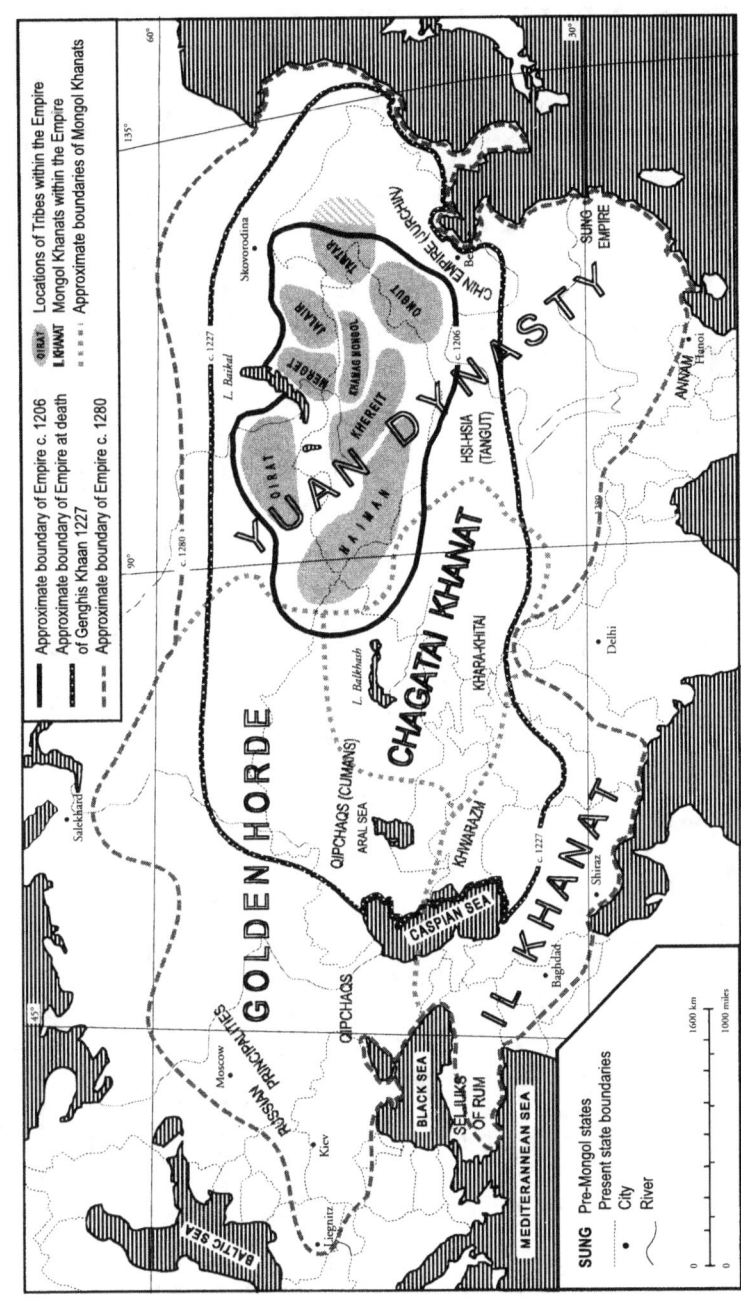

Map 1: The Mongol Empire in the 13th century

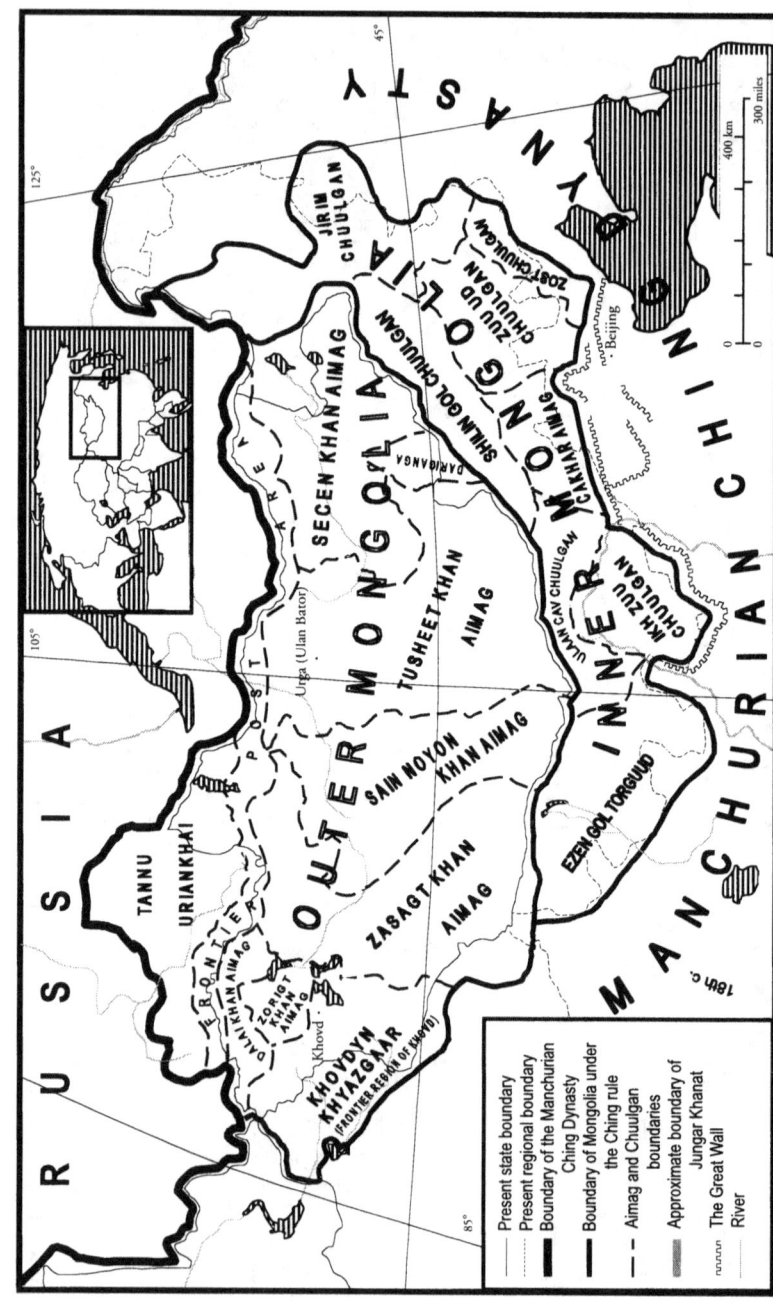

Map 2: Mongolia about 1800

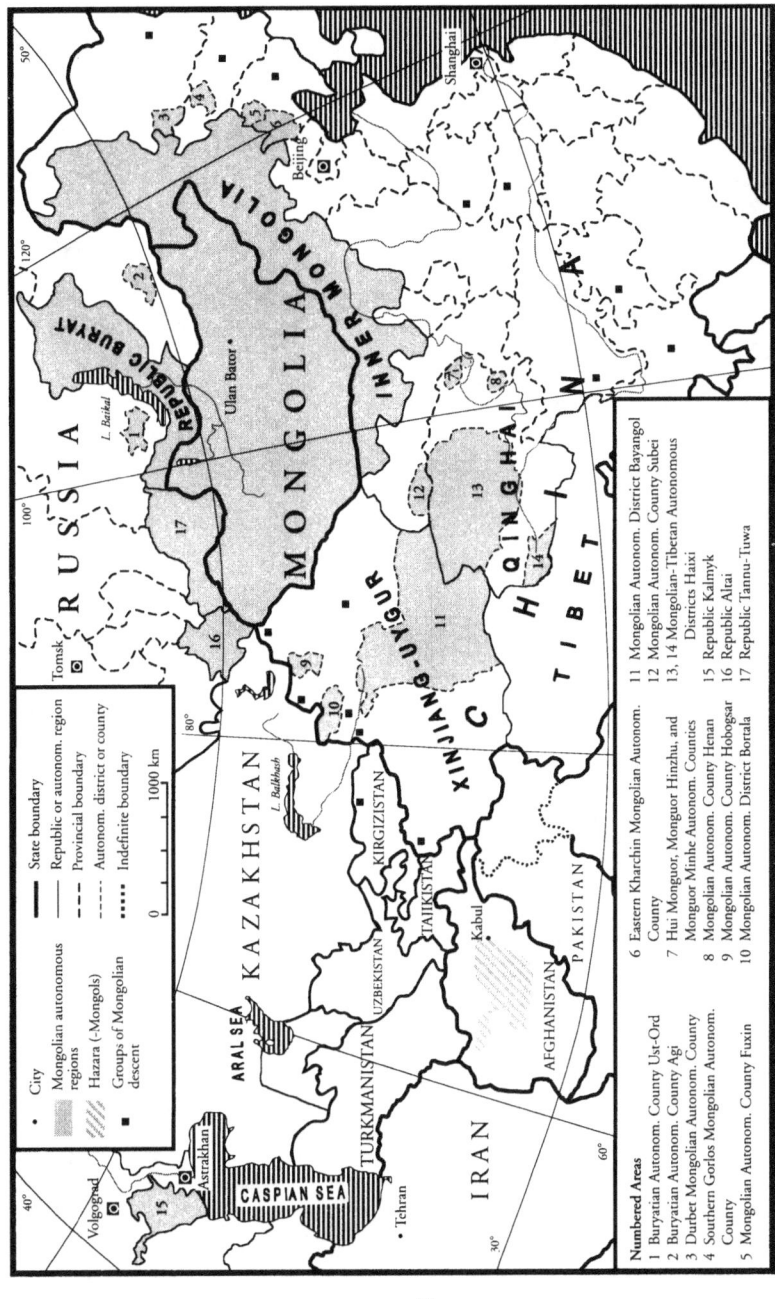

Map 3: The Mongols in Asia today

INTRODUCTION

Until the collapse of the socialist system in Mongolia in 1990 and the consequent decline of the Soviet Union's influence upon all areas of Mongolian society, Mongolian social sciences had been fundamentally schematised in accordance with the prevailing political ideology of socialism. This situation was especially characteristic of the theoretical treatment of Mongolian historiography after the 1930s. Mongolian historians as well as Russian specialists in Mongolian studies, and historians who conducted historical research on Mongolia, have mostly considered this history as an ideological object, i.e. in the theoretical framework of historical materialism, the 'theory of socio-economic formation'. It is therefore now necessary to analyse critically Mongolian historiography and to free Mongolian history from this ideological scheme. In doing this, however, one should not let one's approach be influenced by the present euphoria of radical change or by short-lived political ideas. Rather, it is necessary to apply cognitive norms of analysis to the real historical facts.

Except for very few treatises, there have been hitherto no investigations into this problem. The present work is an attempt to evaluate the course of Mongolian history over a relatively broad period with regard to the structural and developmental characteristics of Mongolian nomadic society. To achieve this, it is necessary to analyse the subject matter from both a theoretical and an empirical perspective. In order to systematise the course of Mongolian history and the available sources and secondary material, we have considered it appropriate to restrict our attention to the period from the twelfth century to the nineteenth century. The following significant facts have guided us in this decision: (a) it was only at the end of the twelfth century that an independent and stable Mongolian social system developed, and (b) with the Manchurian conquest and the growth of Buddhism, the spontaneous development of Mongolia ceased some time about the eighteenth century to evolve according to the predominantly internal dynamics of traditional nomadic society; the long chain of traditional, spontaneously developing nomadic societies thereby ended.

This book contains six chapters, each of which treats an aspect of the nomadic society. In the first chapter, the source material for the history of Mongolia for the period we shall be considering will be described first of all. At the same time, we shall study the various approaches taken by the sources and secondary literature, which have been shaped by various traditional and cultural ways of thinking and theoretical viewpoints. We thought it especially important, however, in connection with the position of specialists in Mongolian studies subsequent to the October Revolution, to give an overview of the development of discussions concerning world history within the framework of the 'theory of socio-economic formation', as well as of the use of the term 'feudalism', or of the feudalism concept, and its modification to the case of nomadic culture. Here, a critical analysis will be conducted on the concept of nomadic feudalism of B. Ya. Vladimircov who, as he wrote in the foreword to his work (1934: vii), submitted his treatise with a view to discussion and criticism.

In the second, third and fourth chapters the structural elements and the essentials of nomadic society, its economic conditions, tribal and politico-administrative organisation and social strata will be analysed. Via a detailed depiction of all areas of Mongolian nomadic society, we shall attempt to show that Manchurian–Chinese policy was the most influential factor in the transformation of the society. Using the conclusions that we draw, we shall then critically view modern Mongolian historiography in terms of the concept of nomadic

Introduction

feudalism. The economic relation to pasture land, the organisation of the Mongolian state as well as social 'class relations', which have all become criteria of 'nomadic feudalism' in Mongolian historiography, will be subjected to examination. In doing so, we shall also draw a comparison between conditions in pre-industrial Europe and in nomadic Mongolia.

The majority of Mongolian and Soviet historians, as well as several historians from other countries, who investigate broad periods of Mongolian history, represent this history in terms of time structures, classifying all areas of society into a rigid periodic framework. As a result, difficulties arise in considering the continuity of the course of history. In this work, we shall avoid such a division into periods.

In the fifth chapter we shall examine the spread of Buddhism as one of the most important factors in the gradual transformation of the entire Mongolian nomadic society. In the sixth chapter we shall attempt to depict the essence, function and evolution of traditional Mongolian nomadic society.

The book is concluded with attempt to depict the internal structure and the particularity of evolution of traditional Mongolian nomadic society.

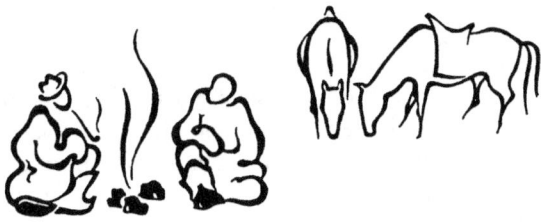

1. STARTING POINT FOR VIEWING THE HISTORY OF THE MONGOLS

WAYS OF APPROACHING MONGOLIAN HISTORY BY MEANS OF SOURCE MATERIAL AND RESEARCH

The history of Mongolia from the twelfth to the eighteenth centuries represents a period which has long been of interest to specialists of Mongolian studies and which has been extensively researched. This does not mean, however, that historians have been able to reach a common opinion concerning this period. There are still a great many of unexplained questions that arise not so much from the scanty empirical material available as from the differing criteria of evaluation. An analysis of these differing means of evaluation is a prerequisite for an exact understanding of the character of the course of Mongolian history. In describing a feature of history, the historian is of course guided by his own objectives. The various viewpoints for the description of the period of the twelfth to the eighteenth centuries in Mongolia are further influenced by two factors. The first is spatial: when a people leaves deep tracks in the history of another people, the former's development must be taken into account in the historiography of the latter. The second factor is temporal: with the emergence of a new politico-historical phase of a people, the way of viewing historical phenomena often changes. On account of these factors the dynamics of this period of Mongolian history is complicated and multi-layered, and it is precisely this which will be the subject of our research.

One of the main causes of the plurality of opinions concerning this period, and in general of the interest in Mongolian history, is the fact that at the start of the thirteenth century there arose a unified, independent Mongolian Empire which had a great influence not only on the further course of Mongolian history but also on the history of other peoples.

The Mongolian Empire of the thirteenth and fourteenth centuries was vast – it extended from what is today Korea to Hungary, encompassed the entire Asian continent up to India, Southeast Asia and Eastern Europe. It existed in this size for more than a hundred years and in some regions for even longer as partial or successor empire. The main difference between the Mongols and earlier conquerors is that no other previous nomad empire has controlled the Asian inner steppe and vast regions of settled peoples.

From the viewpoint of the historian, this had a significant consequence: the history of the Mongolian Empire was considerably better documented than its predecessors. The reason for this is that the settled peoples wrote about the Mongols as part of their own history. Research into the Mongolian Empire has therefore a special character. A complex problem arises from the number of sources – in Mongolian, Chinese, Persian, Arabic, Russian, French, Latin, Turkish, Japanese, Armenian, Georgian, Tibetan and other languages. No single person is able to read more than a fraction of the available sources in the original. In addition to this there is also the cultural problem. The medieval systems in China, in the Islamic countries, in Europe and amongst the nomadic peoples differ from one another considerably. Historical accounts have therefore differing traditional starting points, backgrounds and objectives and are marked by differing mentalities.

As regards the influence of the temporal factor on the judgement of historians, we believe that it is necessary to concentrate on nuances of change in an evaluation of the development of Mongolian society; these nuances arose from changes in global development and their effect on intellectual life. Focusing our attention on just a few aspects, it appears that the eighteenth century was one of the periods when the approach to Mongolian history adopted in European literature began to change (Krader 1966: 21–22; Gol'man 1988: 5), while in the thirteenth–fourteenth centuries, a cliché notion of Mongols as plunderers, barbarians and monsters prevailed. This was connected in general with the start of modern scientific thought and on the whole with the growing interest in the Orient, and in particular in Mongolia, subsequent to centuries of lack of contact. This process was rooted in the development of capitalist politico-economic principles in Europe. At the start of the twentieth century, social consciousness was moulded by the emergence of two fundamentally different systems of society. There thus developed two mutually exclusive theoretical and methodological approaches in the social sciences. Due to these approaches, differing evaluations of Mongolian history arose. Thus research into the history of Mongolia, in particular the theoretical interpretation of the development of Mongolia, has been more or less an arena of ideological argument. For this reason, theoretical consideration of Mongolian history has contained more ideological discussion than scholarly research until the present time.

Chinese sources

Since ancient times, Chinese historians have concerned themselves with the nomadic peoples of Central Asia. Ancient Chinese chronicles contain a wealth of information relating to the nomads in the north of China. There are two reasons why these chronicles deal so extensively with the nomads.

First, the nomadic peoples in the Mongolian part of Central Asia were at times under the rule of Chinese emperors and at times ruled themselves or even the whole of China – for example the Northern Wei (Xianbei: A.D. 386–534), Liao (the Khitans: 916–1125), Jin (Jurchens: 1115–1234), Yuan (the Mongols: 1271–1368) and Qing (the Manchus: 1644–1911) dynasties. Some of these 'official' historical chronicles, such as 'History of the Song', 'History of the Liao' and 'History of the J'in', were thus compiled under Chinese sovereignty and even by Mongolian historians, and some, such as 'History of the Yuan', were compiled under Mongolian sovereignty.

Second, since nomadic movements southwards and eastwards were regarded as threatening by the Chinese, there were usually historians and scholars at the royal court of each Chinese dynasty who were charged with recording events deemed important or suspicious. Such records are called *Shihlu* and/or *Qijuzhu* (veritable records). The official historical chronicles have a common structure which was first established by Sima Qian (145–86 B.C.) and Ban Gu (A.D. 32–93). The histories of the main nomadic tribes living in or around China and their chieftains were usually documented in the volumes *liezhuan* (biographies) or *waiguo* (foreign countries). This Chinese administrative practice of compiling such governmental reports continued until the Chinese Manchu Qing Empire. V. S. Taskin believed with justification that:

> [Chinese] historical works have been vividly compared to shining mirrors which bring the truth of past history before one's eyes. Their task was to give correct answers based on experience to constantly emerging problems of importance to the state...
>
> It is not surprising that Chinese historians, for practical reasons, mainly turned their attention to military-political and diplomatic re-lations with China's neighbours, and thus various aspects of the actual lives of these peoples were for them peripheral and of minor importance (Taskin 1984: 11).

Very little synthesis arose out of the 'veritable records'. Chinese bureaucracy, just the prevailing taxation system, was immovable and normally little influenced by the changing of dynasties. Each new dynasty marked its entrance and the definitive exit of the old dynasty by appropriating the official history of the predecessor. Much the same applies to Chinese history of recent times.[1]

Chinese sources of the period with which we are dealing here, can be classified into three groups:
- official dynastic history
- legal sources
- writings in the form of records (Trauzettel 1986: 11–13)

Official dynastic history

The most important contemporary source in Chinese concerning the early history of the Mongols is the 'History of the Yuan Dynasty' (*Yuan-shi*)[2]. This is an official dynastic history compiled in 1369–70, immediately after the expulsion of the Mongols from China, by a commission of historians after the pattern of the Song history. It was written in Peking by at first 16 and then, in 1370, by a further 14 Chinese historians under the direction of Song Lian (1310–81) and Wang Wei (1322–73), who were scholars of the royal court (Dalai 1992: 19). Sources in both Mongolian and Chinese were used. The main source for this chronicle was the historical book written in the period of the Yuan dynasty concerning the 13 Mongolian kings, *Shih-lu* (True history), which General Sui Da of the newly founded Min state had obtained as booty during the expulsion of the Mongols. In addition, in the year 1370, 20 historians under the direction of Wan Wie were sent north into Mongolia in order to obtain further material for the second version of the chronicle (*Mingshi*, ch. 282: in Dalai 1992: 174).

In spite of this, Mongolian sources were somewhat neglected in the drafting of the *Yuanshi*. Since Chinese aversion to the Mongols was still very strong in the period of the writing of this work, Mongolian history as well as Mongolian sources were accordingly treated with disdain (Cin' Yui-fu 1957: 113). For example, Mongolian scholars and officials who were well known at the time and who had carried out documentation in the course of the Yuan dynasty, such as Kharkhasun, Bayan, Cagaan, Togoon, Ariun, Shaazgay, Alintamir, Dashkhayan, Tugtumur, etc., are not mentioned in the *Yuanshi*. This neglect is also to a certain extent apparent with regard to valuable Chinese sources concerning the history of the Mongols. For example, the Chinese eyewitness accounts of Peng Daya, Chao Hong, Chang Chun and Chan De-hui, which were at the time already known, are scarcely considered in the *Yuanshi*.

Legal documentation

The first Chinese legal sources for the history of the Mongols in the thirteenth–fourteenth centuries originate from the Yuan period. The Yuan dynasty was actually founded and governed by the Mongols. There had been a long tradition of Mongolian khaans[3] creating state laws after the manner of the Mongolian statute book of Genghis Khaan, the Great Yasa (*Ikh Yasag*), which had been used since the start of the thirteenth century. In the case of the Yuan dynasty, however, this was unrealisable for various reasons. Because the dynasty comprised many and to a large extent settled Chinese peoples, it was necessary for the Mongolian kings to form their laws after the patterns of traditional Chinese legal ordinances in order to govern successfully. In addition, Khublai Khaan was very much influenced by Chinese culture. After the death of his father Tului, Genghis Khaan's son, he took over, at the age of 21, Tului's possessions of ten thousand subject families in Xinzhou as well as his mother's possessions in what is today Zhending in Hebei province, where he remained from this time. On the advice of his trusted Chinese minister, Yao Shu, Khublai had the first legislation revised in accordance with Chinese tradition. The most important laws dating from the Yuan period are the 'New Ordinances from the Zhi Yuan Government' *(Zhi Yuan Xinge)*, the 'State Codex of the Sacred Government of the Great Yuan Empire' (*Da Yuan shengzheng guochao dianzhang*', often abbreviated to '*Yuan dianzhang*') and the 'Regulations in Systematic Order from the State Book of the Great Yuan Empire' (*Da Yuan tongzih Tiaoge*).

Legislation of the Manchu-Chinese Qing Empire provides legal sources concerning Mongolia dating from a later period. Even the first Manchu-Chinese rulers decreed laws for the Mongolian region conquered in 1632, which were originally intended for Inner Mongolia but later, in the middle of the seventeenth century, were extended to Outer Mongolia as well. In 1696 Emperor Kangxi (1662–1722) unified all single laws decreed by his predecessors into a codex. They were further revised into the *Menggu lüli* (Statute for Mongolia) in the year 1789 and into the *Lifanyuan zeli* (Statute Book, established by all highest Command, of the Ministry of the Government of the Outer Provinces) in the years 1815, 1826, 1832.

Writing in the form of records
The third group of sources consists of all other published works that were not government commissions, e.g. travel reports such as 'Survey Report on the Black Tartars' (*Hei Da shilüe*) by Peng Daya and 'Complete Description of the Mongol-Tartars' (*Meng Da beilu*) by Chao Hong[4]. Together with the *Secret History of the Mongols* [hereafter abbreviated SHM] (*c.* 1227–64), the *Xiyouji* ... 'Notes of a Journey (of the Taoist monk Changchun) to the West' (1228) and the *Shengwu qinzheng lu...* 'Reports on the Personal Campaigns of the Emperor Shengwu (Genghis Khaan)' published in the period 1260–85, these two works are considered the most significant and extensive early sources concerning the history of Mongolia until the end of the government of Ogadai (1229–41) (Haenisch 1980: vii). The authors practised the traditional Chinese style of report. In this connection W. Banck writes,

> To what extent were the authors committed to a standardised, formal, almost stereotyped Chinese tradition of reporting about foreign peoples? To a tradition which was possibly first established by Sima Qian's ... *Shiji* ... and consequently became more or less obligatory, and which was retained in the early dynastic histories as well as in Ma Duanlin's ... *Wenxian tong-kao* ... and the great encyclopaedias of the Min period until recent times? To a generally accepted and only rarely broken tradition which frequently aided the perpetuation of typically Chinese cliché ideas rather than enabling an objective portrayal free of a genre-bound form and of ethnocentrally conditioned prejudice? (In Haenisch 1980: xx–xxi).

STARTING POINT FOR VIEWING THE HISTORY OF THE MONGOLS

Persian sources
In West Asia, large territories of what are today Iran, Iraq, Afghanistan and the Caucasus were under the direct control of the Mongols in the thirteenth and fourteenth centuries. For this reason there is an abundance of sources amongst the Near Eastern peoples concerning Mongolian history, not only relating to the period of the Il Khanate in West Asia but also to earlier periods. These sources are Persian, Syrian, Armenian, Georgian and Arabic, of which the Persian are the most extensive and detailed.

Persia did not develop an institutionalised official way of writing history as can be seen in official Chinese sources. There did, however, develop a particular 'official history' in the period of Mongolian rule. Most of these chronicles were, even if they are not in all cases of an official nature, to a certain extent commissioned by Mongolian rulers and thus their authors were obliged to take into account the viewpoint of the ruling class and to portray its achievements. Perhaps the character of the Persian histories was partly the result of shock, since the Muslims of western Asia had hitherto not experienced anything comparable to the Mongol conquests.

The most important Persian historical works in the thirteenth and fourteenth centuries are:

- the 'Classes under Nasir' (*Tabaqat-i Nasir*), written in 1260 by Abu Umar Minhag ad-Din Utman Ibn Sirag ad-Din al-Guzgani (often abbreviated to Guzgani);
- the 'History of the World Conquerors' (*Ta'rih-i gahán-gusái*) written in 1252–60 by Alá ad-Din atá Matik al-Guvaini (often abbreviated to Guvaini);
- the 'Collection of Histories' (*Gámi at-tawárih*) written in 1301–11 by Rashid ad-Din Fadl Alláh; and
- the 'Distribution of the Countries and the Course of the Ages' (*Tagziyatu 'I-amsár wa tagziyatu 'I-a sár*) written in 1300–28 by Abd Alláh Ibn Fadl Alláh as-Sirázi (often abbreviated to Wassaf).

These four historians were all high-ranking government officials. The most significant of them was Rashid ad-Din, who for 20 years was the *wazir* of the Mongolian Il Khanate in Persia during the governments of Gahzan, Ulzeitu and Abu Said *bagatur*.

Guzgani was a Ghaznavid historian. He records, amongst other things, the report of the legate Baha ad-Din Razi whom the Khalif an-Nasir li-Din Allah (1180–1225) sent to Genghis Khaan in the year

1215 on the occasion of the Mongolian conquest of Peking, and describes the meeting of the two men as well as the destruction subsequently wrought by the Mongols. He wrote his work as an old man in the safe sanctuary of the Delhi sultanate and it is of particular importance since he was not obliged to temper his language regarding the Mongols. He had himself witnessed the horrors of Genghis's invasions 40 years earlier.

Guvaini spent most of his life in the service of the Mongols, his last 25 years as Mongol governor of Baghdad. He wrote his historical work mostly between 1252–60 in the then capital of the Mongolian Empire, Kara-Korum, but was still working on it from 1260 in Baghdad after his appointment as governor. Although he did not experience the first invasions of the Mongols, he began describing events during the early Mongolian period, for which he had a wealth of information from Mongolia at his disposal. He himself had travelled twice to Mongolia and had gathered a good deal of historical material there. Thus we learn from him not only about the Mongol invasions of the Islamic lands but also about the previous dynasties in the territories which formed the Mongolian Empire, such as Khar Khitai in Central Asia, the Uigurs further east, the Khwarazm-shahs in Persia and the Assassins subsequent to their emergence in Persia at the end of the eleventh century.

Rashid ad-Din (1247–1318), just like the other authors, wrote his work by imperial commission. For example, Ghazan commissioned him to compile a history of the Mongols in Persia. It is possible that Ghazan wanted such a history as a sort of 'manual' in order to record his own wisdom. In this regard it was inevitable that Mongolian rule in Persia was given a very detailed treatment which has as its high points Rashid ad-Din's enormously complex execution of the work and the difficult demands of Ghazan's programme of administrative reform (Morgan 1990: 167). Rashid ad-Din declared in his introduction that the Mongolian Empire marked a new era in the history of the world, one that demanded a written record. In 1318 he was executed as an opponent of the reformist policy of the government. It is obvious from reading these works that Mongolian sources were used in their compilation. While writing his work in Tabris[5] from 1301 to 1311, Rashid ad-Din had at his disposal now lost valuable sources written in Mongolian, such as *Altan debter* (Golden Book), which he used to portray the earliest period of the Mongols. Moreover, several Mongolian historians, such as the well-known scholar Bold-*chinsan*, helped with the compilation of his work. Bold-*chinsan* was one of the intimates of the Mongolian imperial court.

Mongolian sources and research

Autochthonous Mongolian sources date from the period after 1204 when Genghis Khaan commissioned the captive Uigur Tatatunga, custodian of the imperial seal of the Naiman, to adapt the Uiguric script to the Mongolian language (Weiers 1969: 1). Very few historical sources date from the first half of the thirteenth century. The only relatively detailed source from this period is the 'Secret History of the Mongols'. In one respect, however, there is no doubt: as a means of gaining an impression of the daily life, mentality and beliefs of the Mongols in the thirteenth century, the SHM is unique. All conclusions drawn from non-Mongolian sources are thus to be considered of secondary importance. The SHM is the only principal source, which in our opinion gives a realistic appraisal of the Mongols. E. Haenisch, who has studied this work intensively, characterises it thus: 'The wind of the steppe blows through the pages of this book. The events are recorded and the scenes described for us in a special way' (Haenisch 1948: ix). In essence, this is more of an epic than an annalistic work, with long passages of genealogical details. In Mongolian literature it is regarded as a literary work rather than a historical testament (Heissig 1959: 12). It should be noted, however, that the mentality of that time encompassed many forms of consciousness and that the author should not be expected to have written the work in accordance with modern literary conceptions. This means that there is no reason to appraise the information contained in it as historically or scientifically frivolous. According to the opinion of researchers, the work was originally written in Uiguro-Mongolian script in East Mongolia. It has, however, come down to us only in a version written in syllabic Chinese dating from the second half of the fourteenth century (Gaadamba 1990: 218–19). Because the SHM ends with the sentence 'The writing down of this work was completed while the palace was encamped between the places Dolo'on Boldag[6] and Shilgincig[7] at Köde'ü Aral[8] at the Kerulen River in the seventh month of the year of the rat (1240 or 1228: Rachewiltz 1971; Gaadamba 1990: 415–16) during the assembly of the Great Imperial Parliament', the exact time and place of composition of this work is known.

For the period from the fourteenth to the seventeenth centuries, family chronicles predominate as sources, the main concern of which was to provide a genealogical record in accordance with Mongolian tradition. With the start of missionary work of Tibetan Buddhists amongst the Mongols, Mongol rulers were portrayed by Lamaist monks as descending from Indian and Tibetan kings, a fact that was used to promote Buddhist belief (Mostaert 1953: 122). In this connection Heissig writes:

> With the second dissemination of Lamaism amongst the Mongols in the late sixteenth century, the technical prerequisite, arising from a further spread of literacy, was lain not only for the creation of an extensive Buddhist literature consisting of translations and commentaries, but also for an increase in the compilation of histories. (Heissig 1959: 15)

In the eighteenth century, a type of genealogically oriented chronicle, normally arising from the wish of a particular prince or member of the nobility and concentrating on his ancestors, took shape and Mongolian religious historical writing also developed. The authors were from the noble class or Lamaist scholars of noble descent. The cited sources became more and more numerous. The first steps towards a critical selection of the events under consideration and their sources were taken, and out of this, a critical writing of history gradually developed. Thus, for example, Ishibaljir (Bold 1990) and Rasipunzug (Sagaster 1970: 295) were the first Mongolian historians to take historical criticism into account in their work.

In addition to Tibetan history, the great Chinese historical works came to be known and considered through the medium of Manchurian translations (Heissig 1959: 112). Moreover, the incorporation of the Mongolian peoples into the Chinese Empire of the Manchu Qing dynasty was completed in the eighteenth century, a process which had already commenced for some Mongolian peoples in 1636 and 1691. The fact that Mongolian regions belonged to the Qing Empire gave rise to a separate type of traditional source which can be described as Sino-Mongolian, i.e. sources that were based on both Chinese and Mongolian material that dealt with events relating to Mongolian history, and that were written in Peking under the aegis of the Lifanyuan[9] and the Imperial Office of History. The most important of such sources is the reference book dating from the year 1795 written in Mongolian, Manchurian and Chinese, consisting of 120 volumes in each language and entitled 'Reports compiled under imperial command concerning the princes and dukes of the outerlying Mongolian and Turkestani regions',[10] which was followed in the nineteenth century by at least two (1814 and 1839) supplementary versions (Pelliot 1960: 65, note 69).

Mongolian writing of family history of the nineteenth century can be characterised as chronological and genealogical general history. The most important such works of this period are by Jimbadorji, Galdan *taij* and Injannashi (1837–92).

After the People's Revolution of 1921, the first attempts at a historiography to encompass all epochs of Mongolian history were undertaken in the former Khalkha Mongolia. Older generation of historians such as Ch. Demchigdorj (1863–1932), A. Magsarjab (or Magsarkhurc), A. Amar (1887–1939), L. Dendeb (1895–1957), J. Zeveen (d. 1937), B. Buyanchuulgan (d. 1938), C. Batochir (1873–1935) and G. Navannamjil (1882–1924), wrote and published many interesting works. They remained bound, however, to the traditional way of writing history: they referred to Manchurian, Chinese, Tibetan and Mongolian sources and described in chronological order the succession of state organisation in Mongolia and the policies and the biographies of individual rulers.

Research into history was then suspended in the Mongolian People's Republic until a new generation of historians began to view the history of Mongolia from the Marxist conception of the theory of socio-economic formation. The results of theoretical and methodological discussions, which were carried out in the Soviet Union from the middle of the 1920s until the 1940s by proponents of the Marxist conception on the one hand and advocates of other interpretations of Marxist ideas on the other, influenced the writing of history during and after this period. This methodological position is to be found in the consideration of the 'middle epoch'[11] of Mongolia and as a consequence of it the conception of so-called 'nomadic feudalism' developed, which is even today generally accepted.

The first extensive work, in which the results of Mongolian historiography in accordance with the formation theory were brought together, was 'History of the Mongolian People's Republic' (*Istoriya Mongol'skoi Narodnoi Respubliki*, 1954) which was written jointly by Mongolian and Soviet scholars at the beginning of the 1950s. The methodological orientation for further research was here 'established'.

A number of investigations by Mongolian historians, such as Sh. Nacagdorj, Sh. Bira, D. Gongor, N. Ishjamc, B. Shirendev and Ch. Dalai, were directed towards explaining the history of the Mongolian 'middle epoch' in accordance with this orientation.[12] We shall deal with these works in more detail in the course of the next chapters.

European sources and research

In the thirteenth and fourteenth centuries large territories of the Middle East and Eastern Europe, such as the Caucasus and considerable parts of Russia, were under the direct control of the Mongols. The independent Western European powers established contact with the Mongol conquerors. Basically, information which reached the Western countries from the Orient in either written or oral form and was interpreted there formed the pool of knowledge for those who did not travel, yet desired to find out more. Even prior to the Mongolian advance into the West, the first explanations for the Mongolian emergence appeared at the beginning of the 1220s – launched evidently by oriental Christians, Crusaders and Eastern Europeans. In a faraway place, so the story goes, a Christian King David (Genghis Khaan) set out in order to rush to the aid of the Franks at Damietta and to attack the Muslims from the rear (Schmieder 1994: 248). It was both fascinating and informative for Europeans to hear reports concerning the Mongolian Empire from travellers and merchants who came from all levels of society and had much to relate. Usually, European historians wrote little about what was happening in distant Asia and only when they felt obliged to report about certain events, such as the Mongolian invasion of Russia and Eastern Europe in 1237–42. By means of such sources as the *Novgorod Chronicle*, we are able to imagine with what terrified misunderstanding and lack of warning the Europeans had to bear the brunt of the Mongolian attack.

By far the best report is by the chronicler Matthew Paris, a historian from St Albans. It appears that he had access to very good information about the Mongols, as is evidenced for example by his explanation of the fall in the price of herring in Yarmouth being due to the Baltic fleet remaining in port from fear of the Mongols!

The most acute observers amongst the travellers were two Franciscan monks, Giovanni of Plano Carpini (1182–1252) and William van Rubruck (1220–93). The main mission of Carpini was to reconnoitre the country, as his report *Historia Mongalorum* makes clear. He recounts us his travels and his observations concerning Mongolian history and customs. As the first observer not only to see the Mongols for himself, but also to live for some time amongst them, Carpini gained much prestige after his return to Europe. However, he expected critical scepticism from his readers, for which reason he covered himself at the conclusion of his report in 1247:

STARTING POINT FOR VIEWING THE HISTORY OF THE MONGOLS

We ask all who read the preceding report to take nothing away and to add nothing, for we have written down everything as we have seen it or as we have heard it from others whom we considered credible, without knowingly adding anything (Wyngaert 1929: 129–30).

Rubruck's book is a travel description which contains much more information than that of Carpini and is written by a much keener observer. The main part of the book consists of a report about a fictional religious debate between Nestorians, Muslims and Buddhists in the period of Münkhe Khaan.[13] Rubruck, who participates in the discussion, leaves no doubt that he advocates Christianity and not Nestorianism which he opposes. Even when it seems that he makes no reference to the heresy which originally differentiated Nestorianism from orthodox Christianity, he has very little regard for the Nestorian priests and monks whom he meets. In the description of a region of Central Asia he adds:

> The Nestorians there have no education. They say that their central and sacred books are in Syria and written in a language which they do not know ... and this confirms the fact that they are fully corrupt (Wyngaert 1929, quoted in: Dawson 1955: 144).

Twenty years later, when Marco Polo travelled to China, the Mongolian Empire was divided into various smaller empires. The information about China constitutes the most valuable part of his book. Some of his reports about the Mongols are not very reliable because he only recounted what he had heard. Nonetheless, there still prevailed mistrust of reports of genuine eyewitnesses such as Marco Polo; in fact, unreliable travel reports from the Far East, where monsters were expected to inhabit, were more readily believed. Marco Polo confirmed himself as a genuine eyewitness when, on his deathbed and forced to retract his exaggerations, he said: 'I didn't write down even a half of what I saw' (Benedetto 1928: cxciv).

In the West, the Mongols did not even have a common border with the countries which they had ruled until the middle of the fourteenth century. Events in Mongolia disappeared completely from the field of vision of the Near and Middle East as well as of Europe. For this reason there are no more Near Eastern or European sources concerning the history of the Mongols in Central Asia from about the 1470s.

Mongolian studies had no independent significance in Western Europe for a long time afterward and were in principle a branch of sinology. The Frenchmen F. Gerbillon, C. Visdelou, A. Gaubil and M.

Maille played leading roles in the first renewed investigations into the history of Mongolia. They went to China as missionaries in the last quarter of the seventeenth century. As a consequence of the intensified colonialisation policy of France under Louis XIV (1643–1717), the historian J. Guignes became a qualified sinologist. His work laid the foundation for scholarly research into the history of Mongolia in the West in the first half of the eighteenth century. All the above authors are generally characterised by their Sinocentrism, their uncritical approach to their sources, their depiction of historical process as a result of political events, and their disregard of socio-economic and ethnic processes. Most of them, with their Sinocentric viewpoint, divided the peoples of Central Asia into the settled 'cultured' on the one hand and, on the other, the nomadic 'cultureless' barbaric, for whom the possibility of historical development was denied.

After these scholars, research continued and received new momentum from the development in relations between East and West and between China and Europe, and of course from the rapid growth in historical sciences and Oriental studies at the beginning of the nineteenth century.[14] This was above all manifested in the historical investigations of C. M. de Ohsson, J. P. Abel-Remusat, etc. In the second half of the nineteenth century, apologetic tendencies are to be seen in research on the 'middle epoch' of the Mongols. Such tendencies are especially evident in the works of scholars such as F. Erdmann, G. Strakosch-Grassman, R. K. Douglas, L. Cahun, and J. Abott.

From the end of the nineteenth century and at the start of the twentieth century, research was undertaken in two further directions which were more specialised than previous works. On the one hand, Mongolian history was treated and elucidated by travel books, diaries, and reports of Catholic missionaries, researchers, journalists, diplomats and other Europeans and Americans who travelled through Mongolian territory. Amongst the travel reports, the works of E. R. Huc, J. Gabet, J. Gilmour, J. Hedley, J. Roberts, J. Curtin, and W. W. Rockhill are outstanding. The journey of the Finnish scholar G. J. Ramstedt to Buryat and Mongolia, expeditions of the Prussian scholars A. Grunwedel, G. Hut, and A. von Lekok and the journey of the Belgian geographer R. Verbrugge also furnished valuable information.

On the other hand, research came to be more the study of source material and more specialised, e.g. concerning the history of Lamaism and of Mongolian diplomacy.

In general, apologetic tendencies in the treatment of the conquests and the personality of Genghis Khaan and his successors can be seen in connection with growing Eurocentrism and 'Asian despotism' and their consequent conceptions. This was related to the scarcity of factual material and the lack of direct contact with the Mongols. Therefore research was of a coincidental nature and its themes were determined by the relatively insignificant material which was available to scholars (Heissig 1968: 53).

It should not be forgotten that owing to its geographical proximity, its close contact with Mongolia and its having Mongolian-speaking minorities (*viz*. Buryats and Kalmyks), Russia became the homeland of Mongolian studies as an independent branch of research in the nineteenth century. The works of scholars such as J. I. Schmidt, O. M. Kovolevskii, N. Ya. Bichurin, V. P. Vasilev, A. M. Pozdneev and I. N. Berezin relate mainly, however, to the compilation of a chronology of historical events via a reappraisal of available sources, documents and other material concerning the history of Mongolia. This means that these works are essentially an initial reworking of the collections of empirical data intended for further future research.

In conclusion, we should remark that in cases where scholars met with historical and ethnological events unfamiliar to Europeans, they explained them by means of comparison with approximately similar events in European history, such as the French Middle Ages, in order to obtain a general understanding.

CRITICAL ANALYSIS OF THE METHODOLOGY OF MODERN MONGOLIAN HISTORIOGRAPHY

The feudalism concept in relation to the history of Mongolia

In the past decades there has been a prolonged and controversial discussion concerning the question of which social systems have emerged throughout history and how they were formed and have replaced one another.

We restrict ourselves in this regard to how the debate was conducted in the former Soviet Union, since we wish here to investigate the problem of the feudalism concept only in relation to its influence on Mongolian historiography. On the one hand, this debate had a political and ideological orientation; on the other, it was of great scholarly significance.

The first high point of the discussion in the Soviet Union was during the 1920s and early 1930s and was connected with the controversy over the history of the formation of Russia and China. It concerned the phases and principal characteristics of feudalism, slavery and the Asian means of production, as well as questions relating to the conditions for the growth of socialism in a relatively backward country and to the different possibilities and groupings of the movement in China.[15]

M. Weber's concept which dates from the 1920s and concerns the specific social ordering in the East, and in particular in China (Weber 1964: 795–809), had a great influence on historians. This way of regarding the problem became especially significant after the publication of an article by J. Pepper, an American historian, in the newspaper *Pravda* (Pepper 1927).

In this period the main goal of these discussions was to push through the formation theory in opposition to other concepts. This was attempted under the direct influence of the political and ideological need to confirm that socialism's following upon capitalism represents a general line of development of human history in accordance with a law. V. N. Nikiforov, a proponent of this concept, writes:

> Subsequent to the Great Socialist October Revolution, the need for a precisely formulated breaking up of world history into periods from a Marxist viewpoint evoked a broad wave of sociological discussion in the years 1925–35. The international approach to world history made a compact schematised approach to history in the East and the West unconditionally necessary (Nikiforov 1975: 171).

The debate was broken off in the second half of the 1930s. Under the influence of the Stalin cult figure, a dogmatic limitation of the concept of successive formation to a five-step scheme was adopted: primitive society–slavery–feudalism–capitalism–socialism/communism.

At the end of the fifties, a new phase of the discussion began amongst Marxists of the Soviet Union and other countries and was continued into the 1960s. Not only were the themes of the first controversy taken up again, but also general theoretical and methodological questions of historical science were raised. The five-step scheme played, however, a significant role.

In general, this debate, which was still quite widely carried on in the 1970s and into the 1980s without any concrete conclusion, substantially enriched the theoretical means, and at the same time called into question the methodology of the way of regarding history. During the discussion, in addition to concrete historical questions relating to division into periods, theoretical historical problems of the interpretation of Marxist literature came into the foreground. In both points the debate focused above all on Marx's sentence:

> In a broad outline, Asiatic, ancient, feudal and modern bourgeois means of production can be described as progressive epochs of economic formations of society (Marx 1961: vol. 13: 9).

The main point of debate here was whether these epochs should be regarded as a basis for the successive stages of the formations of history or whether a fundamental modification of this concept should ensue based on later works of Marx and recent results from research. As a consequence, two different methodological positions arose.

One line of the discussion gained significance. According to this, previous concepts concerning some of the formation stages between primitive society and capitalism, namely slavery and feudalism, were called into question.[16] This means in particular that it is wrong to interpret the successive stages mechanistically and to regard the history of separate peoples and regions as uniform and, via the theoretical stencil of a 'progressive epoch', even as identical. In the majority of cases, one finds a plethora of differing subjection and exploitation conditions since the final phases of tribal organisation of society. They contain elements of slavery as well as of bondage, serfdom, vassalage and paid labour. In many countries, early class society and patriarchal forms of rule were widely distributed until capitalist colonialisation. How the separate peoples and regions developed, what contribution they made to world development, and to what extent they were influenced by known epochs of progression, all these things have to be concretely identified. This cannot be measured by a theoretical yardstick, and it is not possible to interpret schematically and universally or to regionalise this sequence of formation. Trends in the development of individual countries and parts of continents are different and, to a degree, contrary to one another. Also the progressive centres change during this process even within Western and Middle Europe. What therefore applies generally for theories of historical processes and for the standardisations derived from them, i.e. that they idealise real relations and do not delve into reality itself in all its concrete ramifications, applies also to the theory of successive formation. This, in neither its classical nor its derivative forms, is capable of holding true for regions. The ancient means of production in Greece and Rome was based – at least in its developed form – entirely on slavery. But slavery was not universally a necessary condition for development in all catchment areas of this social system. 'The system of slavery was distributed only along the Mediterranean coast and in cities on important traffic routes and rivers' (Kreißig 1981: 398).

A similar reasoning applies to feudalism. The assumption of a universally existing feudal society implies that the notion of feudalism extends over such totally differing social factors that it becomes meaningless. On the one hand, the notion of feudalism becomes empty, and on the other, one is forced, when confronted by concrete questions, to incorporate into it determinants of other social epochs. This happens, for example, when the characteristics that differentiate the 'feudal societies' of India, China, Mongolia, the Arabic countries and sub-Saharan Africa are analysed. Factors such as state ownership of land, absence of land ownership, low development of private property, continued existence of slavery, marked influence of patriarchal clan and tribal organisations, absence of a strong urban bourgeoisie, etc. are then cited.[17] It is not possible for all this to be grouped under feudalism, together with European medieval society which was structured quite differently and spawned totally different movements. These social systems differ substantially from what marked European feudalism, defined its historically progressive role and made it a stage of progression.

Another line of the discussion followed further the sequential development of formation epochs, more or less rejecting its rigidity and raising questions concerning its temporal and regional differences. Just as in the 1920s and 1930s, the notion and object of the 'Asian means of production' were still discussed. This was now interpreted as an initial class society formation either in the specific forms of slavery or feudalism or in combined forms of primitive society, slavery and feudalism (Bold 1992b: 9), and attitudes to it were at the same time modified (Semenov 1966; Nikiforov 1975). This line accorded with socialism's political and ideological demand for 'confirmation' of the historical inevitability of successive formation, i.e. of the universality of the five formation stages, primitive society, slavery, feudalism, capitalism and communism, which lead to communism 'in accordance with law'. For this reason it was generally accepted as the methodological approach in social sciences research. This applies also to the Russian and Mongolian schools of the history of Central Asian nomadic societies and the history of Mongolia.

Since these five successive formation stages are uncharacteristic of the history of Central Asian nomadism, proponents of this theory conceived models to account for such anomalies. In order to avoid the fact that some formations, such as slavery and capitalism, are not demonstrable in the history of nomads, the curious theoretical term 'by-passing' was coined: the peoples *should have* experienced these phases but in fact by-passed them owing to certain socio-economic conditions. In Mongolian historiography the opinion was proposed that Mongolia, too, had by-passed the slavery phase. This idea might appear logical at first glance, but in essence it is merely playing around with words. In the real history of nomadic peoples there was no such 'by-passing' of this phase. Socio-economic conditions of nomadic society did not allow for slavery, in the true sense of the word. It was and is an attempt to resolve the contradiction between the real course of history of the nomadic peoples, and of Mongolia, and the universal theoretical concept of socio-economic formation.

Another modification of this standpoint is the theory of the 'non-capitalist way of development'. Generations of scholars in all fields of the social sciences endeavoured, up to the collapse of the socialist-communist regime, to define the recent history of Mongolia since the People's Revolution of 1921 and of the Soviet Central Asian countries since the October Revolution in terms of this theoretical modification. There is hardly a research work in the social sciences concerning the recent history of Mongolia that is free from the motto of the 'non-capitalist way of development'.

On the basis of the problems treated in this work, it is reasonable to limit the above-mentioned concept to feudalism. In order to clarify the question of whether the historical reality of Mongolia can be elucidated by the feudalism concept, we should describe this universally disseminated theory in more detail. According to this, the feudal social system is in effect a part of the history of all peoples. Feudal systems had in individual regions differing characteristics as well as general ones. The differences observed in the course of the feudalism process depend of course on natural geographical conditions, but they also arise to a great degree from socio-economic and political conditions existing at the start of the process. Feudal societies, according to the concept, could develop either on the basis of a pronounced slavery society (like the Mediterranean region) or a highly developed, early class society with extreme state exploitation of independently working peasant communities and slave labour, or a disintegrating primitive structure with free peasants. These differing starting conditions resulted in several variations in the development and form of the feudal structure. In general, one distinguishes between feudalism

- in Europe;[18]
- amongst the Scandinavian and many Slavic peoples including the Kiev Russians;
- in the central regions of the Byzantine Empire, in the more highly developed regions of the Caliphate and also amongst tribes of the Arabian Peninsula;
- in China and India;
- in Japan, where the process developed in a similar way to that in Europe (Töpfer 1985: 138–43).

These variants of feudalisation appear in the theoretical generalisation of this line of discussion as follows: the term feudalism (Coulbourn 1956; Müller-Mertens 1966: 52–73) describes first of all a specific *political* relationship, namely a vassal relationship. Then it describes a specific *economic* relationship. European feudalism is feudal in both dimensions, as is at times Islamic and Japanese feudalism. Late feudalism in India and in Byzantium is merely economic and stands in contrast to the existing political structures. Feudalism at the end of the Chou period in China is political but cannot break away from village community bonds. All this, which represents the second standpoint of feudalism – the universal historical clarification – shows us that the feudalism concept is in the end grounded in the fact that agriculture (cultivation of grain and horticulture) was the economic basis for the variability of feudalisation.

> In describing the essence of feudalism in the sense of Marxist historical science, it is assumed that in feudal society, as in all pre-capitalist class societies, land was the most important means of production and agriculture therefore played a dominating role. Thus, agri-cultural working of the land and ownership conditions of land had a defining influence on the class structure of feudalism. (Töpfer 1985: 16)

If one assumes that agriculture is the economic basis of feudalism, there is then no reason to carry over this assumption to nomadism, in which pastoral livestock keeping is dominant and which therefore represents a totally different form of land use.

The concept of 'nomadic feudalism'

A modification of the standpoint of the too generalised feudalism model is 'nomadic feudalism'. The period of Mongolian history which has hitherto been evaluated in an overly one-sided manner, is of interest to us. We are here talking about the period from the thirteenth to the nineteenth centuries, which in modern Mongolian historiography is termed 'Mongolian feudalism' or 'Mongolian nomadic feudalism'. M. I. Gol'man writes in his book *Western Historiography Concerning Mongolia from the Thirteenth Century to the Middle of the Twentieth Century* that on account of the October Revolution, the influence of the ideology of anti-communism and anti-Sovietism on bourgeois scholars intensified and this led to a negative appraisal of Mongolian history (Gol'man 1988: 127). If we, like M. I. Gol'man, restrict the consequences that the October Revolution had on Mongolian historiography to the above-mentioned point, the result would be too simplistic. This historical event ushered in a discussion about the line of development of mankind, the main goal of which, as we have mentioned, was to push through a universal model of the theory of economic formation of society in favour of socialism as opposed to other possible concepts. At the same time this requires world history to be regarded from the standpoint of an oversimplified and idealised model. The consequence was that the history of Mongolia, too, was pressed into the scheme of the successive formations of society as they are in principle characteristic of the European peoples. This methodological position was adopted in the treatment of the 'middle epoch' of Mongolia and, as a result, the theory of so-called 'nomadic feudalism' developed, which is even today accepted as the means of approach. This led to the majority of Mongolian and Soviet historians to attempt to seek out historical facts that would fit into the theoretical model. The facts that did not correspond to the character of the 'classical model' were explained away as 'specific peculiarities' or were underestimated and little investigated.

B. Ya. Vladimircov was the first in Mongolian historiography to designate the period from the twelfth to the twentieth centuries as 'nomadic feudalism'. 'There is no independent synthesis of the Mongolian social system. How is this system to be characterised ...? To which social formation did it belong?' (Vladimircov 1934: 2) With these questions he did not consider the problem in view of the alternative of whether the Mongolian social system can be elucidated by the Marxist theory of social formations or, outside this theory, according to the particularities of its structure. He did, though, see a possible alternative in the framework of the formation theory – in a combined form of primitive society, slavery and feudalism or in feudalism alone. He decided upon feudalism. O. Lattimore wrote in the mid-1930s about Vladimircov's new concept concerning nomadic feudalism:

> It is important to consider the fact that evolution did not develop in a straight line, as for example from patriarchal tribal organisation of society to feudal form, and from feudalism to imperialistic concentration ... Russian authors of recent times who make a considerable contribution to economic research, lose in my opinion the potential value of their research by underestimating the importance of repeating cycles and by attempting to force their opinions into a straight-lined pattern of evolution. (Lattimore 1962: 252)

In this connection the remark of G. N. Rumyancev is also worth mentioning:

> The main error of Vladimircov's concept of 'Mongolian nomadic feudalism' is that the level of development of Mongolian society and of feudalism in Mongolia in the twelfth and thirteenth centuries was exaggerated and was pressed into the 'classical character' of West European feudalism of the thirteenth and fourteenth centuries. (Rumyancev 1958: 81)

The discussion of the 1930s was intensified in the 1950s. An article in the Soviet journal *Voprosy Istorii* bearing the title 'Concerning the Essence of Patriarchal-Feudal Conditions of the Nomadic Peoples' led to new considerations of hitherto collected factual material. Here, it was not so much a matter of the term, which the editor rejected in a final analysis, as of the demonstration of feudal production conditions amongst Asian (i.e. Mongolian and Kazakh) nomads (Potapov 1955; Tolybekov 1955; Zlatkin 1955).

The discussions of the 1970s evinced in part their own character: some Soviet scholars, such as S. N. Wainstein, Yu. I. Semenov and G. E. Markov, introduced the notion of a non-feudal form, or more precisely of a 'proto-class' form in the development of nomadic society (Markov 1976; Wainstein and Semenov 1977). Other scholars even subjected the Vladimircov concept of nomadic feudalism to severe criticism. For example S. E. Tolybekov wrote: '[It is] essentially a repetition of Dühring's reactionary theory of "power".' (Tolybekov 1971: 224)

From the end of the 1950s Mongolian historians participated in the debate (for example Nacagdorj 1958). In the following years, as already mentioned, Mongolian historians occupied themselves with the basic economic and social structure of the Mongols and, like their Soviet colleagues, reached the conclusion that these 'displayed' feudal traits. If we examine the research carried out into the period of 'Mongolian feudalism', we see in essence three factors which became scholarly criteria:

- the emergence of a concentration of ownership of pastoral land and the formation of a system of feudal exploitation;
- the founding of the state in Mongolia;
- the formation of feudal and feudally dependent classes.

We shall undertake a critical examination of these criteria in the relevant sections of this work.

It is clear that the core of the discussion about 'nomadic feudalism' lies in the problem of the existence or non-existence of feudal ownership of land in nomadic societies (Fedorov-Davydov 1976: 40). Thus the discussion is essentially conducted on the theoretical level in terms of what constitutes the main means of production of a nomadic economy.

The scholar who first doubted Vladimircov's theory was S. E. Tolybekov. Referring to the real conditions of Kazakh nomadism, he was of the opinion that feudal ownership of pasture land is uncharacteristic of nomadic peoples and that therefore the main means of production in nomadic livestock economy is the herd (Tolybekov 1971: 220). A similar view was offered by V. F. Shakhmatov (1964: 27). This opinion was criticised by many scholars. In the 1950s, I. Ya. Zlatkin and L. P. Potapov showed that the herd was not monopolised property of nomadic feudal lords and thus ownership of land and not of herds was the means of exploitation. Only via ownership of land could a feudal lord retain livestock keepers at his disposal (Zlatkin 1955: 73). A feudal lord would not have been able to force common livestock keepers, who possessed the herds, to work for him if he were not the owner of land (Potapov 1955: 79; Zlatkin 1955: 78). This opinion was further supported by historians such as S. A. Pletneva, N. Ishjamc, D. Gorgor, G. A. Fedorov-Davydov and E. Werner.

Another group of scholars including Sh. Nacagdorj, A. Minis, G. Sükhbataar, and N. Ser-odjav were of the opinion that both the herd and the pasture land were the main means of production in Mongolia and were the property of feudal lords (Minis 1968: 36; Serodjav 1976: 146; Nacagdorj 1978: 186; Sükhbaatar 1980: 61).

Some scholars, S. I. Wainstein and Yu. I. Semenov among others, were of another opinion: that special production conditions characteristic only of nomadism formed the basis of nomadic society (Wainstein and Semenov 1977: 164). G. E. Markov concluded that in the history of nomadic society no monopolised ownership conditions, whether of herd or of land, developed (Markov 1976: 289–90). This opinion has often been criticised because it is theoretically vague and because it does not determine to which socio-economic formation system nomadism belongs.

The impression arises that the societal structure of Mongolia for the period we are considering cannot be explained via the feudalism model. The concept of feudalism was formulated on the basis of an assumed universality of the special economic, political and social system that was created by the resolution of the contradictions in early social conditions of Byzantine and some European peoples. For this reason feudalism is at total variance to evolved ancient and Asian models. If such a 'feudalism' did not arise in the Mongolian history of the middle epoch, then it should not be believed that there was no social progress amongst the nomads. It is beyond doubt that social progress took place there, but it assumed a particular form.

'Mongolian feudalism' is an inference which 'attests' the universal feudal model by selecting and compiling proofs and confirmations from events of Mongolian history. On account of such an evaluation, phenomena and factors that are in fact irrelevant to the description of the system and dynamics of development of traditional Mongolian nomadic society have been deemed vitally important due to the demand for 'confirmation' of the feudal model. We shall deal with these questions in detail in the next chapter.

The present period of Mongolian history since 1990 has been characterised as a period of radical change. In spite of no less negative consequences, this process is bringing positive trends into several areas of social life. For the first time it has become possible to express new opinions concerning problems of history and tentative attempts have been made to re-examine ways of approaching Mongolian historiography and of critically depicting the country's history. These have hitherto been limited mainly to individual questions about the recent history of Mongolia in the twentieth century.

2. Economic Conditions and Their Development

Origin of Nomadic Livestock Keeping in the Mongolian Part of Central Asia

Ecological and socio-cultural prerequisites for nomadic livestock keeping

In the Central Asian continental regions the climate is hot to moderately warm in summer and always extremely cold in winter. A relatively homogeneous distribution of feed supply exists in predominantly short grass steppe. A low density of forage plants and a short period of vegetation are characteristic. Nomadic livestock keeping is optimally adapted to these limiting natural conditions. Not only does it represent a complete adaptation to the particular ecology of the regions, but is also the only possible economic form of using nature. Therefore nomadic livestock keeping is not only extremely dependent upon land and thereby sensitive to even the smallest ecological changes; it is also a consequence of specific natural ecological conditions. In this respect two questions arise: (a) To what extent has livestock keeping been influenced by ecological changes? and (b) How was its origin determined ecologically? Both questions have been little researched.

E. Huntington was, at the beginning of the twentieth century, the first scholar to propose the hypothesis that climatic changes were the determining factor for the waves of Central Asian nomads moving westward (Huntington 1907, 1914, 1935). There are several research results which show that climatic changes in Central Asia having an adverse effect upon livestock keeping were one of the main causes of the warlike activities of the nomads (Lenk 1974; Fang 1990; Fang and Liu 1992).

Hardly any research has been conducted into the climatic ecological prerequisites for the development of livestock keeping which forms the basis of the origins and evolution of nomadism in the Mongolian part of Central Asia. It is reasonable also to ask upon which socio-cultural and economic basis nomadic livestock keeping was formed. There is a plausible view according to which development in Central Asia conforms to the economic-historical three-stage theory: from hunting and gathering to nomadic livestock keeping to agriculture. This may appear logical at a first glance, but does not accord with the facts.

Under the influence of the Tibetan ice thaw, which in the regions of high latitudes started from 40000 B.C. and had its greatest effect with the total ice meltage in the years 12000–9000 B.C., significant changes in the climate occurred after about 12000 B.C. This marked climatic boundary can be recognised from the floor levels of lakes (Kuhle 1991: 304). The cold, dry climate was transformed into a warm, dry climate, and the process of the shallowing out and reduction of the water reservoirs began (Vipper 1975: 106). Species of forest plants were almost totally wiped out and in their stead steppe grasses spread thickly upwards into the mountains. This set the pattern for the development of steppe to the detriment of the forests. This period lasted about 1,500 years and corresponds to the late European Allerød and the Upper Dryas, to the Taimyr warm period in Siberia and to the Norian Stage of temperature decrease (Vipper et al. 1985: 59).

During the following Holocene period, which in Mongolia is dated from the 10000–8000 B.C. era, the climate was a little cooler and somewhat wet (Vipper et al. 1985: 59; Hövermann and Süssenberger 1986: 184). This period marks the end of the relatively short but intensive process of aridisation.

In the period 7000–5000 B.C. the climate became mild and moist, and yearly and daily temperatures were lower than hitherto. As a consequence, the areas of water reservoirs increased and the quality of soil improved. Forests began to spread rapidly in mountainous zones where steppe terrain had been predominant (Vipper et al. 1985: 60). The favourable climate and the presence of local varieties of wild plants that might have been the forerunners of later cultivated plants such as *paniculate* and *capitate* millet, provided the preconditions for the independent development of agriculture in some regions. In the steppe zone of South and East Mongolia a heterogeneity of plants which resulted from the moist temperatures was characteristic. As a consequence, especially good ecological conditions for agriculture developed, which is shown by recent archaeological research in these areas. It has been demonstrated that the findings from the lower level of the ancient settlement of Shavraga-us in South Mongolia relate to the Mesolithic, while those from the upper level relate to the Neolithic period.

This significant difference in levels was characterised by differing forms of survival. In the Neolithic level there are stone implements for agricultural use – for example in the Shavraga-us settlement fragments of scraping stones have been found (Novgorodova 1989: 59–63). In several places of the Gobi, development of agriculture is also demonstrable. Evidence of this takes the form of fragments of pottery from Shavraga-us as well as from Tögrögiin-Shireet of the Ömnögobi *Aimag* district and the south of the Dornogobi *Aimag* district. Decorative drawings on the pottery exhibit a certain similarity to the decorations frequently found up to the first millennium B.C. on vases from the regions of Northern China, Manchuria and Xingqian, where the existence of agriculture has been ascertained. The other Neolithic site in East Mongolia is the settlement discovered in 1949 by A. P. Oklanidov in Tamsagbulag *Sum* county (7 km east of the *sum* centre) of the Dornod *Aimag*. Archaeologists estimate that it dates from the second Neolithic period in Eastern Mongolia, i.e. from the third millennium B.C. (Okladnikov and Derevyanko 1970).

One of the most important problems in studying the tribes of the Tamsagbulag culture is that of agriculture. Striking evidence of the emergence and full development of agriculture in this region is provided by the numerous specimens of pestles, grinders and graters for grinding grain, hoes for loosening soil, millstones (with biconical centre holes with a diameter of between 10–15 cm) and weights for digging sticks. All available information indicates that agriculture in Eastern Mongolia emerged independently and had its origins in the active practice of food gathering. The implements are clear evidence of the fact that the inhabitants of Tamsagbulag engaged in primitive hoe agriculture. Despite its relatively unsophisticated character, agriculture in the Middle and Late Neolithic periods was, it seems, a more effective source of food than livestock breeding, hunting and fishing (Derevyanko and Dorj 1992: 175).

The borderline between the Atlantic and Sub-boreal periods is dated at 4,000 years ago and is characterised by further heightening of the continental climate. In this period a change in atmospheric circulation and an intensification of the cyclone process have been ascertained. The permafrost line in Siberia shifted in the direction of the Equator, and the deciduous wood forest line reached closer to the sea coasts in Siberia than it does today. The woodland steppe line in Siberia shifted up to 500 km in the direction of the Equator 4,000 years ago. While the courses of the Arctic forest and the permafrost lines are dependent on temperature, and with temperature changes of 1–1.5°C experienced fluctuations of up to 1,000 km, the woodland steppe and the deciduous forest lines vary according to moistness and the continental climate (Klaus 1980: 19). The change in climate formed the basis of a slight increase in forest area and of the heterogeneous character of the steppe vegetation. Thus the raw climate which brought about these consequences prevailed between the years 4000 and 3300 B.C. (Vipper et al. 1985: 62). As a result of the climatic change in this period, a climate of large temperature differences between high and low reliefs and a corresponding vegetational differentiation arose. As a rule, all forms of nomadic pastoral economy developed in regions where, by virtue of mountains, ranges and valleys, the vegetation rhythm of forage plants shows large differences over small areas throughout the year: in such places, the seasonal forage balance can be exploited with relatively short, seasonal migrations. The region of Central Asia thus became climatically and ecologically unsuitable for agriculture as a main form of economy and instead of it a hitherto little developed livestock economy slowly began to dominate.

Attempt at classification

The facts described above stand in contradiction to the generally accepted idea of how the peoples of Central Asia came to livestock keeping. Plausible notions of the origins of nomadism have been derived from various cultural and economic-historical three-stage theories (Vajda 1968: 50ff.; Otremba 1969: 196ff.). According to a view which has pre-Socratic roots and was supported by Adam Smith (1723–90) amongst others, as well as Friedrich List (1789–1846) in his explanation of the development of the productive force in agriculture, the nomad represents genetically a preliminary stage of the agriculturist. This opinion prevailed in the nineteenth century and was until recent times championed by such writers as O. Spengler, F. Flor and W. Koppers and W. P. Schmidt and by the renowned members of the Vienna School who believed they had discovered the origin of nomadism in the Altai. Since the studies of E. Hahn and R. Pumpelly, however, who regard a peasantry engaged in agriculture and livestock keeping as a prerequisite for the emergence of nomadism (Hahn 1891: 487; Pumpelly 1904: xxviii), this notion has been refuted. A concrete proof of this refutation is given by A. Toynbee who, with reference to an archaeological study concerning the Transcaspian Oasis, reaches the conclusion that it was not the hunter but the farmer who developed the art of domestication of wild animals.

> For the art of domesticating wild animals, which the hunter, by the very nature of his occupation, is unable to develop beyond narrow limits, has vastly greater potentialities in the hands of the agriculturists. The hunter may conceivably domesticate the wolf or jackal with whom he disputes or shares his prey by turning the wild beast into a partner in the hunter's own human predatory activities... The agriculturist enjoys a double advantage for this purpose. Unlike the hunter, he is not preying on the wild animals and therefore is not inspiring them with a deadly fear of his presence, and unlike the hunter again, he possesses food supplies which are attractive to ruminants like the ox and the sheep, which would not, like dogs, be attracted by meat or other products of a hunting or fishing life. (Toynbee 1934: 10)

Such notions of origin on the part of other scholars go even further. For example, Werth was of the opinion that the alpine pastoral economy, which emerged from plough farming, and the consequent livestock economy and transhumance – inspired by hunting and its roaming way of life – are the predecessors of livestock keeping nomadism (Werth 1956: 15). According to H. Bobek, however, nomadism represents a branch of clan peasantry.

> This development is explained on the one hand by the existence of extensive pastoral regions which are only usable seasonally and which are not suitable for settlement, and on the other hand by the doubling of economic interest of grain farmers in possession of livestock. (Bobek 1959: 272)

Relevant to this is the fact that such farmers, by emphasising livestock keeping in preference to grain cultivation and vice versa, can easily and rapidly change their way of life. Bobek advocates the process of emergence of nomadism in two phases (Bobek 1959: 273ff.):

> 1. The characteristics of this phase of economic development are the keeping of small animals, close family attachment and rapid, for

example climatically determined, change between agriculture and animal keeping, and the resultant ever-repeating division of livestock keeping and agricultural labour within the same family and the same tribe. This phase lasted until the second millennium B.C..

2. The characteristics of this second phase are, first, the domestication of the horse in the Eurasian steppes (in Turan in 2800 B.C.), which, according to Bobek, led entire peoples to nomadism, and of the camel in the Near East (end of the second millennium B.C.), the greater mobility which arose from this, and the formation of cavalries and of cavalry empires. Second, the emergence of 'prosperous' centres of high culture based on irrigation. These formed the background of the conflicts between settled peoples and nomads which subsequently deter-mined the history of the region.

In this connection it is conceivable that, in the early phase of economic development in the Mongolian part of Central Asia there existed a complex combination of economic forms of agriculture, livestock keeping, hunting and even fishing and thus a climatically determined alternation between agriculture and livestock keeping as main economic activities until 4000–3500 B.C. According to A. P. Okladnidov, hunting in the Tamsagbulag culture even had a specialised character. Together with agriculture, the most important feature of the Tamsagbulag economy was livestock breeding. There can be no doubt that livestock breeding was a fully developed activity (Okladnikov and Derevyanko 1970). That fishing constituted a subsidiary element of the economy is evidenced by finds of fish bones.

The institutionalisation of nomadic livestock keeping was certainly a long-term process during which pastoral migration developed from something occasional and spontaneous into something regular and orderly. Scholars believe that the mobility of livestock keeping that developed is characterised by types of livestock. Livestock keeping which was closely associated with agriculture in the still undivided economy favoured, as bone findings show, mainly draught animals that worked the soil (in particular oxen), while nomadic livestock keeping, i.e. separated from agriculture, favoured mounts and pack animals (in particular horses). From results of osteological, genetic and physio-morphological analyses of bone findings of domesticated animals in Mongolia and the region of Lake Baikal, it can be concluded that the types of animals and the ratios of numbers kept were at that time basically as they are today.

The following points are worth noting as regards the use of horses as mounts and as pack animals. It is closely associated with the demands of longer and more frequent migrations, which means that, on account of the degradation of vegetation reserves by gradual temperature changes, a greater pastoral area than hitherto was required. This accelerated the process of using horses amongst the nomads of Central Asia.

Livestock keeping as a supplementary or complementary economic activity arose earlier amongst the peoples of Central Asia than the institutionalisation of nomadic livestock keeping. Bones of small and large animals similar to today's domesticated animals have been found in numerous archaeological digs. But it is difficult to ascertain whether these are the remains of domesticated animals or not. Additional proofs are the petroglyphs which are quite widely distributed in the mountain regions of Mongolia. The oldest pictures of sheep/goat species and camels are in the Khoit-cenkher cave in the river valley of the Khoit-cenkhriyn Gol in the territory of the Mankhan *Sum* of the Khovd *Aimag* and date from the Upper Palaeolithic period, 40000–12000 B.C. (Novgorodova 1989: 49).

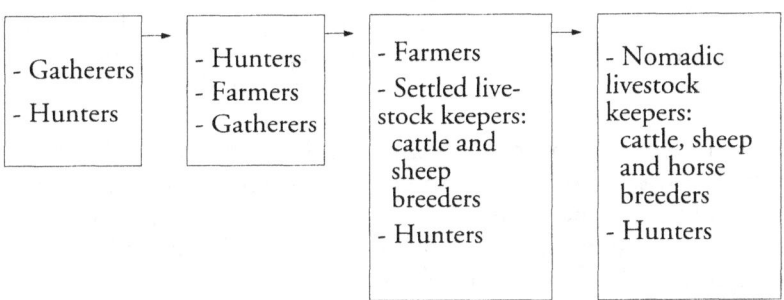

Figure 1: Emergence of nomadic livestock keeping in East, South and Central Mongolia

Other petroglyphs in the region of Gobi Altai which are relevant for the emergence of livestock keeping, are in Aj-Bogd (Bold 1998a). In these petroglyphs camels, goats, wild sheep and horses are depicted. There are also several interesting representations of camels with their young and of camel keepers with camels and their young. This familiarity with camels could only have been gained by their productivity, i.e. by camel keeping, and not by hunting, which was then the only other possible use of the animal. This is indicated by the fact that Mongolian nomads traditionally regard camels not as a source of meat but as a source of milk and hair and as a beast of burden. The (at least three) representations of a camel with young in particular symbolise livestock keeping and dairy production. Moreover, this region is very suitable ecologically for camels and the acclimatisation of camels there a long time ago is demonstrable. In addition, the representations depicting a camel keeper behind a camel with its young can be estimated as dating from a period before the representations of figures with bows, horse riders and carts and clearly demonstrate that domestication of camels occurred in the Pre-Neolithic period. Thus domestication of the Mongolian domestic camel must have occurred on native ground and can, by virtue of zoological, palaeontological and anthropological evidence, be dated to the period 3000–2000 B.C. If one considers the discovery of camel bones dating from the Pleistocene, which was made during a Soviet–Mongolian geological expedition in the south of Mongolia in the summer of 1973 (Volkov and Novgorodova 1974), one can well believe that domestication first took place essentially in the Gobi region in the south of the country, i.e. earlier than in the north.

Thus the emergence of nomadic livestock keeping in East, South and Central Mongolia with regard to the changing of importance of the economic forms, can be schematically depicted (see Fig. 1, on p. 31).

In the west of the country there is however no evidence that agriculture was the predecessor of livestock keeping. On the contrary, livestock keeping and its mobility can be ascertained as having existed earlier. Thus the development phases of mobile livestock keeping in this region can be depicted as follows:

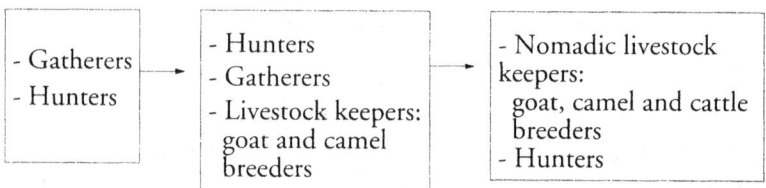

Figure 2: Development phases of mobile livestock keeping in West Mongolia

Economic Conditions and Their Development

Production Character of Nomadic Livestock Keeping in the Thirteenth to Nineteenth Centuries

There is a good deal of information concerning the economic situation of the Mongols in the period under consideration, but it is all of a fragmentary nature and much of it influenced by political interests; moreover it is not sequentially documented. Therefore it is not easy to reconstruct systematically the development of nomadic livestock keeping in Mongolia. If one were to look over historical reports from the thirteenth century concerning livestock keeping, or if one were to compare the oldest reports with the most recent, one would be astounded at how contemporary these reports seem and at how little nomadic livestock keeping in all its forms had changed over the centuries until recent times.

In accordance with verified economic facts of later centuries, we can assume that, even when the Mongols were first designated as a tribal unit in Chinese sources of the early twelfth century, the Mongolian economic structure was based on extensive nomadic livestock keeping of a natural character.

The production process that was characteristic for Central Asian or Mongolian livestock breeding nomads, was socially organised in the framework of households. Households were at the same time production and cooperative units. Such a means of production permitted the division of labour according to sex and age only within the household. It represented a simple form of worker ownership. Production remained limited to basic requirements. Livestock keeping provided for food, transport, clothing and items for exchange in marketplaces. Very few items for exchange were produced in comparison with the case of settled peoples, but such exchange with other peoples did exist in a limited form. This did not lead, however, to an increase in production. For the most part, animals were exchanged for products. Such a form of production remained, in our opinion, virtually unchanged until the start of the twentieth century. I. M. Maiskii writes:

> For the economic system which I was able to observe in Mongolia, the designation 'extensive livestock economy' is still appropriate. It is essentially characterised by the fact that the people have only minimally participated in natural historical processes ... It is an almost ideal embodiment of the famous formula 'laissez faire – laissez passer'. (Maiskii 1960: 119)

Scholars who today talk of an intensive development of the economy or even of an inner development capacity of nomadic livestock keeping, do not take the extensive character of Mongolian livestock keeping sufficiently into account. This extensiveness has as a consequence that livestock keeping can hardly be changed or improved. If livestock keeping were to assume an intensive character, it would cease to be nomadic. As a result, all the traditional institutions of nomadic society would collapse and the way of life would change totally. This can be deduced from the history of the Mongols up until the present time. As regards intensity of economic forms, nomadic livestock keeping is not the most extensive form in comparison to other ancient forms. 'The economy of pastoralism is therefore extensive, but not as extensive as hunting. Its extensiveness is distinguished by the livestock and by the pasture land ...' (Lattimore 1962: 246)

Livestock keeping was conducted exclusively on the basis of private ownership of animals. Ownership conditions in the period under consideration can in general be divided into two forms: private and state (i.e. owned by the royal court). The quantity of livestock under state ownership represented a more concentrated form than that under private ownership, and increased from the end of the thirteenth century. For this reason, an authority responsible for the royal livestock had to be instituted in 1263, which was later often re-organised in the 1320s (*Yuanshi*, vols 89, 90). The imposition of the Chinese-Manchurian political administrative system and the spread of Buddhism in Mongolia resulted in changes in the economic situation of the country from the end of the seventeenth century. Larger quantities of livestock privately owned by nobles, dignitaries and monasteries drastically increased. There was, however, in no case any socially organised production.

Since nomadic livestock keeping is totally dependent on the natural pasture, the economy is all the more sensitive to climatic changes, these resulting sometimes in a drastic reduction in productivity. In the chronicles there are infrequent reports of natural catastrophes, especially of droughts, which brought livestock keepers into dire economic straits. In order to overcome these difficulties, nomads resorted to more distant pasture land, often undertaking large-scale migrations. It should be noted, however, that such opportunities were not always available. In particular, with increased close-meshed territorial-administrative divisions and the consequent marking-out of borders within the country, which had previously been unknown to nomads, free migration was often limited.

In the ancient Chinese chronicles there are references to temperature falls and continual natural catastrophes in the nomadic homeland of the Mongolia of today. For example, the Chinese researcher Wang inferred from such chronicles that in the period from 250 B.C. to A.D. 1900 there were 202 years when winter thunderstorms occurred in the northern part of China (Wang 1980). He hypothesised that a colder and stronger Siberian high resulted in a strong, fast-moving cold front which caused a rapid uplift motion of warm air ahead of it and thus induced more frequent winter thunderstorms. Also duststorms reflect in some way the change of aridity in the nomadic homelands. The Chinese researcher Zhang has reconstructed time series of duststorms in Northern China in the period 470 B.C. to A.D. 1790 based on historical records in local and other chronicles. He studied the sources of the dust and its relationship to climatic change (Zhang 1984), and concluded that the dust originated from the deserts of Northwestern China and Inner Mongolia where the nomadic peoples lived. He proposed that a high frequency of duststorms was associated with a stronger Siberian high which caused a steeper pressure gradient and stronger and in principle drier winter monsoons over Eastern Asia. It is interesting that both these phenomena, winter thunderstorms and duststorms, correspond with accounts in ancient Chinese chronicles concerning periodic migrations of nomads southwards into China.

In the autochthonous Mongolian sources there are no detailed accounts of climatic changes and resultant large-scale migrations in ancient or in recent times. The long drought in 1737 in the Secen Khan *Aimag* and the droughts in the Zasagt Khan *Aimag* during the reign of the emperor Jiaqing (1796–1820) and in the Tüsheet Khan *Aimag* during the reign of the emperor Shan-fung (1851–61), which were especially devastating, have been ascertained. The drought in the Zasagt Khan *Aimag* in particular was so bad that duty from the *aimag* to the government was deferred for 20 years (Nacagdorj 1963: 108). Even in this period the possibility of migrating to distant pastoral regions was substantially reduced on account of territorial-administrative borders which came to be drawn up increasingly from the end of the seventeenth century.

Traditional Herd Animals

Kinds of livestock

Herd animals in the Central Asian region are nature's means of offering indigenous peoples a chance of long-term survival in the form of nomadism under extreme natural and inflicted socio-political conditions. Due to their capacity to produce a highly nutritious foodstuff and refined raw materials out of scanty resources, these animals have enabled the peoples to open up even unfavourably snow-covered mountain regions, endless steppe and the Gobi desert.

According to sources and archaeological finds, the Mongols, just like earlier peoples of Central Asia, have kept camels, horses, cattle, sheep and goats as the economically most important animal species. There is definite evidence that Central Asian peoples have kept these five animal species at least since the period of the Huns (Sükhbaatar 1980: 25). In the *Yuanshi*, one of the most important sources for Mongolian history from the fourteenth century, it is often mentioned that the Mongols bred these five animal species. The term goat, however, is rarely used in the *Yuanshi* and in later chronicles. This is explained by the fact that the Mongols counted goats as sheep. In some regions the yak was or is still kept: in the mountains it is of particular importance as a working and cart animal. Since the yak lives almost only in the high Khangai mountain region, it is not normally reckoned as an independent or sixth animal species. In animal counts it has for a long time been registered under cattle. For this reason we have hardly any concrete reports from ancient times concerning yak keeping in Mongolia.

In early history, the breeding of pigs and fowl was unknown. The reason is obvious: they are unsuited to the nomadic way of life.

The Mongols keep sheep as a source of meat, hides, fat and, to a limited extent, milk. The meat is relished and the most frequently eaten. Mongols consider the sheep an ideal animal on account of its calorific meat and fat content. Peng Daya reported at the beginning of the thirteenth century in connection with the food of the Mongols: 'What of pastoral animals they use in the kitchen, that is as a rule the sheep' (Olbricht and Pinks 1980: 110). The relatively small amount of work required for slaughtering and the possibility of conserving the meat are also advantageous for nomadic conditions. The Mongolian sheep has in general a rough wool which is suitable for the production of felt and coverings for *yurts*. Information dating from previous centuries shows that in those areas where there were relatively few cows, sheep's milk was drunk.

Goats are in general kept as sources of hair and milk. Goat meat is valued less by the Mongols and is not eaten with relish because the fat quickly solidifies. On the other hand the Mongols prefer goat's milk to sheep's milk. Goats and sheep are not usually kept separately; nor was either species kept exclusively in earlier times by the Mongolian nomads.

The Mongols use cattle in many ways. Cow's milk is drunk everywhere with relish and is preferred. In the many regions where no *airag* (*kumiss*) is produced, sour cow's milk is drunk. As *Hei Da shilüe* reports, it was customary for the Mongols to drink it even in the thirteenth century (Olbricht and Pinks 1980: 112). Cattle hides are mainly used as floor coverings for the *yurt* in winter. Ropes (Mong. *sur*), rugs, sacks, etc. are produced from cattle leather for household use and for work. Beef is valued second only to mutton. In most places in Mongolia, cattle are used as beasts of burden and work animals. In addition, dried and crusted cattle dung is of great importance for private household use and in a work environment. In particular, it was the only source of fuel in the steppe and Gobi regions for a long time. From many contemporary reports, such as those of Carpini, Rubruck and Peng Daya, it can be ascertained that cattle and horse dung was the usual and the most important fuel in the thirteenth century, just as it is today (Risch 1930: 52; Olbricht and Pinks 1980: 115). Moreover, it is used everywhere in Mongolia for insulating the winter and spring stalls, and in places with few forests it is frequently used as a construction material for windbreak walls in spring.

The horse mainly serves as a mount, less frequently as a spanned draught animal. In the many bygone accounts of foreign travellers, it is reported that the Mongols did not like to walk and would use horses even for small distances. In spite of its small size, the Mongolian horse is sturdy and capable of bearing heavy loads. It can carry about a third of its own weight and can travel long distances. This was an influencing factor on the success of the Mongolian raids in Eurasia in the thirteenth century. Detailed reports (Jagchid and Bawden 1965) about the role of horses in the Mongolian nomadic way of life and about state policies concerning horses come from the Yuan period, when several large horse herds were owned by the royal court. For this reason the state acquired the best pastures both inside and outside Mongolia. It was in this period that the authority responsible for the royal horse herds was instituted (Dalai 1992: 91). Because horses play a crucial role in nomadic life, a special method of horse keeping was developed. Such a method was already known in the sixteenth century. For example, Yisuji reports:

> The horses are very fat in autumn, and when they are allowed to run fast, they are dead even before they have reached three stages because their fat is not solid. They [the Mongols] thus choose the best horses and apply the method of pulling on the reins: one rides each day 20 to 30 *li* [Chinese unit of length (Mong. *gazar*): one *li* or *gazar* = 576 m] until the horse sweats a little; then one puts chains on its front hooves so that it can't jump or stamp, and one makes the reins so short that the horse can neither eat nor drink. Thus it is tied fast each day from the afternoon till the evening or from the evening till the morning. Afterwards it is set free in the pasture, and on the next day one starts again in the same way. After 3 or 5 days, or after 8 or 9 days, the fat on the horse's back has thickened, its belly is small but strong, its croup is large and solid. Before it was a false fat which [resulted] from the green grass; now the fat has grown solid and thick. [The horse] can gallop at full strength without losing its breath. The horse can participate in battles, can go without sufficient water or grass for 8 or 9 days without exhausting its strength (Serruys 1945: 149).

Horses as a rule are less frequently slaughtered than sheep and cattle. Peng Ta-ya reported in the thirteenth century: 'Horses are slaughtered only at great festivities' (Olbricht and Pinks 1980: 110). In winter, however, horsemeat is eaten on account of its warming effect and high calorific value. The most important product which the Mongols produce from horse milk is *airag*. It often happens that in warm seasons only *airag* is drunk and no meat is eaten for weeks on end. According to the reports of Carpini and Rubruck from the thirteenth century, the Mongols nourished themselves in summer exclusively with horse milk, and meat was eaten only in exceptional circumstances (Risch 1930: 10; 1934, 46). In addition, dried horse dung, just like cattle dung, is of great importance in particular for the people of the steppe and Gobi regions, where it is used as a fuel.

There is little information in the chronicles concerning the camel. According to reports in the *Yuanshi*, the camel was used as a source of hair and milk, as a mount and as a pack and draught animal (*Chen Yuanqin* 1935: ch. 1, 27). As a pack animal it can carry on average 200–240 kg and as a draught animal 400–600 kg. A fully laden camel can travel 30 to 40 km per day (Cerenpuncag 1971). Because camel milk is rich in fat, cheese (Mong. *aaruul*) of good quality is produced from it. Camel meat is in general eaten in the regions where camels are kept. It is also worth mentioning that dried camel dung is the main fuel for the rural people of the Gobi.

Quantity of livestock

The official quantity of livestock can be determined only after the count of 1918. Unfortunately we do not have any facts concerning livestock numbers in earlier times. In official files and in historical documents, there are reports that animal counts were carried out in the eighteenth century and especially in the nineteenth century, but the results of these have only been partially preserved.

Accounts dating from the Yuan period report that livestock under state ownership was counted (*Yuanshi*, vol. 100, 2a). For example in 1320, an animal count took place under the direction of the official Alagtumur, while in 1326 a count of horses under state ownership was conducted. The results of these are however unknown and it may be assumed that the results of horse counts were kept secret. Because every Mongolian warrior was known to have on average 2–5 horses in reserve, the number of warriors could have easily been calculated on the basis of such results. In order, therefore, not to reveal the number of their warriors, it was customary for the Mongols after about the twelfth century not to disclose the numbers of their horses.

Official files report that in Outer Mongolia during the period of the Manchurian rule, Qianlong (1736–95), Daoguang (1821–50), Xianfeng (1851–61) and Guangxu (1875–1908), animals in Mongolia (the four *aimag*s, the largest territorial-administrative units, and *shavi*, i.e. regions belonging to the Buddhist dignitaries) were often counted. The data, however, are unavailable. There is a further report that in 1836 an animal count was carried out in the four *aimag*s. Here it is written that the government office of the Secen Khan *Aimag* reported the number of animals in all four *aimag*s to ministers of the main government of the capital Urga: according to this, Secen Khan *Aimag* had more than 430,000 animals, Tüsheet Khan *Aimag* more than 200,000, Sain Noyan Khan *Aimag* more than 170,000 and Zasagt Khan *Aimag* more than 80,000 (Nacagdorj 1963: 92). Thus there were in Mongolia, excluding the small quantity in the *shavi*, only 880,000 animals. These figures do not in probability correspond to the actual situation. On account of taxes due to the government and to the Manchu emperor per head of cattle, it is likely that less animals were reported than in fact existed. We do have a single, incomplete but reasonably exact document of an animal count in the Secen Khan *Aimag* from the year 1841 (Nacagdorj 1963: 92).

Table 1: An animal count in the Secen Khan *Aimag* from the year 1841

	Camels	Horses	Cattles	Sheep	Goats	Total
1841	26,479	157,327	203,790	837,145	–	1,224,741

The horse is the only type of animal whose numbers in the thirteenth century we can ascertain. Since military campaigns were characteristic in Central Asia during this period, horses were especially important as mounts during battle. Because of this there are numerous relevant reports in the chronicles, which allow us to estimate the number of horses used as mounts and the total number of horses at the start of the thirteenth century as 1,400,000 (Bold 1998a: Table 6). This fact enables us to deduce the number of livestock at the start of the thirteenth century.

Table 2: Quantitative relation between animal types

	Camels	Horses	Cattle	Sheep	Goats
Average percentage of animal types	2.62	9.52	9.77	58.8	19.1
General stable relation of animal types as coefficient*	0.3	1.0	1.0	6.2	2.0

* see in: Bold 1998: Table 1

There are factors which make the relation between animal types stable and independent of time. Apart from occasional social influences, the climatic conditions and the geographical zones of Mongolia determine the distribution of the various animal types. The total dependence of Mongolian livestock keeping on the natural pasture determines not only the distribution of animal types but also their quantitative relation. Moreover, the stability of the relation between animal types arises from the fact that a fixed number of animal types is economically necessary in each individual nomadic household.

If we consider the quantity of stock only from those years in which livestock breeding was not overly disrupted on account of special social and ecological factors, we can arrive at numbers given in Table 2. On the basis of the above estimated total number of horses, we can calculate the total quantity of livestock in about 1220 (see Table 3 below).

Table 3: Total quantity of livestock in about 1220

	Camels	Horses	Cattle	Sheep	Goats	Total
Total no.	420,000	1,400,000	1,400,000	8,960,000	2,940,000	15,120,000
%	2.77	9.26	9.26	59.26	19.44	

ROLE OF PASTURE LAND IN THE NOMADIC ECONOMY

Economic parameters of pasture land

The question of the economic parameters of pasture land is of decisive importance for describing Mongolian nomadic livestock keeping and nomadic society.

In the main sources, such as the SHM, 'Collection of Histories', *Altan tobchi,* etc., it is clear that *nutug* or *nuntug*[1] is the most important term when describing the economic significance of the pasture land in the nomadic economy. If we examine the use of the word *nutug* in the SHM, we find the following alternatives of meaning:

- *Nutug* is first of all used to designate place of residence or migration region.[2]

- *Nutug* designates pasture land for animals, i.e. *nutug* is the natural prerequisite for the nomadic economy (SHM, §§118, 232, 278). In this sense *nutug* can also be equated with the hunting ground.

- The word *nutug* is used furthermore to designate the country, its nomadic population and its entire livestock (SHM, §§207, 255, 279).

- *Nutug* can also mean the quasi-ownership conditions of place of abode, pasture and hunting ground (SHM, §§219, 255). It should be pointed out that these ownership conditions did not relate to property in the economic sense, but rather to access to pasture land.

In addition there are other terms in the chronicles, such as *etügen* and *yurt*,[3] which are connected with the question of the economic parameters of the *nutug* but which essentially do not differ in meaning from this last term (Vladimircov 1929: 43). These terms do not go further in describing the ownership conditions of pasture land.

From the above we can conclude that *nutug* is a term with extensive meaning and includes the country as well as the pasture land, the place of abode, the hunting ground, the inhabitants and livestock. In the consciousness of Mongolian nomads, these components are inseparably united in *nutug*.

The chronicles often relate of one tribe conquering another and taking the conquered *nutug* into its possession. The question can then be raised, to what extent the people strove to have more possessions or *nutug*. Of course, the interest in extending accessible pasture land, amongst other things, comes to play a role here. Many historical investigations of Mongolian and Russian historians have come to the conclusion that we are here dealing exclusively with ownership of pasture land. Regarded from an economic viewpoint, there is no reason to equate the nomadic quasi-ownership conditions of the *nutug* or the pasture land with land ownership under the feudal economy. The history of the nomads is full of military conflicts, the reason of which can be explained by the need for pasture land reserves and the arising need to defend and to conquer. We believe that since ancient times, the basic motivation for gaining possession of *nutug* was to use the conquered people as potential soldiers and not as labourers (Bold 1988). This political mentality remained as long as the people maintained their nomadic lifestyle. Although some political administrative changes took place in the period from the twelfth century onwards, the economic parameters of the *nutug* remained essentially unchanged until the eighteenth century.

As regards rights of access to pasture land, in the pre-Manchurian period the noblemen freely used pasture land within their given territorial administrative areas. Common people were economically independent producers and also were freely able to choose pastoral areas for their livestock within their *khoshuu* region. For example, the 'Mongol-Oirat Regulations of 1640' assert:

> If anybody hammers in a post [in order to move in] on a site [for winter and spring] where the *yurt* of someone else has been broken or should again be put up, he will be punished. If the site belongs to a prince, the culprit will be fined six times nine ani-

mals.[4] If the site belongs to common people, the culprit will be fined nine animals (Dylykov 1981: 106).

The establishment of the Manchurian administration system, which brought about deep changes in nomadic society gradually in the course of the eighteenth century, had as a consequence basic changes in conditions of ownership and of rights of access. At the end of the eighteenth century, land belonged to

1. the Manchu emperor,
2. Mongolian princes and noblemen,
3. common livestock keepers.

The Manchu emperor: Land available to the imperial court was used as pasture for the herds, for cultivation and for hunting.

Mongolian princes and noblemen: The second largest share of the land was reserved for princes and high-ranking Buddhist dignitaries. They too used the land for livestock pasture and in some areas for agriculture. They chose the best regions for grazing their own livestock, but there are also known cases of others using the land in return for payment of duty. There are reports that after about the middle of the eighteenth century princes in Inner Mongolia, and somewhat later in Outer Mongolia, delivered up plots of land for the purpose of agriculture to Chinese peasants in return for tax payment (Sharkhüü 1975: 198ff.). Although this was forbidden by Manchurian law, the practice became widespread. On the other hand we have no evidence of princes or high-ranking Buddhist dignitaries renting out pasture land in return for payment.

Common livestock-keepers: There is no doubt that livestock keepers used land freely since ancient times for grazing their livestock. Under Manchurian law the emperor, the princes and the other noblemen had the right to use pasture land as they chose. There are, however, no specific references about this also applying to common livestock keepers. A free use of pasture land was also substantially hindered by the close-knit character of the Manchurian administrative and territorial network, and they were forced to use pastoral regions of inadequate size.

It can be concluded from this that significant changes in the use of pasture land in comparison to previous times arose in the eighteenth century. We believe that this was due to a number of reasons.

- First, with the establishment of Manchurian military and civil administration in Mongolia, there were at first no fundamental changes – nomadic traditions continued freely so that no alteration in the economic form arose. Gradually however, Manchurian territorial-administrative linkages had an unfavourable effect on the free use of pastoral areas. To this negative effect was also associated the fact that the amount of pastoral region which was made available to the Manchu emperor and to Buddhist dignitaries continually increased, with the result that the pasture land that was available to common livestock keepers correspondingly decreased.

- The second wave of the spread of Buddhism in Mongolia, which occurred at about the same time as the Manchu conquest, had an effect upon traditional Mongolian nomadic society. The ever-increasing number of settled monasteries resulted in an increase in agriculture. Larger and larger fields were built on for the army, the administration and the monasteries. In addition, many Chinese peasants settled in Mongolia from the second half of the eighteenth century. This all led to a more intensive use of the land. According to reports, from the nineteenth century onwards foreigners introduced a new type of land use – the mining of ore, salt, gold, gemstones, etc. (*Lifanyuan zeli*, bk 4). Other forms of land use also arose at about this time.

The territorial divisions which thus resulted in the nineteenth century and which were defined by fixed borders, can be summarised as follows:

1. territory for the personal use of the Manchu emperor;

2. territories for the state services, e.g. area for the army and military households (Mong. *cergiin khüreenii nutag*);

3. territories along the relay station lines (Mong. *örtöönii nutag*);

4. territory of the *khoshuu*, which administratively belonged to the four *aimag*;

5. territory of the border protection outposts (Mong. *kharuulyn nutag*);

6. territory of the property of Buddhist dignitaries (Mong. *shavi-otogiin nutag*).

ECONOMIC CONDITIONS AND THEIR DEVELOPMENT

Pasture land for the personal use of the Manchu emperor

The Manchu-Chinese emperor had the greatest right to pasture land use (*tömör* or *bosoo sürgiin nutag*). The pastoral region of the Manchurian imperial court was spread over many locations in Mongolia: in the present territory of the Sükhbaatar *Aimag*, then the Dariganga region, (*c.* 20,000 sq. km), in the vicinity of cities such as Khüree (Urga), Uliastai and Khovd, and in pastoral areas for breeding animals in the present Dornogobi *Aimag*, then the Mergen-Van *khoshuu* of the Tüseet Khan *Aimag*, as well as in the present Ömnögobi *Aimag*, then the (Gobi-) Tüseet-Günii *khoshuu* of the Tüseet Khan *Aimag* (*c.* 30,000 sq. km). The emperor also had certain regions reserved for hunting. These eleven regions,[5] the use of which was forbidden to others, were in principle located in the *khoshuu* territories (5,000 sq. km).

Pasture land for requirements of the state

Pasture land was reserved for those responsible for the relay post service along relay lines and at relay stations (Mong. *örtöönii nutag*), for the border protection service (Mong. *kharuulyn nutag*) and for army grounds, settlements and military households (*cergiin khüreenii nutag*).

There were in Mongolia altogether 134 relay stations in eight directions[6] in the nineteenth century. This number was preserved without significant change. Each station enjoyed a right to pasture land for its livestock of an area of 50–60 *gazar* long and 30–40 *gazar* wide (28,800–40,320 m by 15,280–23,040 m). By royal decree each station had at its disposal an additional pasture of an area which was 30–40 *gazar* long and 15–25 *gazar* wide (15,280–23,040 m by 11,520–14,400 m). Calculated thus, they amounted to an area of 120,000 sq km. In some *khoshuu* there were many relay lines and in such cases available pasture land became scarce. In one extreme case, the total area of relay stations and lines amounted to one-fifth of the *khoshuu* territory (Bold 1998c). Moreover there were, in addition to the relay lines, internal post lines (Mong. *suman örtöö*) within the *khoshuu*. There were about 400 such stations altogether in Mongolia (*BNMAU-yn tüükh* 1968: 206). Each of these had a right to pasture land of an area of 28–30 *gazar* (Gongor 1978: 280). Thus in the eighteenth and nineteenth centuries all the relay stations had at their disposal pasture land amounting to 170,000 sq km.

Kharuulyn nutag extended about 2,000 km along the northern border of Mongolia, from the northeastern border point (Gürvelzekh) of the present Dornod *Aimag* to the northwestern border point (Khar

Tarvagatai) of the Bayan-Ölgii *Aimag*. Here there were in all more than 70 permanent *yurt* sites and temporary sites. Each site had at its disposal pasture of an area of 30 by 40 *gazar* (15,280 by 23,040 m) (Gongor 1978: 281). The pasture area for *yurt* sites alone comprised 11,000 sq. km (*BNMAU-yn tüükh* 1968: 200).

Regions well available to the *cergiin khüreenii nutag* were army grounds, settlement and pastoral areas for military households. The main bar-racks were located in the cities of Khüree (Urga), Uliastai and Khovd and consisted of large areas. In their vicinity were also large pastoral regions. For example, the barracks in Uliastai had land with an area of 100 by 100 (57.6 by 57.6 km). Their settlements were mainly located in the broad valleys of the rivers Khovd and Buyant, and together they comprised an area of about 50,000 sq km (Gongor 1964: 45).

Pasture land of the religious head of Mongolia

Pasture land and livestock and subject property, the *otog*[7] of the great dignitary *rJe-bcun dam-pa khutagt* (highest religious official),[8] resembled territorially the *khoshuu*. There were also other types of pasture land ownership, *bag*, which existed within a *khoshuu*. They enjoyed a status of independence from the *khoshuu* government, which was characterised by the fact that the pastoral area, *otog*, could only be used by *shavi* subjects of the religious head and that these subjects were not required to render administrative service to the respective *khoshuu* governments. According to statistics from 1918, the eighth *rJe-bcun dam-pa khutagt* (religious state head of Mongolia 1911–24) possessed 198 *otog*s and *bag*s. Most of these were not independent territorial-administrative units but rather pastoral land and livestock and subject property within the *khoshuu*.

Pastoral land for high-ranking Buddhist dignitaries and princes

Although *khoshuu* territory was at the disposal of its governing prince, there was within the *khoshuu* pasture land property belonging to Buddhist dignitaries which administratively did not belong to the prince. The 12 dignitaries of second rank (not including the religious head of the country) with elevated official duties, *khutagt* with seal, had their own pasture land property which territorially resembled the *khoshuu* and existed within the *khoshuu*. Such pastoral regions could only be used by those subjects belonging to the dignitaries.

There were princes of various classes: the princes ruling the *aimag*s and the *khoshuu*s; high-ranking civil servants; non-ruling princes of royal descent, *taij*. They had the right in order of their rank to choose pasture land within their respective *khoshuu*s. In principle, a governing prince had a right to the entire territory of his *khoshuu*. But as described above, there were special regions within a *khoshuu* that were not subordinated to him. Most of the *khoshuu*s had extensive regions for the pasturage of the livestock of the emperor, the state services (*örtöö, kharuul* and *cergiin khüreenii nutag*) and the great dignitaries.

The right of the common livestock keepers to use pasture land
The question whether common livestock keepers had the established right to choose pasture land within their respective *khoshuu* is extremely difficult to ascertain. On the one hand there were no interdicts for livestock keepers to prevent them from freely choosing pastoral regions for seasonal migrations. This was legally prescribed in the statute book *Khalkha Jirum*[9] of the eighteenth century. Here it is written:

> If a *yurt* has already been broken, the *ötög* [site] still belongs to the owner of the *yurt*. If two people seeking an *ötög-buuc* [site] arrive simultaneously at a location favourable for the winter and spring site, then it belongs to him who saw it first. If the two saw it simultaneously, then the site belongs to him who first came and struck the place with his whip (Zamcarano 1959: 45).

On the other hand it was complicated under the circumstances to exercise this freedom. As described above, the most suitable pastoral regions were at the disposal firstly of the emperor and then of high-ranking Buddhist dignitaries and the *khoshuu* princes. In old official files there are indications that the higher-ranking princes sought favourable pastoral regions for winter–spring and summer–autumn, raised marking posts (Mong. *paiz*) which showed to whom the regions belonged, and forbade anybody to move into them of their own accord. Those of lower ranks or the wealthy were then, by virtue of their social standing, able to seek out the next most favourable pastoral regions and demarcate them frequently with stone piles. Common livestock keepers were able to use the remainder of the pasture land, which comprised about 40 per cent of the country's usable pasture. There was, however, a certain difference between the possibility of a free choice of pasture and the real likelihood of reaching a distant, favourably lying pastoral region. Since normal livestock keepers, who were in the majority, did not have at their disposal sufficient number of pack animals, mounts and carts, they often experienced difficulties in making use of distant pastures.

Critical comments concerning the 'feudal conditions of pasture land'

An important viewpoint which demonstrates 'Mongolian feudalism' concerns the emergence of concentrated forms of pasture land ownership as well as of feudal land ownership at the establishment of the united Mongolian empire. Although some scholars mention the particularities of the economic parameters of pasture land which arise from nomadic livestock keeping, they maintain in the end that the conditions relating to pasture land in Mongolia from the thirteenth century to the first half of the fourteenth century were basically similar to the European principle of feudal ownership of land. The so-called ownership conditions in this period can be divided, according to historians such as Vladimircov, Nacagdorj and Gongor, into

- the land of the groups of thousand, the property of the Khaan;
- the land of the members of the 'Golden Tribe' (i.e. Genghisic; Mong: *altan urug*) of the Khaan;
- the land of persons who received special rewards (Vladimircov 1934: 111; Ishjamc 1976: 79; Gongor 1978: 26, 248, 256).

They thus also believed that due to the existence of a private and a state form (of the Khaan) of feudal land ownership in Mongolia, a feudalism peculiar to the country prevailed. With the intention of bringing ownership conditions of pastoral land into line with European (e.g. French) feudal conditions, scholars conclude that in Mongolia there existed such things as 'feuds', 'appanages', 'benefices', etc., which formed the legal basis of the actual feudal production conditions and hence the economic basis of Mongolian nomadic society (Colmon 1987: 26). The majority of research adheres to the principle that land ownership is the economic basis of feudalism and that the economic basis of Mongolia in that period was the ownership of land. In other words, it supports the view that in the production system of nomadic livestock keeping, land was the main instrument of production (Zlatkin 1973: 62; Ser-odjav 1976: 146; Gongor 1978: 325: Nacagdorj 1978: 186). The ownership conditions of traditional Mongolian nomads who conduct livestock keeping in order to produce, are embedded in the relation livestock keeper–livestock–pasture land (Bold 1988). In order to determine the core of 'ownership conditions' of pasture land and livestock, the role of pasture land and of livestock in the production process of nomadic livestock keeping is important. For nomads, however, livestock is of much more fundamental significance. The economic relation to the animal as a means of production is in livestock keeping more intensive than that to pasture. For this reason, animal ownership dominated in Mongolia, land ownership being reduced to a right of access. F. Scholz is quite correct when he writes that

> Private ownership of pasture land does not belong to the nature of nomadic culture ... what is meant rather is fixed use of and exclusive access to pasture and thereby the loss of a freedom of movement which is necessary both for the guarantee of survival and for ecological reasons. (Scholz 1995: 26)

The appropriation of pasture land stands in fundamental contrast to the appropriation of land under the conditions of settled agriculture which carries out production by working the land via human labour. In the latter case, there is an effective involvement with the land in the production process on the part of the producer; in the former case, pasture land has an 'unhumanised' form in the production process and thus does not go beyond being a requisite for production.

We can compare the elements of land usage in pre-industrial, i.e. feudal, Europe with those in Mongolia in terms of their significance, as set out in Table 4:

Table 4: Comparison of land usage in Mongolian nomadic economy with land usage in the European pre-industrial economy

Mongolian nomadic economy	European feudal economy
1. Residential and pasture land	1. Agricultural land
2. Hunting ground	2. Horticultural land for cultivation of fruit, vegetables, pulse, oil-yielding seeds, fibre-yielding plants; also for special cultivation: viniculture, olive trees, commercially useful plants
3. Agriculture	
	3. Meadows for livestock use in winter
	4. Pasture land; forests: systematic and intensive extraction of fuel and building material
	6. Mining and quarry land for minerals
	7. Hunting ground

The table clearly shows the great difference between the economic functions and the extent of expenditure of labour in the two forms of land use.

The logical conclusion of 'confirming' that in Mongolia there existed feudal ownership of land is that the people were shackled to the soil (Nacagdorj 1978: 67) and that feudal exploitation prevailed.

As regards the three forms of feudal ground rent, scholars are of the opinion that there undoubtedly existed payment for labour and produce and that Mongolian princes received payment in the form of duty or service from conquered peoples (Sereeter 1974: 134–37). As mentioned above, there is little evidence in the sources that there existed payments in form of labour or produce, and it seems doubtful that such were important in the nomadic economic mechanism. In the sources there are effectively no references to practices that are identical to the mechanisms of payment in the economic system of feudalism.

In this connection some remarks concerning the structure of ground rent which was characteristic for European feudalism should be made.

Labour. Members of peasant economies were obliged to make their labour available to their lord for working land that was his direct property. Production and appropriation of multiple forms of labour here coincide. The differing forms of labour (socage) are determined by

- the work process into which they are incorporated and what is produced: agriculture, viniculture, use of meadowland, horticulture, use of forest land, processing of agricultural and domestic industrial-commercial raw materials, road, fortress and house construction, maintenance of tools, buildings, fences, etc.;

- whether the socage encompassed all or only part of this labour process;

- with which and with whose working instruments it was carried out;

- whether it was conducted by the respective members of the peasant community independently or in consecutive or cooperative operations with other labourers under the supervision of the local representative of the feudal lord.

Produce. With this basic form, the responsibility of labour has been transferred to the individual peasant economy. This means that all production up to the point of delivery has been removed from the control of the feudal lord or his representative. Such labour which has 'flowed' into produce can relate to all production branches of the peasant economy: grain, wine, hop, livestock, fish, manure, timber, wax-honey, flax-wool and other raw materials of a commercial type.

Money. With this form, labour has 'shed' its natural character by means of trade. In order to pay the requisite duty, the peasant is forced to exchange products for money.

In conclusion, it can be maintained that peasant labour, no matter by which forms of sanction its appropriation is guaranteed, represents the ground rent as material 'income' of the feudal lord. In other words, ground rent is the realisation of feudal ownership of land and of the peasant economy; the status of the peasant is as subject or household enfeoffed, bound and/or personally belonging to the feudal lord. As regards the Mongolian nomadic economic relation, therefore, service and duty that existed sporadically before the establishment of Manchurian economic policy and which cannot be regarded as pivotal in the nomadic economic system do not represent a realisation of land ownership of the kind that forms the core of feudalism.

MIGRATION TO NEW PASTURE AS TRADITIONAL STRATEGY OF PASTURE LAND USE

Ecological determinants of pastoral area and migration patterns

Nomadism has been the most important characteristic of livestock keeping of the peoples of Central Asia. Pastoral livestock keeping and migratory (nomadic) livestock keeping are often equated. Nomadic livestock keeping is however only one form of which grazing is characteristic, since pastoral livestock keeping can be carried out in both nomadic and non-nomadic, i.e. settled or half-settled, lifestyles.

There is a simplified notion that nomads spontaneously migrate to places where there is good pasture. However, in their migrations nomads follow definite rules which are consequences of ecological conditions. Although the prevailing political-economic framework also has a certain influence, it is the ecological determinants which play the decisive role in the development of migration patterns. They enable us to reconstruct the basic pattern of migration in ancient times. These determining ecological factors are climatic conditions, the distribution of forage plants, the distribution of salty soils and the supply of water.

The continental interiors of the temperate arid regions (Middle/Central Asia) are hot to moderately warm in summer, but always extremely cold in winter. The thermal conditions are subject to an altitudinally climatic and exposure-related differentiation on account of the high and dominating east-west extension of mountain ranges. Climatically, the best winter pasturage, on account of the favourable combination of temperature, wind and precipitation, lies in principle in all ecological zones of Mongolia, in the belt between the higher and middle mountain ranges. The winter site is therefore located on a higher southern slope of a mountain or in a mountain cleft away from the wind direction. The spring pasturage on the other hand is located somewhat below the winter pasturage on the southern face of a mountain between a middle altitude and the mountain foot. Although in general the lower the location the warmer it is, snow often remains at the foot of mountains and in the lowlands until May, and nights can be cold and damp. The site suitable for the summer pasturage lies for climatic reasons on the higher ranges, higher than the winter pasturage, on the mountain crest where it is windier. There are of course differences in relation to differing geographical zones. Since the inversion line of the Khangai and Khentii forest highlands lies lower, for example, the altitude of this inversion line is chosen for the winter pasturage. Accordingly the summer pasturage must be situated in the foothills. In order to ensure that the livestock remains well nourished from summer into autumn, migrations are undertaken to a warmer location where the animals can feed more peacefully and can be fattened in autumn in a regular way. Such sites, which even in late autumn are warm and free of snow in comparison with other areas, are characteristically located in deep-lying regions – and as a rule in all geographical zones.

One of the most important factors of seasonal migration is the state of the vegetation: the seasonal division of forage plant resources and the distribution of forage plants. If one compares the types of forage plants according to seasonal need and the distribution of forage plants in the mountain ranges, it becomes clear that the seasonal pasture regions, as determined by the distribution of these forage plants, are connected with the altitudinal conditions. This corresponds in principle with the climatically determined altitudinal planning of seasonal migrations.

Over and above this, salty soils play an important role in the fattening of the livestock in summer and the maintenance of a nourished condition and continued fattening in autumn. Because, in the distribution of salty soils, there exists the phenomenon that the mineral content is lowest in the highlands and highest in the lowlands, the seasonal migration should in the main be determined altitudinally. It can be deduced from Mongolian historical sources that nomads in ancient times migrated in autumn to the steppes or the desert steppes in order to reach regions rich in salty soils, sometimes covering distances of hundreds of kilometres.

Also the location of drinking water plays an important role in migration. On hot summer days, for example, the need for water for cooling down and for intensive nourishment of the livestock is especially acute. Because on summer days there are many mosquitoes, midges and horseflies at the water sites in the lowlands, the summer pasturage is carried out on those windy hills lying near to water. Here the in-adequate cooling capacity of the wind can be regularly compensated by water. When the insect pests disappear in autumn on account of the decrease in temperature, it is possible to move downwards directly to the water. Since a region lying near water is cold in winter, a pasture quite distant from water sites or rivers is then required. In addition, water sources are of great significance for the division and for the divided use of pasture regions.

The effects of all these factors on seasonal migrations are connected with altitudinal conditions. From this fact it follows that seasonal migrations are in principle directed altitudinally between the highlands and the lowlands correspondingly. Such altitudinally directed migrations were carried out as early as in the fourth century B.C. In ancient Chinese chronicles it is written that the homeland of the nomads living in the north ranged from the high mountains, which are covered in snow even in summer, to the boundless steppe, and that they migrate in summer to the south of the Gobi and in winter to the north of the Gobi (Taskin 1984: 267–69, 289; Sükhbaatar 1992: 81).

Historical chronicles reveal a multitude of details concerning the direction, distance and frequency of seasonal migrations. In the SHM there are numerous reports of pasture usage depending on differences in altitude for the cold winter–spring period and the warm summer–autumn period. In the 'Collection of Histories' the terms 'winter site' and 'summer site' are mentioned quite often (Rashid ad-Din 1952: vol. 1, bk 2: 126–27, 136). This can be explained by the fact that in those times the winter and spring sites and the summer and autumn sites were established in adjoining locations, and the migrations from the spring site to the summer site and from the autumn site to the winter site were the longest and most important. *Altan tobchi* (Luvsandanzan 1990), one of the most important sources of Mongolian history, reports that in the thirteenth century Mongolian tribes who kept livestock in the spacious pasture land of the Eastern Khentii Mountains between the voluminous Kherlen and Onon Rivers, often moved in autumn far northeast to the Ulz River. The reason for this was the salty soils. The details of the source show that the summer pasturage was conducted in the somewhat higher region of the upper surrounding area of the Onon River (Luvsandanzan 1990: 18, 23, 26, 30, 31, 38). Between these two seasons, long and important migrations took place. According to reports from later chronicles and official files, this was the case even up to the dawn of the twentieth century.

This view should not however serve as an argument that in Mongolia there are absolutely no planar migrations. On the contrary, livestock keepers make use of planar migrations quite often within a season in order to extend the area of pasturage and to increase feed supply.

As far as ecology is concerned, there are actually two main regions relevant to pasturage: mountain land and the Gobi steppe, in which the mountain land is divided into two subregions according to the prevailing ecosystem, the highlands of the Altai Mountains and those of the Khangai-Khentii Mountains.

As to pasturage, there are three different sorts of migration corresponding to definite geographical zones: the migrations in the Altai Mountains, in the Khangai-Khentii Mountains and in the Gobi-steppe (Bazargür et al. 1989: 104–44). In addition, livestock keepers do not always carry out their seasonal migrations in the steppes of Central and Eastern Mongolia and in the southeast Gobi region in the same manner. This is probably caused by the too narrowly drawn administrative borders, whereby the pasture region required for the entire year was neglected.

In the first two forms, i.e. in the Altai Mountains and in the Khangai-Khentii Mountains, seasonal migrations are quite obviously altitudinally directed according to relief conditions. There is, however, a clear difference in connection with the order of the seasonal pasturage depending on orographical conditions. Such migration patterns have a long tradition amongst the Mongols. Just like in present times, there were also migrations within each season in addition to seasonal migrations. Within the warm season, new pasture is often sought out, and within the cold season, migrations are carried out from the winter stalls to the spring site. Livestock keepers also migrate alone with their stock in order to make use of distant pastures. These changes of pasture depend on the climate of each season and their frequency differs in the differing geographical zones. Russian researchers in the transition period of the nineteenth and twentieth centuries observed that eight to ten migrations per year were customary for a single family. In cases of emergency, nomads migrate more frequently. For example, Maiskii writes that some families migrated up to 25–30 times per year (Maiskii 1921: 116).

Details concerning migration distances are available only from the end of the nineteenth and the beginning of the twentieth centuries. For example, in this period families migrated on average 8–10 km (Bogolepov and Soboleva 1911: 138). In the northwest of Mongolia distances amounted to 15–20 km (Potanin 1948). In Khovd they were 50 km on average. In the *khoshuu* of Achit-Vang of the Zasagt Khan *Aimag*, the furthest migrations amounted to 200 km. In the *khoshuu* of Zorigt Khan, which was located in the region between the Khovd River and Lake Uvs, migrations went as far as 250 km.

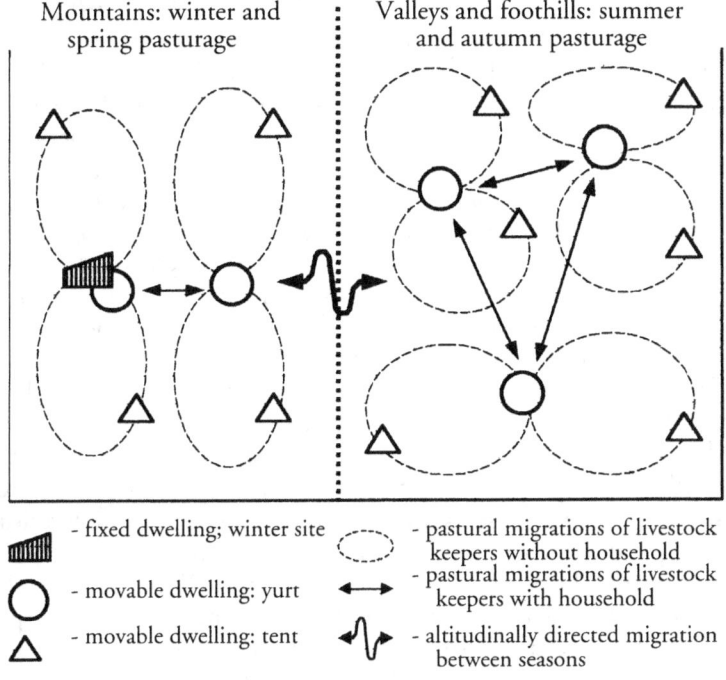

Figure 3: Approximate migration patterns of Mongolian nomadic livestock keepers in the twelfth to nineteenth centuries

In chronicles such as the SHM and *Altan tobchi*, the migration from the winter–spring site to the summer–autumn site is often mentioned as taking place on the 16th day of the first summer month.

This date has probably a long tradition. In the Chinese chronicle *Than-shi*, which dates from the eleventh century and which has preserved reports concerning the nomads from the sixth century, this date, i.e. the middle of the first summer month, is mentioned as a day of sacrifice (Bichurin 1950: 231). I. M. Maiskii remarks that the date of migration to the summer pasture from the long-lasting winter–spring pasturage was at the beginning of the twentieth century also as a rule in May (Maiskii 1921: 115). The migration date from the summer–autumn site to the winter–spring site was at the end of October and start of November. As Maiskii reports, this date applied everywhere at the beginning of the twentieth century.

Pasture land, migration and territorial-administrative divisions

With the help of reports to be found in ancient Chinese chronicles of the second century B.C. to the first century A.D. and of the sixth to the eighth centuries, one can approximately define the locations of the nomadic tribes. The territories of the nomadic peoples ranged over highland and lowland regions. However, to what extent the pastoral areas and the tribal locations corresponded with one another cannot be determined on account of the deficiency of the documentation of the chronicles. More detailed documentation is only to be found in later chronicles, and from reports in chronicles such as 'Collection of Histories' by Rashid ad-Din, SHM, *Altan tobchi*, etc., one can clearly determine the connection between pastoral areas and geographical relief.

The time at the end of the twelfth and the beginning of the thirteenth centuries represents a period of history in which Mongolian-speaking and Turkish-speaking nomadic tribes in Central Asia gradually began to merge – from a phase of dispersion to a reconcentration. There arose more and larger groupings: federations of tribes. From the source material of this period it is possible to determine the locations of the tribal groups. This then enables an analysis of the relation in which the locations of the tribal groups stood with respect to the location of the natural pasture. The ecological conditions of the locations of the then larger nomadic tribes such as Khamag Mongol, Jalair, Khereit, Naiman, Merget, Ongut and the Tartars, were heterogeneous rather than homogeneous. Each tribal group possessed its own region of pasturage which extended from the mountains into the lowlands. If we compare the location of the pasture regions, altitudinally ordered between highlands and lowlands/valleys, with the locations of the tribal groups, we see that they correspond harmoniously on the whole. The numerous tribes, which belonged to a tribal group or to the territory of a tribal group, used the pasture land, viewed as ordered between the highlands and the lowlands, in a linear manner and thus migrated altitudinally. This altitudinal use of natural pasture had certainly been determined by many hundreds of years of empirical experience.

At that time there was no strict bordering between the pasture regions used by the different tribes. The stability of the defined borders and of the right to use a pasture region imparted generally recognised ethical norms such as 'modesty', 'respect', 'friendship', etc. In this respect there was no reason to disturb the harmony between the locations of the tribal groups and the pasture regions, since no livestock keeper could personally choose the seasonal migration paths: rather as a rule these followed the ancient tradition, or the optimal method, of pasture land use.

The development of the territorial-administrative border setting of the *khoshuu* system in this period strongly influenced the gradual breakdown of the above-described correspondence between the locations of tribes and of the pasture regions. In the period of the old Mongolian seven *khoshuu* divisions during the second half of the sixteenth century and the first half of the seventeenth century, there were no strict border lines between the *khoshuu*s. The first three *aimag*s arose out of the seven *khoshuu*s in the first half of the seventeenth century, and with the *aimag* division, borderlines came to be somewhat more marked. It is difficult to determine the degree of correspondence between the location of the pasture area and the then territorial-administrative divisions. Geographical maps which could show the exact location of the above early seven *khoshuu*s and the individual tribes that belonged to them, are still unknown to us. From the maps from the period of the end of the eighteenth century to the beginning of the nineteenth century, one can only in a general way recognise the geographical location of the four *aimag*s. At this time single *khoshuu*s were indeed mapped and it is possible to compare the location of the *khoshuu*s with that of the pasture regions. From the available information, it is clear that at the start there was no complicated *khoshuu* division.

After the conquest of Outer Mongolia by Manchuria, these administrative *aimag* and *khoshuu* divisions were taken over, however in a strongly administered form. With the appointment of 34 representatives of the nobility descended from Genghis Khaan as the first ruling princes at the conference at Dolon-Nuur[10] in the year 1691, the new division of the *aimag*s into *khoshuu*s was completed. Afterwards, during 1691–1755, the number of the *khoshuu*s increased dramatically. In the year 1725 there were 75 *khoshuu*s and in the year 1755, 84 *khoshuu*s were registered. Thus the new situation made the drawing up of borders imperative. This was often done by laying stone piles (Mong. *ovoo*). From approximately this period, the animistic sacrificial ritual of invoking mountain spirits by revering stone piles at high altitudes, which has its origins in Shamanism, was no longer a traditional religious ceremony and the stone piles came to symbolise demarcation of pastoral regions. It is however worth mentioning that there were originally no border markings within a *khoshuu* territory. Only from the second half of the eighteenth century, terms relating to borders between *khoshuu*s came into official and legal use: *nutgiin sav* (owned pastureal region), *nutgiin dees* (pasture land border), *nutag khöökh* (expulsion from pastoral region), *nutag khuraakh* (confiscation of pasture land), *nutag cagdakh* (surveillance of pasture land), *nutag evdekh* (change of right to pasture land), etc. In the light of available files, it can also be seen that land measurements (*nutag deeslekh* and *nutag savlakh*, etc.) had become common. Thus various terms for units of measurement of pasture land which had earlier never been used in practice became widespread: *gazar, beer, on tusakh gazar, eriin gazar, ald gazar* and *khuv' gazar* (Bold 1998c). These originally Mongolian words have, however, a Chinese derivation in the sense of units of measurement of pastoral area.

The following can be found in documents:

- Each *ail* (nomadic family) has the right to use or possess land.

- The size of the land depends on the number of people, 576 m^2 is assigned per person (Gongor 1978: 279).

- Land is not allocated per person; rather the unit of allocation is based on the area of land to which 15 persons are entitled, since each ruling prince has the right to possess a 15-person portion of land.

It is to be noted that the drawing up of borders amongst the *khoshuu*s occurred at different times in the different ecological zones as a result of differing requirements of suitable pastoral area. This can be deduced from the fact that disputes concerning pastoral land arose amongst livestock keepers at different times in the different geographical zones. For example, the disputes in the mountain regions occurred much earlier than on the Eastern Mongolian steppe and in the Gobi Desert on account of the greater population density of humans and animals.

In addition to the establishment of the above-mentioned numerous *khoshuu*s, many smaller units having special status were founded. The vast majority of the newly founded units were formed by the pasture, livestock and subject property of the highest-ranking monk, *otog* (property of the great dignitary *rJe-bcun dam-pa khutagt*) and *shavi* (property of the second most senior monks *khutagt* with Seal), which administratively resembled the *khoshuu*s. The pasture land property of high-ranking Buddhist dignitaries, in particular of *rJe-bcun dam-pa khutagt*, was situated in the best regions of the natural pasture (Album 1987). It can be seen from maps that many *khoshuu*s were unfavourably structured in respect to the location of the natural pasture.

There were also other forms of *otog* and *bag* ownership which existed within a *khoshuu*. They enjoyed a status of autonomy within the *khoshuu* government, which manifested itself especially in the fact that the pasture region, *otog*, could only be used by *shavi* subjects of the monks and that these subjects did not have to perform administrative service in the *khoshuu* government. According to the statistics from 1918, the *rJe-bcun dam-pa khutagt* (the religious head of state of Mongolia 1911–24) had altogether 198 *otog*s and *bag*s. Most of these were not independent territorial-administrative units; rather, they were ownership of pasture land, livestock and subjects within the *khoshuu*. With the territorial-administrative changes after the release of Mongolia from Manchurian rule in 1911 and after the resulting inclusion of several West Mongolian *khoshuu*s into Mongolia, 127 these and similar administrative divisions were defined: namely all together 115 *khoshuu*s and 12 *otog*s and *shavi*s (*BNMAU-yn tüükh* 1968: 445–46).

From the second half of the eighteenth century the problem of pastoral land use erupted mainly for the following reasons:

- Due to the increase in the number of territorial-administrative *khoshuu* units, traditional pasture land use, which is principally characterised by altitudinally directed seasonal migrations between highlands and lowlands, was greatly disrupted. Thus, even if a *khoshuu* covered a large area of pasture, it might still have lacked pastoral regions for particular seasons or a region of a particular ecological type.
- In the course of the intensifying of hierarchy within Mongolian society under the influence of the Manchurian administration, Mongolian princes of various ranks, just like the imperial court

and representatives of the Manchu-Chinese government in Mongolia, appropriated pasture regions for themselves. The awarding of pasture land and subjects to princes for service to the emperor was a wide-spread practice and led to a severe cutting up of territory and complications regarding access to pasture.

- With the second wave of Buddhism, the dissemination of which had begun in Mongolia in the seventeenth century, monks became influential in society. Pasture land as well as livestock and subjects came to be increasingly the property of high-ranking Buddhist dignitaries.

All this resulted in livestock keepers quarrelling with one another on account of the deficit of necessary natural areas for the seasonal pastoral ways. From the observations of scholars who at the end of the nineteenth century and the beginning of the twentieth century travelled through Mongolia and carried out research, it emerges that the extent of the seasonal migrations of this period had already diminished (Potanin 1948: 68).

Official files of complaints about necessary pasture area have existed since the end of the eighteenth century. The State Central Archive for History and the State Library in Ulaanbaatar preserve a vast number of complaint charges of common livestock keepers against members of the nobility and of members of the nobility against one another, not only within a single *khoshuu* but also amongst *khoshuu*s, concerning the illegal confiscation of pasture regions acquired by generations of tradition. Most of the disputes seemed to arise in those *khoshuu*s whose borders did not correspond with the natural strips which normally contain ecologically optimal regions sufficient for the four seasonal pasturages.

In every period there were attempts to regulate disputes concerning pasture land. In official files the terms *niigem suukh* and *niigem nutaglakh* (to use pasture land with equal rights in friendly co-operation) appear frequently (Sharkhüü 1975: 25). In spite of this, disputes became increasingly heated. It often happened that livestock keepers beat and even killed one another in disputes over pasture regions and water sites. In order to force someone out of a region, their *yurt*s were burnt down and their animals stolen or slaughtered. The rising trend of violence can be followed in the files of charges. It is noteworthy that in this situation different sorts of struggles developed: accusations, destruction of the demarcating stone piles (*ovoo evdekh*), etc.

One often sees the reason for these disputes in the fact that in that period, ownership of land had adopted a specific form with respect to nomadic livestock economy. These disputes were in no way a struggle for private ownership; rather, they should be considered predominantly as a struggle for the natural regions required for the four seasonal pasturages. If the traditional and naturally developed seasonal use of pasture land comes into conflict with a division of territory alien to the nomadic life, such disputes could certainly resemble a struggle for the ownership of pasture land (Bold 1997).

Social forms of organisation in migration

Migrations can be categorised into group migrations and individual migrations. Group migrations can be further categorised into large-group and small-group migrations.

Large-group migrations

Migrations organised on a large-group scale, i.e. in tribes, were characteristic in the early history of the nomads. Large-group migrations comprised up to several tribes and thousands of tribal members. Such a migration organisation has been determined amongst the Huns from the first century B.C. For example, it is written in an ancient Chinese chronicle that in the year 87 B.C., 58 *bu*s comprising in all 200,000 people, of which 8,000 were warriors, undertook migrations (Taskin 1973: 31, 81). V. S. Taskin describes the term *bu* as a migrating community. This means that on average, 3,500 people belonged to each group. There are further details from the period of the early Kidan tribes in the fourth and fifth centuries. A Chinese compiler of reports maintained that he once saw a group of 10,000 Kidans migrating with 3,000 carts (Bagana: 48). Such a group migration was called *neben* by the Kidans. The word could well be an original form of the Mongolian word *negün* (move) (Perlee 1959: 21).

On the basis of such reports it is difficult to determine whether people were migrating in order to change pasture or because of some other reason, such as ejection from their homeland or for reasons of safety, etc. The SHM reports in more detail about *khüree* as a large group migration in the twelfth–thirteenth centuries. This consisted of several hundred paternally (*yasan töröl*) and maternally (*cusan töröl*) related members. There are also reports that the *khüree* existed for several generations of the nomad kingdoms before the Mongols (Sükhbaatar 1971: 157). While the *khüree*s are considered in some works as a form of defence against enemy attacks, other works treat them as economic organisations. We believe that the *khüree* was a typical phenomenon amongst the Central Asian nomads and incorporated both military and economic functions. If we follow the meaning of the word *khüree* in the SHM, we can justifiably say that originally economic reasons were decisive for this form of organisation. In unstable, warring times on the other hand, the defence function might have predominated. As the source reports, there were frequent struggles between tribes in the twelfth and thirteenth centuries. These struggles had outwardly an effect upon the tribal structure. In particular, the first quasi-administrative restructuring, which occurred with the establishment of the Mongolian Empire at the beginning of the thirteenth century, severely shook the tribal form of the traditional *khüree*.

B. Ya. Vladimircov reports that in the fifteenth century there was another form of migration group in Mongolia – *khoroo* (*khoriya*) (1934: 128). As he maintains, *khoroo* differs from *khüree* in that familial relations played no important role. The *khoroo* comprised several thousand people (Uspenskii 1880: 98ff.; Pokotilov 1893: 109 145). It may well be asked why large-group migrations were adopted again. Such a migration organisation had not been mentioned in the chronicles from the middle of the thirteenth century to the end of the fourteenth century. This could be explained by the fact that, with the gradual loss of significance of the military-administrative organisation in Mongolia, the traditional form of livestock keeping such as *khüree* resumed its importantce for tribes. After the establishment of the Yuan empire and the change of capital of the country from Kara-Korum to today's Beijing, Mongolia lay on the periphery. With the collapse of the Yuan dynasty (1271–1368), political unity in Mongolia was lost and at the end of the fourteenth century, Mongolia resembled the country before the period of Genghis Khaan. In addition, the struggle for succession to the throne intensified between Genghisic noblemen and other princes. The need for defence might well have been pushed into the foreground. However, we have no detailed information concerning *khoroo* migra-tions. In all probability this migration form did not last long, at the latest until the end of the fifteenth century. *Khoroo* was the final stage of *khüree*, a transition from *khüree* to small group migrations, and existed only in some locations.

Small group migrations
Migrations occurred not only in large groups but also in small groups, i.e. in family groups. According to Vladimircov, in the eleventh and twelfth centuries poor families migrated in groups while rich families migrated individually because the keeping of livestock in too large

quantities was an impediment to the use of pasture land (Vladimircov 1934: 37).

Individual migrations

Otor is a form of individual migration of nomads which is widespread even today. Livestock keepers migrate mostly alone and with only one species of animal in order to make use of feed reserves in distant pastures, while the family remains at a site with the rest of the animals that are not strong enough to endure a migration or do not need extra pasture, and can thus make use of close-lying pasture. *Otor* migrations are conducted in all four seasons, their lengths and durations depending on feed reserves. In times of scarce feed reserves, such as in droughts or in cold winters with heavy snowfalls, livestock keepers have to migrate for several weeks and cover long distances. They take tents or small *yurt*s along with them. *Otor* migration is a method of using pasture land in which close-lying pasture is held in reserve and distant pastoral regions are used without a cumbersome moving of the entire household. Livestock keepers allow their animals to graze at a location until the pasture is exhausted, and then they move on. This form of migration has been known since at least the thirteenth century.

PRODUCTION ACTIVITY OF LIVESTOCK KEEPERS

General livestock keeping work

Expenditure of labour

The close connectedness of nomads to nature via their herds and the pasture influences their expenditure and time of labour. In general, expenditure of labour in nomadic livestock keeping is low. In the case of some activities it is not clear whether they should be reckoned as production labour or as familial work. The difference between free time and working time is relative. In comparison to the production activity of peasants engaged in agriculture or horticulture, the work of nomadic livestock keepers is very specific. In the eyes of Europeans, or of agricultural workers, such work is incomprehensible. For this reason, words such as 'primitiveness' and 'laziness' occur frequently in the reports of travellers familiar with peasant culture. A classic example of this is I. M. Maiskii, who dealt with this theme at the beginning of the twentieth century. He writes:

> The main characteristic and the basis of the mentality of the Mongols is undoubtedly passiveness. This is a result of the natural

environment and of the people's history ... Passiveness, which from the viewpoint of Europeans is somewhat strange and incomprehensible, is to be seen everywhere. When one considers their state or economic organisation, their religious belief or their laws and customs, one finds everywhere, literally everywhere, submission and indifference. It could be that these characteristics are more marked in the area of livestock keeping than in other areas ... The form of Mongolian livestock keeping at present is extremely primitive. In the true sense of the word, it is a prehistoric form which requires hardly any human labour ...

With the passiveness of the Mongols another characteristic, namely a basic laziness, is connected. One cannot maintain, however, that Mongols are not capable of work. When brutal reality demands work (e.g. when they are underway in caravan), they can work long and hard. But in principle they do not like working because they dislike every sort of agitation and prefer idling. The German proverb 'work makes life sweet' does not apply to them, they are absolutely not in the position to even understand it. (Maiskii 1921: 32ff.)

We believe that he should rather have described the situation in relation to the milieu of the nomads. In this connection Maiskii writes:

The value of time in such a way of life is zero, even less than zero, sometimes it is an unknown dimension. The famous American proverb 'time is money' is fully comprehensible for Europeans, the reverse seems however to be the case for Mongols. For them it is: 'time is not money'. (Maiskii 1921: 35)

Maiskii does not regard the behaviour of nomads in terms of the particularities of nomadic livestock keeping as compared with agriculture; rather, he seeks to define the general character of the people. However, the milieu of the people has to be taken into consideration. Production activity in livestock keeping can indeed be best described as being both effective and ineffective.

Expenditure of labour differs depending on the season and the separate types of activity. The image of a shepherd sitting near his grazing sheep, chatting the day away or snoozing, does in fact represent nomadic livestock keeping work, and such images are characteristic. The search for lost or stolen animals (mostly horses or camels) takes a long time and the livestock keeper can be gone for weeks on end. As the SHM shows, this was also true in early times (SHM, §90). Bringing animals to the market (Mong. *mal tuukh*) has been a form of work for centuries in

Mongolian livestock keeping. All this is livestock keeping activity and has economic significance.

Labour relating to production in Mongolian livestock keeping can be categorised according to day and season. The daily work programme of nomadic livestock keeping – keeping watch, watering, driving, milking, etc. – requires, in comparison with agriculture, little physical exertion. But livestock keeping has no seasonally dependent suspension of the work programme as occurs in agriculture. If one considers the amount of exertion required by Mongolian nomads, then one finds many situations that require physical work, for example putting cows out to pasture, putting calves to pasture separately from their dams, putting small animals to pasture, checking on large animals grazing overnight, fetching cows and calves, fetching small animals and driving them into stalls, etc.

Seasonal labour consists of shearing wool, cutting hair, tending young animals, making dairy produce, breaking in horses, gathering hay, building stalls, migrating to the summer, autumn, winter, spring sites, etc. Within each season, in addition to daily and seasonal work, other activities demanded by the season are also carried out.

Division of labour according to age and sex
Children and youth

The main burden of the daily tending of animals rests on children and the youth among Mongolian nomads. Owing to the high economic value of the labour of children and young people in general in nomadic cultures, there is a close relation between polygamy, abundance of children and abundance of animals.

Children gain at an early age a basic knowledge of nomadic practice and are incorporated into the working process. As young animal tenders they carry out a perilous task in view of the threat of predators and also of thieves. At which age they perform which tasks, especially boys, depends on the nature of the animals – their age, size and docility – as well as on the degree of difficulty of tending and on the labour potential of the nomadic community. Small children from about the age of 4 onwards accompany their older siblings for short periods to the closest pasture and help in the caring of the animals in the vicinity of the *yurt*s. Boys and girls between 5 and 7 years of age keep watch over sheep, goats and calves at first in hearing distance of the *yurt* site, later on more distant pastures. Because children learn to ride at a very early age, they have no difficulty in accompanying others to distant pastures and in bringing back small animals and calves. They learn to ride as early as the age of 3 and from the age of 4 can ride alone. This is a longstanding tradition. As chronicles (e.g. *Yisuji, Hei Da shilüe*), the traveller's reports of Carpini and Rubruck, etc. relate, this was customary even in the thirteenth century (Risch 1930: 105; Serruys 1945: 153; Olbricht and Pink 1980: 165). From about the age of 8, boys are normally entrusted with the grazing of small animals and also regularly tend cattle. Boys from the age of 10 help in the keeping of calves and in milking. Later, when they are stronger and more experienced, they help in the tending of foals. This was also the case in early times, as is illustrated by the depiction in the SHM of a young man milking mares (SHM, §90), and can also be inferred from other chronicles (Risch 1930: 105). Collecting dried dung is almost exclusively children's work.

Men's work

Because children carry out the daily tending of animals as a rule, adult men or heads of family participate in this activity only under exceptional circumstances, for example when there is a shortage of labour or when physical strength is required. Not infrequently, men milk camels and mares. In early times men were in principle responsible for this task. In his travel report dating from 1245–47 Carpini writes about the Mongols that the milking of mares was solely the affair of men (Risch 1930: 105). Their main tasks are as a rule the planning, organisation and control of the production process, digging wells, the *otor* migration when necessary, leading caravans and driving animals to distant markets. The working time of men in the economy is difficult to ascertain because, as we have already mentioned, expenditure of labour in some activities is low, and it is sometimes doubtful whether such activities actually constitute work or not.

Women's work

Women play a secondary role in the tending of animals. They have important tasks within the site in addition to household chores, for example, the making of clothes and the caring of young animals. They are also responsible for the milking of animals, the processing of hides and the production of felt. As a rule, women milk all animal species: cows, mares, camels and ewes. The milking of mares in the thirteenth century, however, was not women's work. Because men are often away searching for lost horses, camels or cattle, women often also have to perform men's tasks. It is not unusual for women to pitch *yurts* and load camels and horses, but only rarely do they catch and break horses. The difference between economic and household tasks of women is in some cases negligible.

Early form of social organisation of labour

A peculiarity of nomadic livestock keeping is revealed in its organisation of labour. In order to ensure the autarchic way of life of roaming tribes, it was necessary that groups were sufficiently large and structured in an appropriate manner. Although the family community changed its character through time, it survived as a way of life. Such a migrating community was indivisible as a type of workers' cooperative.

In the course of the long development of traditional nomadic livestock keeping, a social structure was formed which optimally ensured production in the face of conditions that are totally dependent upon the natural environment. This structure had however different forms and names in the various periods of history.

Social differentiation in the tribal society of Mongolia enabled the emergence of a sort of community composed of small groups that possessed their own stock independently of the tribe. In order to ensure the independent way of life of migrating tribes, it was necessary that they be divided further into migration groups which were structured so as to preserve the form of livestock keeping. Such migration groups were at the same time workers' cooperatives. Chronicles, which report on the oldest of such workers' cooperatives, speak of the *khüree* as a migration group of the twelfth century: this consisted of several hundred paternally and maternally related members. There are also reports that the *khüree* existed before the Mongols for several generations of the nomad kingdoms (Rashid ad-Din 1952: vol. 1, bk 2: 94; Sükhbaatar 1971: 157). The gradual differentiation of family ownership of stock and of family household played a decisive role in the breaking up of the *khüree* community into *ail* – a nomadic family[11] of separate families. After the middle of the thirteenth century, the *khüree* is no longer mentioned in the sources. Instead of it we find *ail*, whereby a smaller migration grouping is meant. Probably the *khüree* began to lose its significance from this time. According to some scholars, the first forms of the *ail* existed already within the *khüree* (Vladimircov 1934: 37). Owing to the strict tribal structure, however, they certainly would have had no independence within the *khüree*. Only after after the middle of the thirteenth century was the *ail* the predominant form of the organisation of labour. The meaning of the term *ail* then differed from what is meant today by the word – a family. To the *ails* of that time belonged a group of families which possessed common property and were characterised by close family relations (SHM, §§98, 99, 100).

Khot-ail *as social organisation of labour*

With the establishment of Manchurian policy, Mongolia was administratively, territorially and economically subordinated to the Manchurian system. This led gradually to a social and economic crystallisation of pastoral nomadism, whereby it was attempted to retain the classical traditional *ail* grouping in the economically and quite strongly institutionalised form of *khot-ail*.[12]

Many research works conducted in the last few years convey the impression that agricultural, socio-economic institutions of nomadic livestock keeping in Mongolia are structured in a logically increasing manner: *ail* (livestock keeping family); *khot-ail* (group of livestock keeping families); *saakhalt-ail* (neighbouring group of livestock keeping families); and *neg-usnykhan* or *neg-nutgiinkhan* (livestock keeping families from a region), the last being the largest institution. This representation may appear systematic but does not correspond to reality. In our opinion the last two terms, *saakhalt-ail* and *neg-nutgiynkhan* or *neg-usnykhan*, do not describe socio-economic units of livestock keeping at all. They were, and are today, rather abstract terms only used ethnologically and do not represent an institutionalised social and economic union of livestock keeping families. Despite the fact that Mongolian nomads have been organised militarily-administratively or territorially-administratively as a result of certain policies throughout their history, their socio-economic organisation has been quite simple as a rule. In this respect *khot-ail* has been the main and sole effective socio-economic institution since the 1850s.

The term *khot-ail* however did not appear until the middle of the nineteenth century. Instead there was another term which in principle can be equated with it. The word *khot* (or *khotong*) had long been used as an ethno-linguistic concept to describe the *yurt* site and the stock fold. For example, *khot* was used frequently in important chronicles from the thirteenth to the seventeenth centuries. In the code of laws 'Mongol-Oirat Regulations of 1640',[13] the terms *otog*[14] and *aimag* (Alinge 1934: 55; Dylykov 1981: 8, 14–17, 23–37) appear frequently and without doubt are directly connected with the description of small nomadic groups (see also Bold 1996: 71ff.).

In this regulation the term *ail* no longer had anything to do with the group of livestock keeping families in its original sense, but had clearly come to signify small family associations (Dylykov 1981: 12, 23, 37) consisting of separate families *örkh* (Dylykov 1981: 76–77). Belonging to a group was not only necessary for the livestock keeper for economic reasons, but also served the interests of the state since as a result of increasing connections, the tax obligations of livestock keepers to princes and the state could be better supervised. For this reason livestock keepers had to be organised as groups. The regulation states:

> If an individual livestock keeper of his own accord leaves his *khoshuu*[15] for a neighbouring one and settles between the two *khoshuus*, he must be brought back. If he does not belong to an *otog*, let him belong to an *otog*. If he does not belong to an *aimag* (in the *otog*), let him belong to an *aimag* (Dylykov 1981: 117).

In the course of the development of Mongolian nomadic society, the interior network of the *khot-ail* union attained a new dimension, in which both the economic and individual dependence between common livestock keepers and steppe princes increased. In statute books, such as *Khalkha Jirum* (Statute book of the Outer Mongolia), the term *aimag* was no longer used in the sense of a nomad group but rather in the sense of a larger territorial-administrative unit in a rural area. It is interesting that in *Khalkha Jirum* the terms *khot* in the sense of a family group and *khotyn akh* (leader of the family group) appear for the first time (Zamcarano 1959: 10). In legal files from the end of the eighteenth century, which contain complaints about pastoral areas, the term '*khot* people' (Mong. *khot khün*), which also means nomad group, can be found. For example a livestock keeper of the Delegdorz *khoshuu* of the Sain Noyan Khan *Aimag* uses very frequently the expression '*khot* people' in his charge of October 1791 (Sharkhüü 1975: 21, 23, 26).

The *khot* unit reflected the basic politico-economic changes of the country in the course of the eighteenth century.

The social function and significance of the *khot-ail* unit can in general be described as follows:

- *Economic relations* between livestock keepers, such as constant or seasonal co-operation in times of migration, marketing of products, construction of winter and spring stables, laying in of the hay supply, digging of wells, shearing of wool, etc. Moreover, it may be assumed that the improvement of stock pedigree by

means of selective breeding was part of the economic co-operation between livestock-owning families.
- *Family relations* of different degrees. These created an environment where members were ethically strongly bound to one another, being reliable and responsible for one another. This guaranteed the stability of the community household. Mutual obligation and responsibility are important prerequisites for livestock keepers to be able to continue with their livelihood.
- *Communication function.* Khot-ail was also an important social environment for the exchange of information and experience and for the training of future livestock keepers. There were various forms in which this exchange could take place, such as get-togethers of various sorts, common seasonal pastures (summer and autumn pastures), etc.
- *Demographic equilibrium.* Khot-ail was a socio-demographic unit. Because the co-operation of labour of mobile livestock keeping formed the basis of the *khot-ail* union, the suitable demographic organisation of labour, i.e. the labour of men, women and children, was not without significance. By means of this, the structure of the sexes and of age of the rural population, and also its growth were regulated.
- *Socio-psychological function.* Traditional, ethical relations amongst live-stock keepers made for a peaceful living together in the use of pastoral regions, etc. Various problems could arise in the use of pasture land; these could be regulated by the traditional ethical norms of the nomadic way of life.
- *Political significance.* Military, administrative, territorial, economic, etc. regulation of livestock keepers.

Economic background of the khot-ail *union*

The main principles of the existence and activity of the *khot-ail* unions were above all based on economic interests. The inclusion of additional labour of this or that form within a household had at all times great economic importance in Mongolian nomadic livestock keeping. The livestock economy was extensive, for which reason a large amount of labour was required. The prerequisite for co-operation within a *khot-ail* was therefore determined by economic interests, of which the quantity of livestock formed a basis. The spectrum of such interests according to the supply of livestock can be represented in the following way:

1. The interests of livestock keepers with a large quantity of stock: the larger the household, or the larger the size of the herds, the greater are the problems of labour. This means that families who own much livestock very often suffer of a shortage of labour and are therefore anxious to co-operate with families with few animals and thus having labour to spare.

2. Families of average wealth have co-operated with one another for the most part in the area of livestock supply, since the amount of required labour within a family has corresponded in general to the size of the family household. This form of *khot-ail* co-operation has not spread to a great extent. Many average families manage alone or support one another occasionally during the difficult seasonal periods of livestock keeping. There are also other interests for those joined in this manner. The mingling of stock creates favourable conditions for grazing and tending for all parts. There is a good deal of experience amongst livestock keepers of the mutual hygienic influences and nutritional effects when different types of animals mix, as well as of the need for the regeneration of vegetation resources in the pastoral regions. Thus an optimal mix of animal types is one of the motivations amongst livestock keepers of average wealth behind a common household or a bringing together of livestock. This sort of *khot-ail* co-operation is in our opinion more desirable today.

3. Poor families were almost always connected to wealthy families in a *khot-ail*. This system was extensive until the 1950s. When poor families possessed a small quantity of livestock sufficient for their livelihood, they stood only in an economic relation to the wealthy families. In this case their labour obligations to the wealthy were accepted under limited conditions. When poor families were not able to subsist by themselves, due to an insufficient quantity of stock, they were linked with the wealthy families both economically and privately.

Family relations within the khot-ail

In research investigations two opinions in essence are proposed concerning the nature of the *khot-ail*:

- Family membership formed the core of the *khot-ail* and was closely linked with traditional family ordering. This opinion prevailed amongst scholars in the 1930s.
- The grouping was more a form of economically determined organisation of labour. Investigations since the 1950s concluded

that the *khot-ail* was shaped more strongly by economic influences.

These different opinions show that in descriptions of the *khot-ail*, the problem of whether to emphasise the economic or the social side arises. In our view the *khot-ail*, just as the *khüree*, should be characterised by both its economic and its social functions, although the economic motivation was the essence of a *khot-ail* union. This economically motivated co-operation between livestock-keeping families was as a rule built upon the basis of family relations under the conditions of traditional nomadic livestock keeping.

There were three variations of amalgamation within a *khot-ail*:

1. *khot-ail* based on family relations;

2. *khot-ail* based on a core of related families to which additional unrelated families had linked;

3. *khot-ail* composed essentially of unrelated families: although some families might have been related this played little role in the community.

Although all these variations existed more or less at the same time, it can be seen that on account of prevailing economic and political conditions, one or the other came to predominate. They also represent the continual loss of significance of family relations within the *khot-ail*. The first variation predominated in the first half of the nineteenth century. The significance of traditional, descendant family groupings grew ever smaller in the course of time. In the nineteenth century both descendant and collateral relations were to be seen in family groups. The inclusion of Mongolia into the field of influence of international finance and the country's development in the period from the second half of the nineteenth century to the beginning of the twentieth century as a source of raw materials and as a market for capitalist powers such as Tsarist Russia, the USA, Great Britain, Japan and China, intensified the country's economic crisis. This had an effect upon the economic situation of the *khot-ail*. High taxes of various sorts, other obligatory contributions and growing economic pressure to increase the supply of livestock and the resulting demand for labour all forced livestock keepers within the household co-operation of the *khot-ail* to give priority to economic concerns. It therefore happened that the second and later the third variation of *khot-ail* spread. In these second and third variations there was, however, quite often a connection of friendship. It is nonetheless worth mentioning that there were individual livestock-keeping families not associated with any cooperative household until the formation of the collectives at the end of the 1950s.

Family relations of a traditional sort have today been loosened. Rural social structuring is no longer determined by close blood relations. There is hardly a single social segmentation unit that consists of descendant groupings – if there is such a group, then its inner structure and function bear no resemblance to the traditional form.

Within a *khot-ail* union one family played a leading role in the end. The head of this family was normally the leader of the *khot-ail*. There were, however, various criteria to determine who should be the *khot-ail* leader.

Birth. In the *khot-ail* union until the nineteenth century, in which descent strongly predominated, the son and heir took over the responsibility of the *khot-ail* leadership. As a rudiment of this tradition the name *akh* (older brother) was used amongst livestock keepers of the Khangai Mountain regions until the Negdel period at the beginning of the 1930s. In later times this epithet had hardly any connection to traditional descendence. The names *akh* and *akhlagch* (leading brother, leader) had the same meaning and were both used, the difference residing only in the size of the unit. For example, *akh* was used for the designation of the leader of a small group and *akhlagch* for a larger group. Even in the seventeenth century these different meanings existed. This is shown by the fact that the terms *ailyn akh* and *aimgiin akhlagch* frequently appear in the 'Mongol-Oirat Regulations of 1640' (Dylykov 1981: 98, 111, 120).

Wealth. Since wealthy families mostly formed the core of a *khot-ail*, the head of the economically leading family came also to be the leader of the *khot-ail*. A social precondition for this was that either family relations had been increasingly neglected or that the families were not at all related.

Experience and authority. In a case where neither of the above situations applied, a leader was chosen by the influential persons in the *khot-ail* according to his experience, competence, affability, loyalty, etc.

Appropriate size of a khot-ail

From the research material of the 1930s it is possible to estimate the size of a *khot-ail*. The number of families in a *khot-ail* depended upon prevailing natural conditions. In the mountain and the mountain steppe zones, a *khot-ail* with six or seven livestock-keeping families in summer and autumn, and with two or three in winter and spring, was regarded as appropriate. In the Gobi region a *khot-ail* consisted mostly of two or three families, in which respect the ecological conditions of the Gobi had a determining effect. On account of the sparse vegetation per unit of pasture area and of poor soil fertility, it was preferable to make use of pasture land in separate families or small family circles. Also livestock keepers were obliged to migrate constantly since quite large pasture areas were required, and it is more suitable to do so either separately or in small family groups. For these reasons large *khot-ail* unions are not characteristic of the Gobi region. This all indicates that the number of families belonging to a *khot-ail* stood in close relation to the extent of available pasture land.

Thus the number of families in a *khot-ail* was essentially determined by the following factors:

- an economic interest in optimal labour co-operation and the least possible expenditure of labour in livestock keeping;

- the extent of the prevailing pastoral region: in order to limit the number of migrations within a pastoral area which provides a sufficient yearly feed supply, the number of connected families had to be optimised according to this pastoral region;

- the need for a certain type and quantity of stock: for an optimal use of pasture land with respect to the types of animals, for the food supply, for the creation of favourable conditions for breeding stock, for the availability of pack animals for migration, etc., the type and quantity of stock of the connected families had to be considered;

- optimal adjustment of the distribution of the sexes and of age of the available labour to the sort and expenditure of the required labour of the respective *khot-ail* also played a great role.

Right of a khot-ail *to use a pastoral region*

Traditionally the *khot-ail* used definite pastoral regions for their seasonal migrations. Suitable pastoral region of a *khoshuu* was divided amongst the *khot-ail*s. Official files show that from the end of the eighteenth century until 1932 throughout the various parts of the various *khoshuu*, assemblies of livestock keepers took place in the presence of those responsible for the respective *khoshuu*, during which pastoral regions were divided amongst *khot-ail* unions. These files also show that, with this division of pasture land, borders were determined by mountain crests, stone piles and rivers. Livestock keepers at first mutually respected their pastoral regions and in principle did not cross the borders. But with the increase of territorial-administrative units in the nineteenth century, whereby the pasture area necessary for the yearly seasonal migrations was not always zonally well considered, the traditional use of pasture land became problematic. This is indicated by the fact that from the second half of the nineteenth century the winter site was designated in most cases by the name of its owner.

In legal regulations there are two different designations for pasture land: *ötög-buuc* (winter–spring site) and *bilcheer-us* (summer-autumn pasturage). In the *ötög-buuc* one had a permanent abode at one's disposal. Despite the fact that livestock keepers sometimes grazed their stock at a distant site alone for weeks on end, in principle they remained stationary at the *ötög-buuc* the entire winter. In *bilcheer-us* – the pasture sites were often changed. A *khot-ail* therefore had *ötög-buuc* as well as *bilcheer-us*. The distances in this respect between *khot-ail*s were different in the differing geographical zones. At the beginning of the 1930s, the Soviet scholar A. D. Simukov reported in his study of the Southern Gobi region that the distances between the *ötög-buuc* of the *khot-ail* amounted to 7–10 km, in some cases 15 km (Simukov 1933; 1934; 1935; 1936).

Probably only the horizontal distance between the *khot-ail* was considered here. Because the *khot-ail* traditionally used pasture land directed altitudinally between the highlands and the lowlands, distances between *khot-ail*s would have been much greater. There is, however, only poor research material concerning this question, and such distances can only be estimated by the lengths of the annual migrations of the *khot-ail*s.

Other Economic Forms

The most important economic activities of livestock breeders apart from keeping livestock were hunting and gathering. All this was organised in the framework of familial production forms. Only a complex co-operation in hunting, which at the same time was a prerequisite for readiness for battle, went beyond the framework of the household. Economically regarded, this activity was, however, not the principal production form. Archaeological finds demonstrate that agriculture also existed, even if it was not universally and continuously carried out. Handicraft in the form of the production of necessary household apparatus and tools has always played a role amongst the nomads. All these economic forms, which for a long time existed side by side amongst the Central Asian peoples, were determined by nomadic livestock keeping. Those economic forms that were necessarily combined with nomadic livestock keeping, were able to develop continuously and were functionally adapted to the nomadic way of life. In this respect it should be noted that livestock keeping was only supplemented by the other economic forms, which thus bore the character of auxiliary economic activities.

Hunting

Nomadic livestock keeping was the predominant but not the sole economic form amongst the Mongols. From the sources we know that for thousands of years pre-Mongolian and Mongolian peoples, especially those who lived in the north of the Central Asian region near the border to Siberia, principally carried out hunting (*Iletkhel Shastir*, bk 63; Vladimircov 1934: 40–42; Shagdarsüren 1988: 113).

As we have already mentioned, hunting was only a secondary economic activity in comparison with livestock breeding in the Central Asian region. It was almost always combined with nomadic livestock keeping and served in times of need to satisfy requirements for food, clothing, etc.

It took two forms: individual hunting and hunting in large groups. The former was carried out in order to obtain meat and hides, the latter served in addition as a sporting activity and also as means of training for battle.

After the collapse of the great empire, the Mongols lost their unity of organisation and there was thus no longer a need to hunt in large groups in order to train for battle. Hence this form of hunting gradually declined.

There are hardly any references to hunting in large groups in Mongolia after the Manchurian conquest. From the eighteenth century there are some known reports concerning hunting co-operation between Buryats and hunting co-operation in the name of the Manchurian emperor. From the nineteenth century onwards hunts in large groups were remembered as historical heroic deeds (Vladimircov 1934: 192). Individual hunting on the other hand continued in addition to livestock keeping.

Agriculture

As mentioned above, archaeological finds demonstrate that before the development of nomadic livestock keeping, agriculture was carried out by Central Asian peoples, even if not universally and continuously. After the institutionalisation of nomadic livestock keeping as the principal economic activity, agriculture became a sideline occupation, mainly because extensive parts of the Central Asian highlands were rendered unsuitable due to climatic changes and the resulting soil composition and short period of vegetation. Climatic conditions such as extremely hot weather and low precipitation do not favour agriculture. Only areas near rivers and lakes can regularly support this land use. Sources dating from the eleventh and twelfth centuries give information about where millet, barley and wheat were cultivated in Mongolia: along the Selenge, Khalkha, Kherlen, Orkhon and Zavkhan Rivers and in the vicinity of Lake Buir (SHM, §152; *Mengu-u-mu-tschzi* 1895: 402, 438–39; Perlee 1960: 32; Perlee 1961: 91–92). In the SHM it is written that in the Mongolian Empire agriculture was carried out in order to guarantee food supplies for the troops (SHM, §279). This was further developed in the course of the Yuan dynasty (1271–1368) (*Yuanshi*, vols 21, 24, 26).

Unfortunately we have little information about how agriculture developed from the second half of the fourteenth century up to the seventeenth century. There is evidence that agriculture revived after the seventeenth century (Posdne'ev 1883: 188; Buyanchigulgan 1934: 14; Buyanchigulgan, man. vol. 1, ch. 5; *Iletkhel Shastir*, bk 45: 17–18; Nasanbaljir 1961: 14, 52).

At the start of their rule, the Manchu did not support the development of agriculture in Khalkha Mongolia in any way. Shortly afterwards their policy changed. We know from the sources that in 1715 the Emperor Kangxi (1662–1722) commissioned the 4th Tüsheet Khan of Khalkha Mongolia, Vangjaldorji, to prepare suitable regions of his district for agriculture. This was carried out without hesitation and evoked neither astonishment nor displeasure (*Iletkhel Shastir*, bk 45: 17–18). It is also known that the Qing emperor maintained barracks in Khalkha Mongolia until 1911, and thus millet, barley and wheat were cultivated there. Products such as tea, rice, etc. were imported mainly from neighbouring Chinese, Muslim and, from the second half of the seventeenth century, Russian regions, mostly in exchange for live animals and animal produce or for silver.

Handicraft

It may be assumed that the Mongols have carried out handicraft since ancient times in order to produce objects and tools for their own needs. For this, simple forms of the division of labour developed that were both necessary and possible in the nomadic way of life. As V. Ronge characterises it: 'They are compelled by their specialised economic form to keep their households to a minimum and to adapt their material culture functionally and rationally to the requirements of an essentially mobile way of life' (Ronge 1986: 125). All the items required for daily use were made from wool, leather, horn, felt, wood, bark: i.e. from available natural raw materials. Saddles, bows and arrows, simple furniture, storage receptacles, *yurt* frames, etc. were fashioned from wood. There are sources that report that since about the tenth century, objects for household use were made of iron and bronze (Kazakevich 1934: 10; Bichurin 1950: 344). After the establishment of the Mongolian Empire, the production of household objects was extended and gradually assumed the character of a more or less organised form of production. The *Yuanshi* reports, for example, about the specialisation of the production of weapons (*Yuanshi*, vol. 98).

Archaeological finds from Kara-Korum demonstrate that a handicraft centre was located there and a large number of foreign craftsmen worked in it, prisoners (Chinese, French, Hungarian, Russian and Persian) amongst them. Prisoners from German-speaking countries, for example, were forced to mine for gold and to produce weapons for the Mongols (Rockhill 1967: 137). During the Yuan dynasty, the handi-craft trade played a similarly important role. In 1262 Khublai Khaan provided for the establishment of a state felt factory which is thought to have employed 29,000 workers and whose task was to supply the court with felt carpets.

After the collapse of the Yuan dynasty in 1368, there was no continuous development of the organisation of handicraft. Depending on political circumstances in Mongolia, it slackened off or revived. As long as nomadic livestock keeping was the dominant economic form, the development of handicraft remained dependent upon it.

In considering the development of handicraft, the influence of Buddhism should also be taken into account. Specialised craftsmen, artists and master builders constructed buildings in the style of monumental art. It should be understood that under the influence of Buddhism, handicraft gradually began to play a large role in the nomadic way of life.

3. Socio-Political Organisation in the Development of Mongolia

Features of Mongolian Tribal Organisation
Mongolian Tribes and Their Relations

Reports about Mongolian tribes are too inadequate to describe past reality in full. Nevertheless, it is possible with the help of records and reports such as the SHM and 'Collection of Histories' to learn something about the character of Mongolian tribes from the twelfth century onwards.

The words *obog, omog* and *urug* are often encountered in the SHM and are used as generally known terms. The first two are actually synonyms, owing to a possible confusion of the consonants b and m in Mongolian orthography (Gongor 1978: 6). *Obog* or *omog* designated a group that was related by blood. *Urug* denoted a group that was related mostly patrilinearly, sometimes bilaterally (Vladimircov 1934: 59–60; Ramstedt 1935: 451; Nominkhanov 1975: 69–70). As a result *obog* and *urug* are used almost interchangeably in the sources.

Also the terms *khari* and *jida* (foreign) are encountered in the SHM and relate to *obog* and *urug*. They are also synonyms in their principal meaning (Gaadamba 1990: 109, 238; Ardajab 1986). According to the SHM, an *obog* or *urug* used these words to express its relationship to a foreign group (SHM, §§40, 42, 43). However it could well be that this meaning merely reflects the subjective viewpoint of the author.

The essence of the Mongolian *obog* can be characterised as follows:

- The ancient Mongolian tribe or *obog* usually consisted of patrilinear descendants, *yasan töröl*. It was thus an agnatic kinship group.
- Each tribe had its own name which was its symbolic characteristic. As a rule the name was connected with the totem of the way of life, activities, deeds of battle and other features.
- Each tribe lived in its own region, whereby the region was not understood as its 'property' but as the natural region where it had led its nomadic existence since ancient times.
- Each tribe had its council which was known by the names *ey-e*, *eyedekhüi* and later *khurildai*. The council nominated a leader, khaan, who stood at the head during large-scale migrations and raids and in times of war.
- Each tribe worshipped the sky and certain natural objects, for example a tree or a mountain, and various animals. This type of belief has been described by historians as a form of Shamanism. The shamans, *böge* or *bögechi*, had a great influence on tribal matters. The Mongolian word *böge* or *bögechi* is always mentioned in connection with the *onggod*,[1] the spirits, in local dictionaries.
- The inner unity of a tribe was expressed by certain symbols, for example *takhilga* (offering), *süld* (genius) and *tug* (banner) (Gongor 1978: 9). It was typical for each tribe that *süld*s and *tug*s were evoked for protection in battles as well as for other purposes, for example for help in hunting.[2]
- The members of a tribe formed an ethnic, moral and linguistic unit. Accordingly they had common dances, songs and nuptial and funeral customs.
- It can also be assumed that each tribe had its own seal (Perlee 1976: 8).

Anda

It is written in the SHM that peaceful relations of an *obog* with another *obog* or between members of different *obog*s or *urug*s were described as *anda* or *andagar* (brotherhood or blood brotherhood). In order to create this connection a ritual was carried out according to Shamanistic and ethnically traditional custom. At the conclusion the person concerned drank a drop of the other's blood as a symbolic sign of the brotherhood. This ritual was conducted for example at the formation of the *anda* between Vang Khan and Temüjin. As a token of genuine brotherhood valuable objects were exchanged (SHM, §§116, 117, 178). During the formation of the *anda*, an oath was sworn (SHM, §177), in which mutual assistance was guaranteed (Barkmann 1991). A relationship of friendship comprised peacefulness, assistance in the event of enemy attack, and also support in combat during revenge raids or conquests. The fact that the last attribute of the anda is mainly mentioned in sources dating from the eleventh and twelfth centuries, is in our opinion due to the historical conditions of this period.

Ösh

In contrast to *anda*, *ösh* was a hostile relationship between individual persons or tribes. The cause of such relationships has its roots in the course of history of Central Asian nomadism: a tribe that had conquered another forced the latter into a federation and via its demands laid the foundation for further hostilities. Such an enmity existed for example between the Mongols on the one side and the Tartars on the other (SHM, §199). Under certain conditions revenge between members of a blood brotherhood was also possible.

Elchin

According to reports from the SHM, there were envoys who conveyed messages between both friendly and enemy tribes. For the long time the function of envoys was to relay messages, call for a common battle against enemies, demand support for raids, and advise on economic problems. In the SHM, two forms of conveyance of messages are described, viz. the speech and the song (SHM, §§107, 129, 132, 141, 177, 181, 199, 265).

We have unfortunately little information from which we can infer conditions of ownership and social differences within tribes. In the early twelfth century, a tendency of dissolution of large tribes into smaller units emerged. On account of this, the ruling class, the steppe aristocracy, increased in number. This class was ethnically determined and can be described more as a blood-related union than as a socially or economically defined grouping. Mongolian tribes, however, were not merely groups of related people. At the same time they formed quasi-political units, just as earlier Central Asian nomadic tribes had done.

As the old patriarchal tribal organisation gradually ceased to be a quasi-political unit in the course of time, the term *obog* remained as a family name or patronym.

The tribal federation

The term *aimag* is often encountered in sources such as the SHM and the 'Collection of Histories'. In our opinion this word is connected with the transformation of the social structure of nomadic society. However an *aimag* cannot be regarded as the next chronological stage of tribal amalgamation. The existence of a tribe or of an *aimag* in nomadism has no direct connection with the ordered transition of tribal organisation into tribal federation in the path towards class-organised society, as has frequently occurred in history. Several research investigations, which have methodologically followed a linear development model, for example the theory of socio-economic formation, have attempted to show that the emergence of the *aimag* was a transition from primitive society or tribal organisation to the next development stage.

The meaning of this term has changed in the course of history. In the twelfth century an *aimag* was understood as a group of *ails*, which were essentially blood-related, and of related tribes (Vladimircov 1978: 27). In addition, *ails* and individual persons, who normally would have been members of another kinship group, could also have belonged to an *aimag*. The *aimag* was an extended form of a tribe or a transitional form to a tribal federation. We are of the opinion that tribes were spontaneously formed by close kinship relations, while tribal federations were formed more or less 'compulsorily'. There existed smaller *aimag*s, like the Khori-Tümed, the Khonkhirad and the Aukhan, as well as larger ones such as the Gurvan Merget, Dörvön Oirat, Kereit, Ongud, Yesen Tartar and Khamag Mongol.[3] A large *aimag* can be described as tribal federations that represented a considerable step towards political unity.

At about the start of the twelfth century, the Tartars lived in the extreme east of today's Mongolia in the vicinity of Lakes Buir and Khülün. The Kereit lived to the west of them, in the region containing the Tuul and Orhon Rivers, the upper Onon and the Kherlen. Further westward, between the Selenge River and the Altai Mountains, lived the Naiman. North of the Khereit and the Naiman were the borders of the regions of the Oirat and the Merget.

The Mongols had no obvious influence in Central Asia before the twelfth century. Their name before the period of Genghis Khaan had an extremely limited area of use and was only applied to the members of a small tribe that lived southeast of Lake Baikal as far as the Khentii Mountains. At the end of the twelfth century however, the Mongols conquered several tribes and formed the first ever federation. Out of this federation the united Mongolian Empire developed at the beginning of the thirteenth century.

The most important features of a tribal federation are set out below.

- In terms of general social structure, there was hardly any difference between a tribal federation and a tribal organisation. It should be noted that tribal federations were not states and the elected khaans were not rulers. They had no powers that could be inherited (Vladimircov 1934: 110). The charisma of rulers was one of the main phenomena of Central Asian history.
- Each federation had its own name. As a rule, this was the name of the tribe that formed the core of the federation. Thus arose, for example, the name 'Monggol' (Mongol)[4].
- A federation had no official documents (Lin Kun and Munkuev 1960: 141) and no written laws (Rashid ad-Din 1952: vol. 1, bk 2: 102).
- Some historians conjecture that each tribal federation had a com-mon language. However, it may be queried whether a common language would have been necessary between tribes if their federation were not economically and culturally connected and if they con-ducted their own affairs independently except in times of war.
- The tribal federations of this period had no standing army.

Ey-e and *khurildai*

The development of a governmental regime is also an important factor in analysing the evolution of political conditions of a society. In the period before the eleventh and twelfth centuries, the Mongols were organised in a politically simple way, partly democratic and partly military. This quasi-democratic form of government is manifested most clearly in the *ey-e* (meeting), in which the majority of the members of the related groupings participated. Unfortunately we have little information concerning the *ey-e* or *eyedekhüi*. For example, in the SHM the word is mentioned only a handful of times. The strengthening of a tribe led to an increase in the size of the ruling class in the *ey-e*. Thus, with the ever growing strength of Mongolian tribes, the *ey-e* was replaced by a larger form of quasi-political assembly, the *khurildai*. All important questions were discussed in the *khurildai*. For example, the Khaan was nominated and decisions concerning raids were made by the *khurildai*. As can be read in the sources, the democratic nature of the *khurildai* revealed itself in the fact that in addition to persons who belonged directly to the

Khaan's family, representatives from the other tribes, all of socially different standing, also participated. The *khurildai* was, however, conducted under the direction and rule of the Khaan. Its democratic character declined in the course of time, which culminated in the golden family (or golden tribe: Mong. *altan urug*) – Borjigin finally exercising absolute power. According to the sources, the *khurildai* continued to meet after the period of Khotul Khaan[5] (*c.* 1130–50) until the sixteenth century.

CHARACTER OF POLITICO-ADMINISTRATIVE ORGANISATION IN THE THIRTEENTH AND FOURTEENTH CENTURIES

Decimally structured administration

The Mongolian system of rule was an attempt to combine the military power of nomadic horsemen with a federal administration founded on fortune, personal charisma and Mongolian traditions which had been adapted to the Central Asian bureaucratic military system of the Huns, Turks, Uigurs and Kidans in an ad hoc manner.

A further attempt to reconstruct the state occurred with the establishment of a central chancellery (*zhongshusheng*) under the direction of the former Jin official, Yelü Chucai, who was appointed in autumn 1231 by Ogadai Khaan in Kara-Korum and was granted a hereditary official title. This was a time when Mongolian rule over the occupied northern Chinese territories was still unstable and the situation demanded a new form of administration. However, the Mongolian and Chinese systems could not be harmoniously united. Attempts to apply principles of nomadic federation to the Chinese led only to confusion and chaos. To the director of the central chancellery, two chancellors, one to the left and one to the right, were thus assigned. The two men appointed to these positions (one from the Khereit tribe and the other from the Jurched tribe) had been, just like Yelü Chucai, secretaries, an office which had been established by Genghis Khaan. The central chancellery represented therefore two functions: to maintain and reconstruct Mongolian institutions and to adapt them to Chinese institutions. Nevertheless the extensively conceived restructuring programme of Yelü Chucai failed. The main cause of this was the steppe tradition of the Mongols which was deeply imbricated with all their customs and habits.

In terms of organisation, the administrative system in Mongolia was structured into groups of ten, hundred, thousand and ten thousand, with a direct conveyance of orders from above to below.

Some researchers believe that this division not only applied to troops but was also a form of administrative organisation for the general populace, an opinion with which we concur. After the split of the Mongolian Empire, this military form of politico-administrative organisation gradually lost its significance. Sources from the seventeenth and eighteenth centuries show clearly that it was civil and not military administration which then took priority. In order to clarify this development, we shall analyse some of the administrative units in more detail.

The decimally structured military administration which was introduced by Genghis Khaan after the establishment of the federation, is the basis for further development of politico-administrative organisation in Mongolia and remained intact throughout the thirteenth century and into the fourteenth century.

The group of ten and the group of a hundred

The group of ten (Mong. *aravt*) and the group of hundred (Mong. *zuut*) were the smallest military-administrative units. They consisted not only of 10 and 100 warriors respectively, but also of a group of nomad families from which the respective warriors could be mobilised. The sources relate no further information about them.

The group of a thousand

The group of a thousand (Mong. *myangat* or *myangan*) was the most important unit. On account of its size, it gave Genghis Khaan an optimal control over his troops. As the SHM reports, Genghis Khaan originally ordered his troops into 95 groups of a thousand. In the period after the establishment of the united Mongolian Empire, this number was increased to 105 (in the year 1206) and to 109 (in the year 1227) (Saiishiyal 1987: 1, 118). With the division of all conquered tribes and tribal federations into 95 groups of a thousand each, Genghis Khaan took into consideration tribal membership and the original homeland. The groups of a thousand, which were divided according to tribal groupings, were designated as *yazagur myangan* (basic groups of ten thousand) (SHM, §§213, 221, 222, 223), to which the members of Genghis Khaan's family belonged. The majority of the groups of a thousand consisted of small tribes or remnants of tribes and were designated as *gadagad myangan* (outer groups of thousand) (ibid.). The group of one thousand was not a purely military unit, but rather a civil one which was obliged to mobilise at least one thousand warriors. After the Yuan dynasty (1271–1368) there is little information about these groups. This is probably connected with the fact that the significance of this form of direct military organisation gradually declined.

There was another form of organisation which had the same rights as the groups of thousand *myangan*, namely the *khishikten* (guards and best warriors). It should however be noted that the *khishikten* differed from the other forms of organisation in being a purely military and permanent establishment. As the sources report, these permanent troop units existed within tribes and tribal federations even before the foundation of the Mongolian Empire. During the Mongolian Empire the *khishikten* consisted of 8,000 *torgud* (strong men) (Drevnetürkskii ... 1969: 588–89) and 2,000 *khorchin* (archers) and *khebtekul* (night-watchmen). After about the end of the thirteenth century there are no more reports about the *khishiktens*. We do however have reports that under Batumünkhe Dayan Khaan[6] in the second half of the fifteenth century there was a unit in the then three eastern groups of thousand that was known as *Khishikten otog*. One may conjecture that this was a remnant of the *khishikten* established by Genghis Khaan.

The group of ten thousand

The group of ten thousand (*tümen* or *tümet*) was the next stage of military-administrative unit and comprised ten groups of one thousand. In none of the sources is it reported exactly how many groups of ten thousand existed in the period of the Mongolian Empire. Some researchers maintain that the 95 groups of thousand were ordered into 10 groups of ten thousand and five groups of one thousand (Saiishiyal 1987: 1, 118). Three of them, namely the eastern, central and western groups of ten thousand had a special significance for Genghis Khaan.

Later sources, which report of so-called *döchin, dörben khoyar* (forty and four) in the second half of the fourteenth century, show that there were 40 eastern and central Mongolian and 4 west Mongolian groups of ten thousand.

The criterion of feudalism in the formation of a feudal state in the thirteenth century

Many presentations of Mongolian history take the stand that the united Mongolian Empire established by Genghis Khaan bore the character of a feudal state. The reason for this is that in the feudalist model of the Marxist formation theory, the feudal state is one of the main elements of feudal society. The question may here be raised, whether the nomadic quasi-state of the thirteenth century should be regarded as a feudal state and to answer this it is first necessary to attempt to define what is meant by a feudal state. In dealing with this problem, one arrives at the basic question of how to understand the term 'state' from the viewpoint of the theory, before a clear notion of the feudal state as a criterion of feudalism can be formed. In research into the emergence and development of the state in Mongolia, this theoretical aspect is not dealt with in depth. Some definitions are oriented towards phenomena such as the formation of a quasi-state apparatus and towards the resulting obligation of independent groups of people to organise themselves so as to defend their region against attacks and to attack other regions.

All this is connected with the basic notion of when the start of the institutionalisation of Mongolian nomadic society should be dated. In research investigations it is assumed that there were two periods during which Mongolian history moved forward.

First, the emergence of the state is regarded in connection with the appearance of the Mongols on the historical stage. In this respect there are two contrary opinions: some scholars identify the emergence of the state with the empire unified by Genghis Khaan at the end of the twelfth century (Munkuev 1970); other scholars link the emergence of the Mongolian state with the Khanate (Nacagdorj 1978: 46–47) that was formed at the start of the thirteenth century. These little differing opinions, however, regard the emergence of the state in the framework of the period when the Mongols established an independent regime, which was a historical event in Central Asia.

Another way to approach the emergence of the Mongolian state is via the period of the Xiongnu dynasty in the third and second centuries B.C. On the basis of research which shows that the Xiongnu dynasty ethnically and linguistically had both Mongolian and Turkish elements, some scholars discuss the question of the emergence of the state in connection with the state organisation of the Xiongnu dynasty. In many investigations the attempt is made to confirm that in the Xiongnu dynasty a state had indeed formed (Ishjamc 1956: 17–38; Dorjsüren 1961: 73–94; Sükhbaatar 1980: 90–91; Taskin 1984: 36). On the other hand, there is also the contention that the society of the Huns was patriarchal (Bernshtam 1951: 129) and took the form of a confederation of *aimag*s (Gumilev 1960: 71–83). Others maintain that the dynasties established by Modun (209 B.C.–A.D. 176) and Attila (ruled A.D. 445–53) and Genghis Khaan failed to achieve the level of state organisation, the last being an old and simple form of transition prior to the emergence of a state. Such opinions are prevalent in research which compares the emergence and development of states and the social evolution of peoples (Herzog 1988: 9).

Some recent research into the formation of state organisation amongst different peoples attempts to describe generally valid features of a state:

- The most important basis for the existence of a state is that one part of the population rules the other. This begins at the time when the former expresses its wishes to the latter as orders. If one regards this condition in isolation from other basic conditions, however, it loses its significance because such a phenomenon exists even before the emergence of a state.

- Another criterion is the level of the ruling class. In other words, an extensive system develops in which many groups with differing duties are gradually organised. Some researchers attempt to demon-trate that the independent manorial system which existed in Europe was a state unit (in the sense of magnitude) or a small-scale manifestation of state.

- Another basic idea, which has dominated research in recent years, is in connection with settlement. Because the organisation, the tasks and the forms of rule of states that existed in the history of settled peoples were more systematic than those of the states in the history of nomads, the theoretical ideas concerning the definition of a state do not apply to the nomadic state.

- The appearance of a state is also to be regarded in connection with its internal sovereignty. This enables the ruling stratum to have power over other groups within strict limits by means of the use of force.

- An important criterion is also that the ruling group has clearly defined functions. Some researchers characterise, according to a comparative analysis of the manifold organisation of a state, economic functions like the cultivation and irrigation of land and socio-economic policy such as defence as imperative functions of a state. Other scholars again do not regard these functions as services belonging unconditionally to a state system.

The above criteria do not represent a complete theoretical explanation of the state but are merely opinions which have been proposed in the course of considering the problem. We believe that it is doubtful that a general theoretical definition is possible.

A general theoretical definition that considers features and events which on the one hand are common to all states and on the other hand appear in different periods, becomes merely an abstract idea. It is too narrow and constrictive. For this reason contrary opinions will always exist. H. Krüger mentions in his book *Allgemeine Staatslehre* that the state in its role as social institution was formed only at the start of the nineteenth century in Europe and afterwards extended throughout the world (Krüger 1964: 39). Some scholars, however, hold a contrary view: 'Everywhere, where a group of people is joined in a binding system and is subject to no other group, i.e. is sovereign, it can be spoken of as a state, at least in a rudimentary form' (Berber 1973: 9).

Taking the above into account, in establishing the criteria according to which 'Mongolian feudalism' arose together with a feudal state, we encounter the following difficulties:

First, the attempt to find a theoretical definition of state applicable to all peoples is questionable. Such a definition can only be achieved in a conventional way.

Second, the attempt to show that feudalism actually existed in Mongolia is directly connected with the attempt to demonstrate, via the Marxist formation theory, that rapid social progress and development were characteristic of the evolution of Mongolian history. If one considers that feudalism was merely one system in the process of social progress (Eder 1980: 104ff.), then there is no need to insist that a feudal state existed in Mongolia. Thus the question whether social progress in Mongolia was achieved via the establishment of a feudal state, may not be amenable to research. R. Herzog writes:

> The reader might ask why seriously-intentioned scholars do not recognise the empires of nomadic peoples – and the empires of Attila and Genghis Khaan to boot – as states and why other scholars define the beginning of the era of states only in modern times, hardly four hundred years ago. If he or she considers the problem, he or she will realise that the notion of state is not unequivocal, and it is not merely the research methods which do not produce exact results – the object of research is not exactly established. (Herzog 1988: 9)

Therefore it should be accepted that the problem of the development of political conditions in Mongolia, just as in pre-Mongolian nomad empires, cannot be investigated from the standpoint of the emergence and development of a state in a general, theoretical sense, but rather as a 'nomad phenomenon' (Orkhon 1992: 10).

The state system in Mongolia in the period of the Yuan dynasty

Due to inadequate reports in the chronicles, it cannot be clearly determined whether the politico-administrative system in the Mongolian homeland adhered to the old system of the former Mongolian Empire or to the administrative structure pertaining to the Chinese part of the regions subject to the Yuan dynasty. In this period Mongolia was not only strictly administered but also became, due to various reasons, a neglected region.

From the end of the thirteenth century to the beginning of the fourteenth century, it was not possible for the government of Khublai Khaan to administer the Mongolian homeland in a politically unified and peaceful manner. Until the final collapse of the resistance of the Mongolian princes to Khublai Khaan in 1310, Mongolia was the battleground of Khublai Khaan, who lived in the capital city Dadu (Peking), and the princes of Genghisic origin in Mongolia, such as his brother Arig-Bukh (d. 1266) and Ogadai's grandson Khaidu (1235–1301). After the final defeat of the main opponent Arig-Bukh, Khaidu was a powerful opponent as the successor of the deceased Khaan Münkhe. Khublai Khaan knew well that the struggle with him would not be an easy or short-lived affair. In fact the Mongolian Empire had expanded to such an extent that Khublai Khaan and his successors were forced to wage intense battles in the years 1286, 1289, 1291, 1300 and 1309, and for a long time the government, consisting of heterogeneous elements, was unable to rule in a unified and central manner. Yesunkhii, Nomgon, Khublai Khaan's youngest son Chingim (d. 1285), Khublai Khaan's third son Gamal (1258–1303), Chingim's oldest son Ölziit-Tömör (1265–1308), Yesun-Tömör (1276–1328) and Badamregzeebuu, Yesun-Tömör's son, who in the years 1260–1328 were responsible for the government of the Yuan dynasty in Mongolia and had their seat in the former capital Kara-Korum, were unable to administer Mongolia successfully because they could not deal with disputes with local Mongolian princes, and indeed with one another, for succession to the throne and exercise of influence in the royal court in Dadu. While those ruling in Kara-Korum were appointed from the royal family and received a special title – *jinvang* – and with it a special right (*Yuanshi*, vol. 115) in the period 1265–1328, Mongolia no longer had any significance in the succeeding period. In 1312 Mongolia was renamed 'Lingbei' (province on the other side of the pass) (*Yuanshi*, vol. 24).

Moreover, there was a growing sympathy among some members of the royal court for the Chinese tradition of state administration, and the struggle between the Chinese-oriented and the Mongolian-oriented parties furthered the decline of Mongolia. After the death of Ölziit-Tömör in 1308, there emerged a conflict of succession in which, for the first time in the history of the Yuan dynasty, two groups came into existence, one supporting the steppe tradition, the other opting for a ruler who would be oriented to the Chinese tradition (Trauzettel 1986: 235–39).

Until the end of the 1320s, the steppe traditionalists managed to suppress the conflict with difficulty. The death of Yesun-Tömör in September 1328 resulted in a second conflict concerning basic political principles between the 'Chinese' faction and the faction of traditional nomadism. In 1329 Yesun-Tömör's eldest son Khoshila (1300–29), pretender to the throne and representative of the traditionalist faction, died, and his brother Tug-Tömör (1304–32), who was a candidate of the Chinese faction, took power. Chinese influence in the political arena thus increased considerably. However, with the death of the ruler in 1332, the old mechanism of cliques grouped about families revived. After the two-month rule of the 6-year-old son of Tug-Tömör, Irinchinbal, the traditionalist line was again taken up with the accession of the 13-year-old Togoon-Tömör, the eldest son of Khoshila, in the year 1333. He ruled until the fall of the Yuan dynasty in 1368. Struggles for political influence between the Chinese faction, the Mongolian traditionalist faction and an ever-growing third group Se-mu-jen, whose members were mainly Muslims, continued however until the end of the Yuan dynasty.

In terms of organisation, administration in Mongolia was simple. Mongolia was one of the 12 provinces (including the central province) of the Yuan dynasty (*BNMAU-yn tüükh* 1966: 305). Just like the other provinces, Mongolia was governed from the provincial chancellery (*hsing zhongshusheng*), which was located in Kara-Korum. In the west of Mongolia, in the southern Altai Mountains, an additional chancellery was later established. The prince to the throne first had to govern in Kara-Korum as the sovereign of Mongolia before he could accede to the throne in Dadu. Chancelleries were led by trusted persons having the high-ranking official title *chinsan*. Thus in Mongolia there were two *chinsan*s – the *chinsan* in the west and the *chinsan* in the east. In 1308, Kharkhasun was appointed *chinsan* of the chancellery in Kara-Korum. Until 1328 the *chinsan* directed the chancellery under the supervision of the sovereign in Kara-Korum, although in this period the latter position was no longer continuously filled. From 1328, after the administration of Badamregzeebuu, princes to the throne were no longer appointed sovereigns of Mongolia in Kara-Korum. In the period of Kharkhasun, Yuchijar was the *chinsan* in the West Mongolian chancellery. The best-known successors were Majirdai and Shirmen in the east and Coros Batula (d. 1416) in the west. These two chancelleries or *chinsan*s continued until the beginning of the sixteenth century. To the eastern part of Mongolia belonged the largest part of Mongolia of today: Central and East Mongolia.

The provincial internal administrative sub-divisions such as *fu*, *chou*, *syan* and *lu*, which were introduced into the Chinese part of the Yuan Empire, did not exist in Mongolia. The term *lu* was used to refer to Kara-Korum and its vicinity: 'Yuanjunlu' (Dalai 1992: 64). Within Mongolia the old military-administrative decimal structuring continued in a somewhat loosened form.

The term *aimag* was frequently used in Mongolia in the period of the Yuan dynasty to describe a sort of administrative unit. While in the eleventh and twelfth centuries an *aimag* was formed from *ail* groups that consisted of related families and tribes, in the Yuan period it had another meaning, although family relations were still taken into consideration. According to the *Yuanshi*, the word *aimag* was used in connection with *olon vang* (many princes), generally in order to emphasise that *aimag* belonged to *olon vang*. *Olon vang* were the people who had close relations to the golden tribe (*altan urug*) of Genghis Khaan, Borjigid, and the term probably arose from the fact that the original title *jinvang* gradually came no longer to be limited to the princes to the throne but to be assigned to high-ranking princes of Genghisic descent. It is reported in the *Yuanshi* that there were 60 *olon vang*s in all (Nacagdorj 1978: 118), of whom 45 were high-ranking princes (*Yuanshi*, vol. 89, 6a). They were divided into three ranks to which the *aimag*s were subordinated according to order of rank, so that each *aimag* bore the name of the nobleman who ruled it. This shows that the *aimag*s were first of all administrative units which were characterised by belonging to noblemen. The continued familial relations within an *aimag* demonstrate that in the nomadic way of life they survived every administrative change.

In the following period, during which Mongolia was named six groups of ten thousand (*zurgaan tümen*), the term *aimag* came to mean a combined form of tribal and quasi-administrative unit within a group of ten thousand.

Administrative Structure from the Fifteenth Century to the First Half of the Seventeenth Century

After the fall of the Yuan dynasty, the weak political unity of Mongolia continued to dissolve. The struggle for the throne intensified. Between the years 1388 and 1466, up to the period of the rule of Batumünkhe Dayan Khaan[6] (1464–1544, ruled 1470–1544), there were 14 khaans, all of whom were either assassinated or fell in the struggle for succession. In this period the throne was often not occupied, and nobody was in a position to bring political unity to the country. At the beginning of the fifteenth century, clashes between East and West Mongolia broke out. The period after the West Mongolian leader Batula-*chinsan* is characterised by such clashes.

In this period the chronicles use the two official titles *chinsan* and *jinon* (prince to the throne) interchangeably. The word *jinon* is a phonetic transformation of the word *jinvang* (Yui-Bayan 1958: 60). This traditional Chinese title was assigned to Mongolian princes in the period of the Yuan dynasty. Probably princes to the throne, who had to first govern in Kara-Korum, were called *chinsan* in Mongolian. After the fall of the Yuan dynasty, the word *jinvang* was no longer used, and in the course of time the word *chinsan* came to be used very seldom.

There are few concrete reports in the chronicles concerning the general state structure in this period. From the end of the fourteenth century there appear general designations for Mongolia such as period of 'the small kings' and 'the northern Yuan', and for the larger internal divisions such as 'forty Mongolian groups of ten thousand' and 'four *oirat* groups of ten thousand' which were probably connected with the name 'forty and four' for a short period during the rule of Esen Khaan in the years 1452–55. There are other designations in the same period concerning the division of Mongolia into east and west, namely 'six Mongolian groups of ten thousand' and 'four *oirat*' or 'four groups of ten thousand', and from this arose, as the eighteenth-century chronicle *Gangiin Uruskhal* reports, a further term 'ten groups of ten thousand' (*arvan tümenulus*) (Gombojab 1960: 63–64). We believe that the use of the term 'six groups of ten thousand' for only the East Mongols was wrong. The reason for this is probably that the term 'six groups of ten thousand', which arose from a later period and applied to both East and West Mongols, was wrongly applied to the preceding period and only in connection with the East Mongols.

It is only after the middle of the fifteenth century that one encounters more precise details, such as 'six groups of ten thousand' or 'six ulus' (six states). The 'three eastern groups of ten thousand' appear in the chronicles also as 'Khalkha', 'Cakhar' and 'Uriankhan'[7] groups of ten thousand or *Ulus*, and the 'three western groups of ten thousand' as 'twelve *tümed*', '*ordos*' and a group of ten thousand from the tribes 'Yunsheebuu', 'Asud' and 'Kharchin'[8]. The term 'group of ten thousand' no longer meant the same as it originally had in the first half of the thirteenth century. We have no definite evidence of whether the term referred to troop units or civil units which were obliged to mobilise ten thousand warriors. However, it appears that the division had an orientation similar to the earlier formed tribal groupings.

Nobody knows exactly when the terms 'group of ten thousand' and *ulus* were first used synonymously. A possible explanation would be that the word *ulus* was used for a long time to designate larger groups of people. It should be here noted that, contrary to modern usage, *ulus* and state had in that period differing meanings. In research investigations *ulus* and 'state' are often equated. Then, however, the word *ulus* had nothing to do with the formation of a state but rather referred to regions with herds and keepers. With the introduction of the military-administrative organisation, the term 'group of ten thousand' became common. With the gradual collapse of this organisation, which was caused by the policy of Mongolian khaans being directed more to inner unity amongst the Mongols than to conquest, the use of the term became questionable. In the fifteenth and sixteenth centuries Batumünkhe Dayan Khaan and Bodi-Alag (1506–47, ruled 1546–47) crushed several groups of ten thousand because they wanted independence. These measures demonstrate that the civil character of groups of ten thousand had become more significant in the administration system. During changes in the civil administrative system, the membership of tribe and *aimag* was always taken into serious consideration (Nacagdorj 1978: 143–44).

The next period of administrative system in Khalkha Mongolia is marked by the emergence of the *khoshuu* and *aimag* as quasi-administrative units. Batumünkhe Dayan Khaan divided Mongolia, which with great difficulty had been brought into unity, amongst his sons. The youngest son of his eleven children, Geresenz (1489–1549), received Khalkha Mongolia, i.e. the 13 *otog* units of the Khalkha tribes, and ruled them as feudal lord in the period 1513–49. Before his death, Geresenz further divided Khalkha Mongolia amongst his seven sons. These seven regions bore the name 'Khalkha seven *khoshuu*'. It is not clear why the word *khoshuu* was used. In addition, other quasi-administrative designations came to be applied. In the chronicles one encounters terms such as *aimag, otog, khoshuu* and *chuulgan*, which are important for explaining the politico-administrative organisation of this period.

Aimag

In the period when Mongolia was called 'six groups of ten thousand', the term *aimag* meant a combined tribal and quasi-administrative unit within a group of ten thousand, similarly to what it meant even in the Yuan period. At the start of the seventeenth century, the meaning of the term changed. Geresenz's grandson, Abtai (1554–88), one of the successors of the *khoshuu* rulers, had, in accordance with tradition of earlier Mongolian emperors, good relations with the Dalai Lama and often had meetings with him. In 1577 the Dalai Lama awarded him the honorary title of 'khan' and he therefore came to be called Tüsheet Khan. With this self-appointment to khan of the most influential of the successors of the seven sons of Geresenz, there arose from the seven *khoshuu*s the first three *aimag*s in Outer Mongolia during the first half of the seventeenth century: Tüsheet Khan *Aimag*, Secen Khan *Aimag*, to each of which one *khoshuu* belonged, and Zasagt Khan *Aimag*, to which four *khoshuu*s belonged. Thus, shortly before the Manchurian conquest, the three large territorial-administrative units were formed in Khalkha Mongolia.

Otog

The word *otog* was used in ancient Turkish, Sogdian and Mongolian for homeland, home, hearth and family. *Otog* was probably initially a rarely used foreign word to describe family relations and then later came to be used to designate an administrative unit. It is however clear that the groups of ten thousand were divided not only into *aimag*s but also into *otog*s. It can be inferred from sources such as *Altan tobchi* (Lu), *Erdeni-yin tobchi, Khalkha-yin üyisen nom Cagaz, Khalkha Jirum* and the 'Mongol-Oirat Regulations of 1640', that this expression came to be used frequently only in the fifteenth and sixteenth centuries. In the SHM and the 'Collection of Histories' the word *otog* does not appear, which implies that before the Yuan dynasty it was not used to designate an administrative unit. From information contained in the sources the following can be ascertained:

- An *otog* consisted of *ail* groups that were related to one another, family relations, however, not being the decisive criterion for the union.
- An *otog* was a unit that was obliged to mobilise a definite number of warriors and to collect taxes (Zamcarano 1959: 50).
- An *otog* was at the same time a quasi-administrative unit ('Mongol-Oirat Regulations of 1640', articles: 122, 125).

After the conference of Dolonur in 1691,[9] *otog* kept its earlier meaning only in connection with the *shavi*[10] of *rJe-bcun dam-pa*,[11] and from the middle of the eighteenth century it was no longer frequently used. The reason for this lay in the Manchurian administration policy in Mongolia.

Khoshuu

Khoshuu is another term for an administrative unit that stands in close relation to *aimag* and *otog*. It is also unclear exactly when this term first came to be used. According to W. Barthold, it originally meant a military unit of 1,000 warriors in Cagadai Ulus (Barthold 1966: vol. 2, sect. 2: 50). The leader of this unit was called *khoshuuchi*.

After the period of Batumünkhe Dayan Khaan one frequently encounters the expressions 'Khalkha seven *Otog*' and 'Khalkha seven *Khoshuu*', in the sources used in conjunction with each other. There are further reports about successful warriors being distinguished with the rank of *khoshuuchi* and *darkhan* by Batumünkhe Dayan Khaan. But it should not be believed that a *khoshuuchi* stood at the head of a *khoshuu* or *otog* or that he governed (Nacagdorj 1978: 152). He was merely the leader of the warriors from a *khoshuu* or *otog*, as research investigations have concluded.

Some researchers assume that the expression *khoshuu* was used in connection with military affairs while *otog* was used more for civil matters. Gradually *khoshuu* came to designate the largest administrative-territorial units, until the *aimag* became the largest unit. It could well be maintained that in this period a *khoshuu* represented a unit that was politically and administratively quite independent and which comprised a large territory and a large population. For this reason *khoshuu* remained relatively stable for some time. D. Cedev writes that the structure of the seven *khoshuu*s existed until the middle of the seventeenth century (Cedev 1964: 24). After the formation of the *aimag* units, however, the *khoshuu* units lost some of their significance.

After the conquest of Mongolia by the Manchu and the subsequent introduction of the Manchu-Chinese *banner* system, the word *khoshuu* was once again used as an administrative unit. However, the Manchu used the word to refer to a *banner* located within an *aimag*, which, in comparison with earlier *khoshuu*s, comprised neither a large territory nor a large population.

Chuulgan

A moment of political significance for the Mongolian state system was the conferences of this period known as *chuulgan*. After about the middle of the sixteenth century until the seventeenth century, the use of the word *chuulgan* increased. This conference form was no doubt an extension of *khurildai*, which we have already discussed. Since the sixteenth century was characterised by a turn towards decentralisation, the sovereignty of the Great Khaan decreased and the rights of other princes increased. *Chuulgan* could well be a reflection of this shift of power.

The sources contain reports about all the *chuulgan*s of 40 groups of ten thousand and four groups of ten thousand and about 18 conferences of the Great *chuulgan* of princes from 'Khalkha seven khoshuu' (*Mongol ba töv ...* 1974: 6). We have however no concrete references concerning the structuring of the conferences. We only know that general questions concerning all Mongolian peoples were discussed in the *chuulgan*. For example, important Mongolian legislation of the seventeenth and eighteenth centuries such as the 'Mongol-Oirat Regulations of 1640' and 'Khalhka Jirum' were discussed and passed in the Great *chuulgan*.

The *chuulgan* was taken over by the Manchu after the conquest of Mongolia, however not as a form of conference but as a territorial-administrative union.

A reasonably clear picture of the evolution of politico-administrative organisation in Mongolia can be formed from the above. Until the start of the Mongolian Empire, there existed comparatively small groupings on a tribal level in accordance with the nomadic way of life. With the establishment of the Mongolian tribal federation, this form of organisation was gradually replaced by a military-administrative system which reached its pinnacle with the founding of the Mongolian Empire. From the end of the thirteenth to the end of the fourteenth centuries, this administrative system existed in Mon-golia in a more or less loosened form.

After the fall of the Yuan dynasty, the military-administrative organisation was gradually superseded owing to the weakness of the central power. Its place was taken by a quasi-civil administration, which from the end of the fourteenth until the start of the seventeenth centuries aimed for political unity in the ever-declining country. From the end of the seventeenth century, the strict Manchurian-Chinese administrative system was introduced, which was unsuitable for many areas of the nomadic way of life.

Table 5: Transformation of the most important administrative terms in the course of Mongolian history.

	12th/13th century	c. 14th/17th century	post-18th century
Group of ten	Smallest military unit	Little mentioned term	Administrative military unit
Group of hundred	Next largest military unit	Little mentioned term	Administrative military unit
Group of thousand	Main military unit	Term is no longer used	
Khoshuu	Not verifiable	Small civil-military administrative unit	Civil (military) administrative unit
Otog	Not verifiable	Term sometimes used synonymous with 'group of ten thousand' and *ulus*	Small civil unit
Aimag	Tribal federation (formed from several *ail*)	Largest civil–military administrative unit	1. Main civil administrative unit in *ulus* 2. Small civil unit (smaller than *otog*) 3. Religious administrative unit in Yeke Khüree (Urga)
Group of ten thousand	Little mentioned term for military unit (formed from *obog* and *aimag*)	Large civil–military administrative unit (formed from *otog*, *khoshuu* and *aimag*)	Term no longer appears
Ulus	Quasi-political state		State

The transformation of the most important administrative terms in the course of history is summarised in Table 5.

In this respect the following should be noted:

- In the course of this evolution family relations continued to play a role, but the politically determined restructuring of society resulted in their loss of importance. It may be maintained that an economy that keeps its nomadic character is marked by family relations.

- The politico-administrative conditions of Mongolia from the end of the fourteenth century until the Manchurian period should be considered in the caution. The administrative network had no clear-cut form. For this reason there are no categorically clear-cut definitions for the terms *khoshuu*, *otog* and *aimag* before the seventeenth century. Because the administrative network contained elements of familial, military and civil systems in a combined form, all these elements should be considered when using these terms.

THE MANCHURIAN-CHINESE ADMINISTRATION SYSTEM FROM THE SECOND HALF OF THE SEVENTEENTH SENTURY TO THE NINETEENTH CENTURY

After the conquest of Inner Mongolia[12] in 1636 and of many other territories, the Manchu had the difficult task of governing the conquered region and its population who, for the most part, lived under nomadic conditions. In particular, the nomadic tribes living on the northern border of the empire had great significance for the empire's stability since peace with them meant, and had meant since ancient times, safe northern borders. Because the traditional Chinese governmental structure with its six ministries had until this time been oriented only towards China and its provinces, the Manchu established the ministry for governing the outer provinces, the Lifanyuan, in Peking in 1638. When the conquest of Outer Mongolia was completed in 1691, it too was placed under the control of the Lifanyuan.

Coordination of the manifold Mongolian affairs lay in the hands of the Lifanyuan. Later, with the expansion of influence of the Chinese-Manchu Qing Empire, relations with Tibet, Chinese Turkestan and Russia fell within its jurisdiction. The Lifanyuan had in 1661 four departments and offices, the number of which was extended to six in 1761, and it remained in this latter form until the fall of the Qing Empire in 1911. The departments and offices were subordinated to the general committee to which a president and three vice-presidents belonged. One of the three vice-presidents was a Mongol, and more than 140 Mongols occupied the 233 posts of the ministry (Veit 1986: 445).

The Lifanyuan was responsible for everything – confirming, promoting, demoting and discharging Mongolian office bearers and dignitaries; publishing decrees; registering and forwarding reports; translating, receiving and paying tribute delegations and new year delegations; regulating legal cases; conducting educational affairs; and supplying grain in times of natural catastrophe. It also bore responsibility for recording maps which showed changes in *khoshuu* borders, compiled genealogical lists of princes which had to be regularly updated, and issued entitlements for Chinese merchants to trade in Mongolia (Legrand 1976: 161–65).

The next level of Manchurian administration in Outer Mongolia led by high-ranking Manchurian officials consisted of the four chancelleries and in the Outer Mongolian settlements Uliastai, the capital Khüree, Khovd and Khiagt. Regarded historically, the establishment of these chancelleries is related to the introduction of the *aimag* and *khoshuu* system. Because the *aimag*s and *khoshuu*s were subordinated to the four chancelleries, we shall first treat the systematic basis of these chancelleries.

On account of the restructuring of the *aimag*s and *khoshuu*s, the need arose to create administrative directing offices for the entire Khalkha Mongolian region. Thus in 1723, the chancellery of the grand marshal was established in Uliastai (*Uliastain janjin ambas*) in the Western Mongolia, this settlement being suitable for an administrative office due to its central location. This chancellery was generally responsible for the coordination of military affairs in Outer Mongolia and specifically for the civil affairs of the Zasagt Khan *Aimag*, the Sain Noyan Khan *Aimag* and the Uriankhai tribes in the regions Khövsgöl Nuur and Tagna. It had a grand marshal (*janjin*), an assistant grand marshal (*tuslagch janjin*) and four departments. In terms of office, it ranked higher than the chancelleries in Khüree, Khiagt and Khovd.

The chancelleries in the capital Khüree and in Khovd were led by grand dignitaries (*said*s or *amban*s) and were in terms of administration more oriented to civil affairs than the chancelleries in Uliastai and Khovd. In the beginning, the chancellery in Khüree was established with the appointment of at first a Mongolian minister in 1751 and, shortly afterwards in 1761, a Manchurian minister. It was generally responsible for all affairs of the eastern part of Mongolia, namely Tüsheet Khan *Aimag* and Secen Khan *Aimag*. In addition, the affairs of the subjects (*shavi*) of the religious head of state in Mongolia, *rJe-bcun dam-pa*, also came under its jurisdiction. It consisted of a large number of officials – 170 officials worked in its office in 1885 (Sonomdagva 1961: 36).

After the conquest of West Mongolia, the Manchu incorporated the West Mongolian region of Khovd[13] into Khalkha Mongolian administration. This region was for some time formally subordinated to the grand marshal of Uliastai, but owing to its expansiveness and lack of administrative apparatus, it proved to be ungovernable. Thus the need arose to create an additional administrative directing office in Khovd. With the establishment of the chancellery there and the consequent appointment of a grand dignitary in 1762, the establishment of Manchurian administration in Khalkha Mongolia, as well as in all Outer Mongolia, can be regarded as complete.

In 1727 a similar establishment was created in the settlement of Khiagt which lay directly on the Russian–Mongolian border. While the office of Khüree controlled the two eastern *aimag*s, the chancellery marshal in Khiagt assumed responsibility for the *khoshuu*s of these *aimag*s located about Khiagt. Moreover, the chancellery controlled all the Russian trade that crossed the border and performed a blocking and regulating function in favour of Chinese merchants. In 1777 the marshal in Khiagt was subordinated to the grand dignitary of Khüree in the wake of the centralisation of Mongolian administration.

To this level of Manchurian administration there also belonged another administrative apparatus. In addition to the abovementioned chancelleries, there existed in the cities of Uliastai, Khovd, Khüree and Khiagt representations, called *suurin jisaa*,[14] of all four *aimag*s. These bore the individual names '*Jisaa* of four *aimag*' in Uliastai, 'Khalkha jisaa' in Khovd, 'Settled and mobile *jisaa*' in Khüree and 'Zaisan *jisaa*' in Khiagt. Their role was to advise in problems dealing with the administration of border patrols, the army, the relay post, the keeping of the imperial livestock and the cultivation of grain. In general, these four representations played the role of intermediaries between the *aimag* and the Manchurian regional centres in the four settlements of Outer Mongolia, while the four chancelleries were intermediaries between the imperial court or the

Lifanyuan and the Outer Mongolian regional centres. Apart from the representation in Khüree, to which representatives from only two *aimag*s, Tüsheet Khan and Secen Khan, were sent, the representations in the other cities had representatives from all four *aimag*s. As a rule, each *aimag* had to send their representatives for 3–6 months' service. The representative groups of all *aimag*s consisted of 2–4 officials plus specialists.

The third level of Manchurian administration in Mongolia was the *aimag* and *khoshuu* system. The Manchu, who in comparison with the Chinese were a semi-nomadic people with no experience in governing a large settled population, preferred after their conquest of China to retain the local system and only later undertook slight changes to Chinese administration. After conquering the Mongols, they were confronted with the other extreme. Here they had to deal with a people who lived a completely nomadic way of life. Undoubtedly it was easier for the Manchu to set up an administrative system founded on their own experience and which accorded with the local conditions. A complete restructuring of the system of the nomadic Mongols, however, proved to be impossible. As a consequence, the Mongolian administrative units *aimag* and *khoshuu* were formally retained. Under such conditions, the Manchu established their administration in Khalkha Mongolia according to the following principles:

- The administration assumed a dual character. First it had to be a means and a framework for registering, recruiting and training Mongolian soldiers and second it had to meet justly the demands of a civil administration.

- The Manchu realised that a nomadic people could only be governed by means of a close-meshed administrative network. In the setting up of such a network, moderately sized and small administrative units were more appropriate, a requirement which the *khoshuu* system with its structure of *khoshuus*, *sums* and groups of ten adequately met.

- In order to consolidate their rule, the Manchu had first to phase out all former power centres of the country gradually and carefully. The positions of the Mongolian high-ranking nobles, the khans and *rJe-bcun dam-pa* were thus destabilised. With the increase in the number of *aimag* from three to four, in which Tüsheet Khan played the leading role, and the division of the *aimag*s into *khoshuu*s the *khoshuu*s into *sum*s and the *sum*s into groups of ten, the policy was completed. (Barkmann 1986: 48–49)

In dealing with the *aimag*s, the Manchu took decentralising measures, with the result that the power of the most powerful of the Mongolian khans, Tüsheet Khan, was totally abolished. The position of this khan had already been weakened by the division of his *aimag* into *khoshuu*s, by the appointment and promotion of ruling princes, as well as by the merely formal subordination of *rJe-bcun dam-pa* and his subjects to his rule. However, a total split of his *aimag* appeared more appropriate to the Manchu. In 1723 the emperor decreed that the subordination of *rJe-bcun dam-pa* be rescinded. This was a large loss of prestige for Tüsheet Khan, since he was now deprived of about 17,000 subjects. In 1725 another split of Tüsheet Khan's *aimag* occurred by imperial decree. Nineteen *khoshuu*s were removed from the *aimag* and formed into a new *aimag*. Jin Vang Dashidondub, who had proved loyal to the Manchu, was appointed Sain Noyan Khan and became ruler of the new *aimag*, which was called Sain Noyan Khan *Aimag*.

In the year 1728 another important measure was taken to undermine the authority of the princes of Genghisic descent who governed the *aimag*. By imperial decree (Sonomdagva 1961: 49), four *aimag*s of Khalkha Mongolia were renamed *chuulgan*s and formed into four *chuulgan* unions which were referred to by the names of the locations of their assemblies: *chuulgan* of Kherlen-Bars-*khot*, the former Secen Khan *Aimag* with 23 *khoshuu*s; *chuulgan* of Khan-Uul, the former Tüsheet Khan *Aimag* with 20 *khoshuu*s; *chuulgan* of Cecerleg, the former Sayn Noyon Khan *Aimag* with 24 *khoshuu*s; and *chuulgan* of Biderye-Nuur at the mouth of the Zag River, the former Zasagt Khan *Aimag* with 19 *khoshuu*s (*Lifanyuan zeli*, bk 30: Holding of the *Chuulgan*). It is noteworthy that the assemblies did not always take place at the same location but at a place decided on by the *chuulgan* head. The word *chuulgan* means here both the union and the assembly of the union. In Mongolia, however, the term *aimag* continued to be used even though *chuulgan* was used in official documents. Instead of the leaders of the *aimag* there were now the *chuulgan* leaders (*chuulgan-y tergüün*), soon afterward called *chuulgan* heads (*chuulgan darga*). Initially these posts were filled by successors of the *aimag* khans, but this did not continue long. By a new decree of the Manchu emperor, suitable *khoshuu* princes could be appointed to the office of *chuulgan* head (Sonomdagva 1961: 50). Every three years the *aimag* princes elected a new head of the *chuulgan*. As soon as the princes had agreed upon a new head, the suggestion was conveyed to the Lifanyuan in Peking, and it was only after a confirmation by the emperor and by the Lifanyuan that the head was appointed to office. In his function he was head of the *aimag* and thus took over the political function of the khan. With the creation of the *chuulgan* system, the Manchu sent supervisory officials into Mongolia for the first time. As one can see from the further course of history, the immediate influence of Manchurian officials on *aimag* affairs came to be normal procedure.

In addition to the head of the *chuulgan*, there was a high-ranking official assistant marshal (*tuslagch janjin*) who had equal rights as the head and who was solely responsible for military affairs.

Beside the head and the assistant marshal, the *chuulgan* (or *aimag*) had a chancellery called *jisaa*: *chuulgan darga-yn jisaa* (abbreviated to *da jisaa*) and *janjin-y jisaa*, which played the role of intermediary in civil and miltary affairs between the *chuulgan* head office and the *khoshuu*. The officials and specialists for civil and military affairs in these chancelleries were sent from their respective *khoshuu* for 3 months' service.

The introduction of the *khoshuu* system as *banner* system, a Manchurian military-administrative system, occurred as a consequence of the conference at Dolonur (or Dolon Nuur) in 1691. In the Tüsheet Khan *Aimag* there were at that time 16 *khoshuu*s, in the Secen Khan *Aimag* 11 and in the Zasagt Khan *Aimag* 7. The Manchu meant by the term *khoshuu* in Mongolia the Manchurian military-administrative unit *banner* (Manch. *gusa*), which comprised neither a very large territory in comparison with the original *khoshuu* nor many inhabitants. Afterwards, in the period from 1691 to 1755, the number of *khoshuu*s increased dramatically. In the year 1725 there were 75 *khoshuu*s, and in 1755 84 *khoshuu*s were registered. According to information from official files and laws, the *khoshuu* territories were differentiated into

- traditionally formed *khoshuu*s (Mong. *khev olson khoshuu*);
- *khoshuu*s formed by decree (Mong. *danst* or *togtoolt khoshuu*).

The majority of the *khoshuu*s were formed by imperial decree. In the northern (in Oirat) and southeastern (in Dariganga, Barga) regions, many *khoshuu*s were created after the Manchurian conquest and, as far as the appointment of *khoshuu* princes was concerned, service to the Manchu emperor rather than Genghisic lineage was of importance.

SOCIO-POLITICAL ORGANISATION IN THE DEVELOPMENT OF MONGOLIA

The size of *khoshuu*s differed considerably. It can be read in official files of the Tüsheet Khan *Aimag* from the year 1858 that 36 families, or 160 inhabitants, and about 500 animals belonged to the smallest *khoshuu* of the *aimag*, while the largest *khoshuu* had 5,400 families, or 25,000 inhabitants, and 57,000 animals (Sonomdagva 1961: 75). On average a *khoshuu* comprised about 1,000–1,500 families and 10,000–15,000 animals.

A large civil service as well as *khoshuu* and *sum* chancelleries were subordinated to the governing princes of the *khoshuu* (Mong. *zasag noyon*), as the codex of 1789 shows. In the codex there are various official designations of Chinese origin for the *khoshuu* leaders of Khalkha Mongolia, such as *vang, beile, beise, güng* and *taij*. Beneath the *khoshuu* leaders were officials such as *janjin, meiren, zalan* and others (Alinge 1934: 139–40).

The lowest level of Manchurian administration in Mongolia was the *sum* system. With the help of the governing princes, who after 1691 were directly subordinated to the Lifanyuan, the *khoshuu* were divided into *sum*s and groups of ten. According to the codex of 1789, the organisation of the *sum* followed exclusively military principles (ibid., 139–41). A *sum* was obliged by law to muster 150 able-bodied men in the age range of 18–60, of whom 50 were permanently in active service and 100 were in reserve (*Lifanyuan zeli*, bk 9). The *sum* bore responsibility for the financing and manning of the army, the border patrol and the relay posts. In 1830 there were 239 *sum*s in Mongolia: 52 *sum*s in the Tüsheet Khan *Aimag*, 40 in the Secen Khan *Aimag*, 20 in the Zasagt Khan *Aimag*, 31 in the Sain Noyan Khan *Aimag*, 36 in the Dörvöd *Aimag*, 27 of the Uriankhai in the Altai region, 4 in Zakhchin, 2 in Ööld, 2 in Myangad, 5 in Torguud, 16 of the Uriankhai in the Tagna region and 4 of the Uriankhai in the Khövsgöl region. The number of *sum*s, however, changed constantly as a result of increases or decreases in the population. In addition there were half *sum*s, called *khondogo* (or *khondogo sum*), which on account of their small populations were unable to muster 150 able-bodied men. Because the sizes of the *khoshuu*s differed, some *khoshuu*s contained only one *sum* while others had more than 10. In each *sum* there was a *sum* chief, who bore the main responsibility, plus other officials, such as the *orlon khöögch* (deputy *sum* chief) and six *baga khöögch*s (specialists). The *sum* were divided into the final military units, the groups of ten. One of the able-bodied men led a group of ten.

At the end of the nineteenth and beginning of the twentieth centuries, Mongolia was greatly splintered on account of the territorial-administrative network of the Chinese-Manchu Qing Empire. In addition, there were the *otog*s and *shavi*s, the religious grand dignitary's property within the *khoshuu*, which however were administratively independent of *khoshuu* administration. In Mongolia there were 86 *khoshuu*s in the four Khalkha *Aimag*s, 16 *khoshuu*s in the two Dörvöd *Aimag*s, 7 *khoshuu*s of the Uriankhai tribe in the Altai region, 1 *khoshuu* of the Uriankhai in the Tagna region, 5 West Mongolian *khoshuu*s (2 Torguud *khoshuu*s, 1 Ööld *khoshuu*, 1 Myangad *khoshuu* and 1 Zakhchin *khoshuu*) – which belonged to the chancellery in Khovd, and 12 *otog*s and *shavi*s.

In conclusion it can be maintained that, after the establishment of the Manchurian political system, Mongolian politico-administrative organisation became complicated, while until the second half of the seventeenth century it had remained traditional, simply structured and almost unchanged. Administrative structure before and during the Manchurian period in Khalkha Mongolia is shown in Figure 4.a.

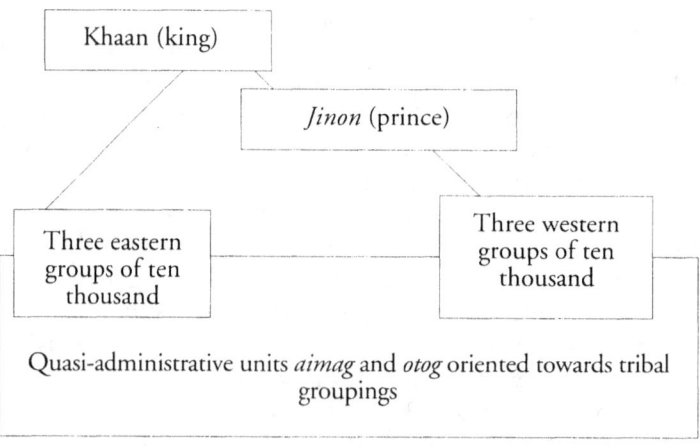

Figure 4.a. Administrative structure of Khalkha Mongolia before the Manchurian period in the seventeenth century

SOCIO-POLITICAL ORGANISATION IN THE DEVELOPMENT OF MONGOLIA

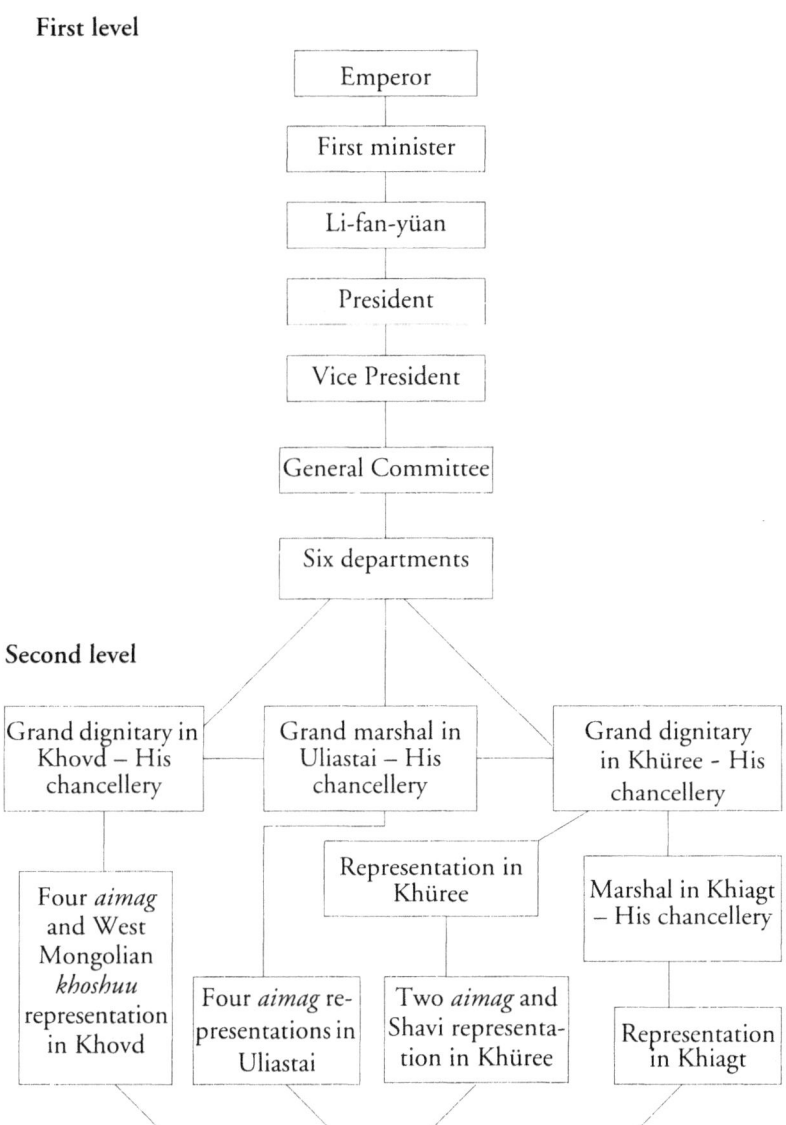

Third level

```
        ┌─────────────────────────────────────────┐
        │   Assembly of princes (chuulgan) of     │
        │   the four aimags of Khalkha Mongolia   │
        └─────────────────────────────────────────┘
                           │
        ┌─────────────────────────────────────────┐
        │     Chancellery of the aimag chuulgan   │
        └─────────────────────────────────────────┘
              ╱                           ╲
   ┌──────────────────────┐      ┌──────────────────────┐
   │  Khoshuu (division)  │      │   Otog (regiment)    │
   └──────────────────────┘      └──────────────────────┘
               ╲                         ╱
                ┌───────────────────────┐
                │    Sum (squadron)     │
                └───────────────────────┘
                           │
                ┌───────────────────────┐
                │     Group of ten      │
                └───────────────────────┘
```

Fig. 4.b. The Manchurian-Chinese administration system during the nineteenth century

4. SOCIAL STRATA OF MONGOLIAN NOMADIC SOCIETY

SOCIAL DIFFERENTIATION IN THE THIRTEENTH CENTURY

The 'class structure' of Mongolian nomadic society from the thirteenth to the nineteenth centuries has been analysed in the research of e.g. Vladimircov (1934), Ishjamc (1976), Gongor (1978) and Nacagdorj (1978). It should first be noted that, in consideration of information contained in the sources, the use of the term 'class structure' is not necessary in treating traditional nomadic society, at least in the thirteenth century. In order to clarify this question, terms used for designating social strata in the first half of the thirteenth century in the most important autochthonous chronicle, the SHM, should first be analysed. In this work, terms such as *nökhör, darkhad, cherbi, khürged, ütü dürü-iin kümün, böö (bögechi)*, blood relatives of the tribal head, *irged, kharc, arad, bool, zaluu (jilagu), geriin kümün* and *inji* appear frequently. The social differences amongst persons or groups of persons designated by these names are not always clear: in some cases it is difficult to determine whether they belong to aristocratic circles or are common livestock keepers.

Nökhör

A group that belonged to aristocratic circles was the *nökhör* (retinue or attendants, entourage). The leader of a tribe or the khaan of a tribal federation granted fiefs to his followers and strengthened his authority via a military retinue whose members had the same ideals and notions of loyalty, represented common interests and were related to the leader. This retinue, the bodyguards of the ruler, was probably a characteristic institution of the Mongols, as of earlier nomadic peoples of Central Asia. The members of the retinue functioned as supervisors, envoys and messengers. They enabled the ruler to hold the common livestock keepers in rein and to undertake raids. These personal attendants were theoretically able to change freely from one ruler to another. Whether they swore any form of oath of allegiance or not cannot be definitely proved. It is certain however that they were bound to their ruler as friends and advisers in a strong relationship of trust. They were analogous to the Anglo-Saxon *hus-carl*, the Angevin *comitatius* and the *druzennik* of early Kiev. According to the SHM, members of the retinue came from various social strata of the tribe. Such a post was gained by leadership and fighting qualities, strength and skill. This was evident in the new social stratum of the retinue of Genghis Khaan (Gongor 1978: 154).

Darkhad

The term *darkhad*, the plural of *darkhan*, is often encountered in the SHM. According to conjectures of some scholars (Gongor 1978: 157), *darkhad* were those who performed outstandingly in battle and were thus rewarded by the ruler with special rights. The *darkhad* were allowed to keep war booty and members of conquered tribes. In addition, they had the right to fetch back lost tribal members and be their masters. It has been shown that such positions existed early in the Central Asian nomadic empires of the Juanjuan in the fifth to sixth centuries and of the Türk in the sixth to eighth centuries (Sükhbaatar 1973: 173; Shinekhüü 1975: 138–41).

Cherbi

The SHM uses the word *cherbi* to designate people who were appointed leaders in military campaigns and who, in times of peace, were responsible for the supervision of the herds and for the organisation of households. The first six *cherbis* – Dodai, Dagolkhu, Ögele, Tolun, Bucharan and Süikhetü – were appointed by Genghis Khaan (SHM, §191). As the exact designations such as 'Ögele *cherbi* of tribe Arulad',

'Süikhetü *cherbi* of tribe Khonkhotu' and 'Dagolkhu *cherbi* of tribe Manggud' in the SHM show that the *cherbi* came from different tribal-social backgrounds.

This term was used before and after the fall of the Great Empire of the Mongols, and it could well be that persons who performed military and administrative services had been so named from earliest times.

Khürged

These were men who married women from tribes of good background in order to form valuable connections and friendships. The *khürged*s (sons-in-law and brothers-in-law) were as a rule of aristocratic origin. In the course of time they came to be mediators for the political federation of different tribes. For example, Genghis Khaan appointed each *khürged* to leader of a group of thousand. Ogadai invited all *khürged*s on the occasion of his accession to the throne. In sources of later times, the term *khürged* was replaced by the term *tabunang*, although the political meaning remained the same. A *tabunang* formed good relations with his ruler and always served in an important office. There exists a report according to which an *otog* was created under the leadership of a *tabunang* (Rumyancev 1965: 91, 111–15). This means that *tabunang*s sometimes ruled over about 100 livestock keepers or estates.

Ütü dürü-iin kümün (persons of free standing)[1]

This term appears in the SHM four times in all: three times as *dürü-iin kümün* and once as *ütü dürü-iin kümün* (SHM, §§191, 224). It has been variously reconstructed and transcribed by scholars from the original form written in Chinese script. The frequently used transcription is *urtu duruyn kümün*, which is literally translated as 'person of long freedom'. We believe that the transcription *ütü dürü-iin kümün* (person of simple standing), which has been concluded by the Inner Mongolian specialist in Mongolian studies E. Ardajab, is convincing (1986: 583). In decoding the meaning of both transcriptions, however, the same results are obtained.

In the SHM these words were used in connection with the military organisation of Genghis Khaan's troops. Such persons were probably appointed to high positions on account of their services at war. Their relatives as well as unrelated groups of livestock-keeping families and even some attendants were to them subordinated.

Böö shamans[2]

Sources such as the SHM, early travel reports and also reports from later Mongolian chronicles show that there were a small number of people who carried out shamanistic practices. The shaman was a member of the aristocracy and sometimes had a leading position, often as a ruler of tribe (Heissig 1970: 305). Above all he was a person who had contact with supernatural powers. There is a fascinating story in the SHM about a conflict between Genghis Khaan and the leading shaman Khökhöchü, one of the seven sons of Menlik, in the period subsequent to Genghis Khaan attaining acknowledgement of his supreme power at the Khuriltai of 1206 (SHM, §245). The impression is given that Genghis Khaan may have been faced at this juncture with a priestly challenge to his authority and that the shaman was aiming to establish himself, as the effective power behind the throne at the very least.

If one studies the reports mentioning *böö* in the SHM, one sees that in the period of Genghis Khaan there were very few shamans. The number of shamans increased in the middle of the thirteenth century. The reports of Rubruck give the impression that shamans represented a hierarchic social stratum of great authority. He writes:

> There are many such seers, and they always have a head, a high priest as it were, who always pitches his residence in front of the main tent of Münkhe Khaan, approximately at a distance of a stone's throw ... The other priests live behind the prince's tent at definite sites which are allocated to them. People who believe in their craft come to them from the most varied parts of the world. (Rubruck 1925: 141)

Blood relatives of the tribal head

The group which formed the core of the steppe aristocracy was the family, the blood relatives, of the tribal head. With the victory of one tribe over another, the standing of all blood relatives of the successful tribal head increased. In the Mongolian tribal federation, Borjigin or Khiad Borjigin was the central tribe. The Borjigin tribe consisted of the descendants of Bodonchar,[3] whose sixteenth-generation forefather was the leader of the Khiad Börtü-Chinu tribe and who, with his wife, moved in about the eighth century from Ergüne-Khun, the region of today's Lake Dalai-nuur and the Argun River, and settled on Mount Burkhan-Khaldung in the Khentii Mountains. In the period of Bodonchar, his Borjigin tribe played the leading role amongst those of Khiad descent. Genghis Khaan was his eleventh-generation descendant. The closest family members of Genghis Khaan are designated in the sources *altan urug* (golden family or golden tribe). Members of the

Borjigin tribe held very influential positions in all *aimag*s of Outer Mongolia up to the nineteenth century.

Irged

This term is frequently used in the SHM. The original meaning of the word is interpreted in different ways by historians because *irged*, the plural form of *irgen* (simple people), encompasses many things in the sources. According to the SHM, *irged* essentially means the following:

1. Members of a livestock keeping family *ail*, of an *ail* group, of a tribe, of a tribal grouping, of a Khüree grouping (SHM, §§5, 8, 28, 90) or of a tribal federation (SHM, §§58, 62, 177, 185, 186, 208, 239, 240, 241);

2. *Irged* are individual persons who do not permanently belong anywhere (SHM, §§110, 214).

Based on this, it can be maintained that there is no reason to regard the term as a designation for a subordinated class. We believe that this word has no direct relation to social structure but rather to ethnic and familial structures. This meaning remained also in later sources. It is noteworthy that from about the seventeenth century the word was used to designate the Chinese – *irgen* or *irgen khümün*.

Kharc

The group which was designated *kharc* (*kharachu*) probably formed in the period between the eighth and tenth centuries. The first reports about the line of succession, which began with Khabich Bagatur[4], son of Bodonchar, date from this period (Perlee 1956: 6). The word *kharc* might have been derived from the Mongolian *Kharbodun* (black Bodun tribe) of a Turkish people. The natural condescension of the nobility to commoners is reflected in the root of the word *kharc* – *khar* means black. Customarily, the Mongols value white as the pure, superior and lucky colour, while black has the opposite connotations. Thus the nobles referred to themselves as the *cagaan yastan* (white bone lineages) and to the ordinary people as *khar yastan* (black bone lineages). The original translation of *kharc*, according to the Chinese from the SHM, was 'low people, subordinates' (*xiamin*). The Mongolian term is roughly the equivalent of the Chinese term *qianshou* or 'black-headed ones' (Jagchid and Hyer 1979: 283). Common steppe people who stood in contrast to the aristocracy, were designated *kharc* (SHM, §§21, 111, 200, 254). The *kharc* were not an economically determined class but rather a socio-ethnic stratum.

Arad (aran, haran)

This term was also used in connection with the social standing of a group of inhabitants of the steppe. In the SHM the terms *arad, haran*, and *aran* are used synonymously. A series of research investigations has shown that they represent morphophonetic variations (Poppe 1941: 104–5; Damdinsuren 1957b: 127). According to the SHM, the term applies to ordinary inhabitants of the steppe who were under the aristocracy, for example warriors and guards (SHM, §§100, 111, 129, 136, 146, 161, 169, 219, 246). It should however also be noted that in some sources the term was used by the ruler or head of a tribe for tribal members who were originally from another tribe in order to refer to their foreign background (SHM, §§129, 146, 169, 219). Today the word *aran* or *haran* has disappeared, and only the plural form *arad* is still in use and has the meaning 'common people'.

Bool (Bo'ol)

According to reports in the chronicles, *bool* refers in general to members of a conquered tribe who were obliged to serve the victorious tribe by, for example, tending the herds, beating during hunts, etc. Some *bool* were entrusted by their parents to a lord even as children. This handing over, however, was voluntary. According to the SHM, people who had a similar status to house slaves were *bool*, but so also were people who obtained special powers from the Khaan, for example Genghis Khaan's trusted commanders Jelme and Mukhulai were called *bool* (SHM, §§137, 211). If one investigates the origin of the word, one sees that it was used positively, sometimes even as a form of praise. In some works of Russian and Mongolian historians, *bool* was equated with slave. The group of *bool* is described by Vladimircov as vassals-serfs but not as slaves (Vladimircov 1934: 64, 96). The reports in the SHM touching on *bool* show clearly that *bool* can in no way be equated with slaves (Irinchin 1980: 1–5). They cannot be imagined as producers in a social production system as the class of slaves was in the coastal regions of the Mediterranean.

In some research works there appear various word groupings such as *ütegu bool, ongu bool, unagan bool* and *ütele bool* (Vladimircov 1934: 96; Phillips 1969: 26–27; Zlatkin 1977; Jagchid and Hyer 1979: 284). In the SHM none of these is encountered. There is, however, some evidence that *ütegu* and *bool* referred to persons who were *bool* in accordance with their being *ütegu* (SHM, §§78, 117, 125, 189, 227, 230, 260, 278; Munkuev 1970: 360–69; Gongor 1978: 77). The meaning of *ütegu* or *ütege* can be inferred from the chronicles as 'ended', 'separated' or 'released'. In his 'Collection of Histories' Rashid ad-Din mentions the term *ü-ne-g-u bool*, by which he means a *bool* who has been released for various reasons, mostly on account of his services. P. Pelliot writes that the word *ü-ne-g-u* is an error in the copying of the word *ü-te-g-u* in most of the versions of Rashid ad-Din's work because *ne* and *te* differ in the Persian script only by an easily misapplied diacritic (Pelliot and Hambis 1951: 85). This falsely written term was variously decoded and transcribed, and thus the wrong impression arose that many different *bool* groups existed in Mongolia.

For example, the term *unagan bool* emerged from I. N. Berezin's translation of the 'Collection of Histories' from Persian into Russian. Berezin transliterated *ünegu* as *ongu* and then compared *ongu* with the term *unagan albat*, which appears in some Mongolian chronicles. *Unagan albat* denotes the tribal members whose ancestors were servants (Kovolevskii 1849). Berezin then used his new term *unagan bool* in connection with *ongu bool* (Berezin 1858: vol. 1: 33, 227), and this has been accepted by specialists in Mongolian studies as an original term. For example, Vladimircov was of this opinion (1934: 64), and many researchers later cited him. In the new Russian version of the 'Collection of Histories', L. A. Khitagurov took over the transliteration *ongu* in the course of his reworking of the first book of the first volume (Rashid ad-Din 1952: vol. 1, bk 1: 93) and thereby saw in *ongu* an explanation of *ötegü* (Munkuev 1970: 360–61).

In historical investigations, *bool* has frequently been explained as a manifestation of slavery amongst Mongolian nomads. This, in the end, is related to the 'attestation' of the universalistic five-stage scheme of social development in the history of nomadic peoples. However, *bool* did not, as we have already mentioned, represent producers in a social production system, as the slaves did in the coastal regions of the Mediterranean.

The problem which has always had an influence on the historical consciousness of Mongolia and disseminates the notion that slavery in the true sense of the word existed amongst Mongolian nomads, arises in equating the words *bool* and slave. This is a consequence of the Russian word for slave, *rab*, having been used by Berezin to translate *bool*, and this form was taken over in the literature. This often leads to a wrong notion about *bool* and to attempts to find characteristics of slavery there.

Zaluu (jilagu), geriin kümün and *inji*

In the SHM the following groups are encountered: *jilagu* (young man), *geriin kümün* (approximately servant) and *inji* (servant given as dowry). There is evidence that certain members of these groups served in the households of aristocratic families. In the sources there are not enough references to the *jilagu* and *geriin kümün* in order to explain their social background more precisely.

The group *inji*, however, is very frequently encountered in the SHM, the 'Collection of Histories' and even in the statute book of the eighteenth century, *Khalkha Jirum*. In the thirteenth century it must have been customary that nobody from a man's family had the right to possess of these 'dowry servants'; only a woman's descendants could possess them. The *inji* performed services in the household.

The various groups described above, which existed in the period of the twelfth and thirteenth centuries, defined their relationship to one another by means of wealth and family membership. They were not socio-economically determined classes or stations. We believe that these groups should be evaluated according to familial, ethno-social and quasi-administrative principles.

SOCIAL STRATA OF MONGOLIAN SOCIETY BEFORE THE MANCHURIAN CONQUEST

The establishment of the union of all Mongolian tribes at the start of the thirteenth century was undoubtedly the trigger for a further differentiation of the ruling group. A ruling system developed on an aristocratic warrior stratum and an administrative apparatus. Social differences amongst the population deepened after the period of the Mongolian Empire. However, the tracing of the further development of social groups up to the start of Manchurian rule is difficult because there are insufficient contemporary sources which could give us detailed information. There are only isolated records which have relevance to this problem. In general, social structure kept its traditionalist character, with tribal membership playing a large role. The general division of the population into members of the golden family (*altan urug*) of Genghis Khaan, non-Genghisic nobles and subordinates, common livestock keepers can clearly be discerned. The *Erdeni-yin tobchi* indicates that, towards the end of the fifteenth century, nobles were greatly interested in restoring lost dependency relations and in subordinating independent common livestock keepers. Using the well-known phrase of the *Erdeni-*

yin tobchi, 'How can and may common people live without masters?', some scholars like to argue that dependency relations were at that time strong (Vladimircov 1934: 158; Nasanbaljir 1960: 206). On the contrary, the phrase implies rather that traditional relations between nobles and subordinates had become endangered – if relations had been normal, there would not have been such concern.

We have no information about economically determined dependency relations between ruling and subordinate groups. Social conditions of this period did not allow the formation of classes in the face of increasing socio-economic differentiation.

Records dating from a later period, for example from the seventeenth and eighteenth centuries, enable us to understand better the social structure before the Manchurian conquest. In the 'Mongol-Oirat Regulations of 1640' and *Khalkha Jirum* it is mentioned that the Mongols in general were divided into two groups: the descendants of Genghis Khaan on the one hand and the entire populations of Mongolian tribes on the other. As regards the dependency relations between the two groups, it can be inferred from isolated facts that membership had become stricter and that subordinated persons were not permitted to cross administrative and territorial borders without the permission of their lords. In the 'Mongol-Oirat Regulations of 1640' it is written:

> If an individual livestock keeper of his own accord leaves his *khoshuu* for a neighbouring one and settles between the two *khoshuu*, he must be brought back. If he does not belong to an *otog* [pasture and livestock keepers belonging to a nobleman], let him belong to an *otog*. If he does not belong to an *aimag* [group of families in an *otog*], let him belong to an *aimag*. (Dylykov 1981: 117)

> If anybody leaves his allotted *nutug* [pastoral area], then he will be punished. If it is an *aimag* people in question, the *akhlagch* [group leader] will be fined nine animals. If it is a single man [a person or a separate family] in question, who leaves without the knowledge of his leader, he will be fined nine animals. He who brings back someone who has left his own *otog* and *aimag*, will receive a horse from the *aimag* leader and a sheep from each of the member families of this *aimag*. (Ibid., 120)

The population, with the exception of the highest ranking nobles, such as the nobility of Genghisic lineage, were divided into three groups: *sain khün* (good people), *dund khün* (average people) and *muu khün* (bad people).

Descendants of Genghis Khaan are known in legal sources by the names khan (grand prince), *jinon* (prince to the throne), *noyan* (princes), *khuntaij* (successors) and *taij* (princes of Genghisic descent of differing rank). Amongst them there were differences in degree of authority which, however, did not always correspond to the order of nobility. As a result there were differing titles and ranks such as *ikh noyon*, *bag*a *noyan*, *tavnan* (*tabunang*), *mergen*, *daichin*, *otog-iin said*, etc.

To the so-called 'good people' belonged, according to the 'Mongol-Oirat Regulations of 1640' and *Khalkha Jirum*, high-ranking nobles of non-Genghisic descent and other high-ranking official princes of ordinary descent (Golstunskii 1880: articles: 10–11, 20–21, 26, 35, 59, 128; Nasanbaljir 1961: 4, 31, 42–44, 49, 71, 78). The vast majority of them did not have the right to obtain offices by inheritance. They are known in the chronicles by the names *darkhad*, *tabunang*, *khonjin*, *shigchin*, *aimgiin akhas*, *tüshmel*, *zaisan*, *shuulenge*, etc.

To the group of 'average people' belonged, according to the above statute books, rich people and those who performed moderate or lowly civil and military services (Golstunskii 1880: articles: 11, 20, 55; Nasanbaljir 1961: 198, 199, 202), for example *lubchitan*, *dugulgatan*, *demch*, etc.

To the group of so-called 'bad people' belonged, according to the 'Mongol-Oirat Regulations of 1640', the ordinary subjects (Golstunskii 1880: articles: 11, 15, 39, 44, 46, 59, 69, 100).

The above-described social differences were taken into special account when punishment was exacted. In some sources there are, interestingly enough, also indications that these differences played a role when definite battle stations were allotted. Thus it is written in the 'Mongol-Oirat Regulations of 1640' that the 'good people' received the safest and most favourable battle stations; the 'average people' were well armed in the course of war; while the 'bad people' were armed only with swords and bows (Golstunskii 1880: articles: 39, 44, 46, 59, 69).

SOCIAL CLASS STRUCTURE IN MONGOLIA AFTER THE MANCHURIAN CONQUEST

The position of the Mongolian nobility

It is possible to learn more about class differentiation in Mongolia only after the Manchurian conquest. This is not because more records and official files are available but because in the course of the establishment of

Manchurian rule more changes in class relations occurred than ever before.

Changes in the standing of the Mongolian nobility were connected with the appointment of the 34 governing princes at the conference of Dolonur in 1691, because the Mongolian nobility was then divided into *khoshuu* governing princes and non-governing noblemen, the number of the latter being far greater than in the pre-Manchurian period. The governing princes were appointed from the most influential Genghisic nobility. In selecting them, the Manchu allowed them to retain their traditional regions. The preservation of the former ruling conditions was in the Manchu's best interests since it was a stabilising factor of their own rule in Khalkha Mongolia. However, while the Mongolian prince had been the direct owner of his land in the pre-Manchurian period, the Manchu-Chinese emperor was now lord of Khalkha Mongolia. The *khoshuu* had become only a fief for the Mongolian prince and thus his legal position in relation to the land he governed played no special role. In other words the Manchu emperor had taken the Mongolian nobility into his service. Reduction in the latter's previous rights was compensated by gifts or new privileges. Thus it came to be that the nobility in the emperor's service, his officials, not only worked for him but were also paid or at least 'given presents' for their services. The governing princes had obligations to the foreign holders of power but they, and indeed the entire Mongolian nobility, were awarded many privileges, too. At the Dolonur conference, the princes were awarded titles corresponding to their backgrounds and services to the Manchurian imperial court in the following order:

1. Governing *khoshoi ching vang*;
2. Governing *doroi jung vang*;
3. Governing *doroi beil*;
4. Governing *beis*;
5. Governing *güng* assisting the State;
6. Governing *güng* protecting the State;
7. Governing *taij* 1st class;
8. *Taij* 2nd–4th class.

The privilege of marriage to a Manchu princess was, as already mentioned, generally connected with the receiving of a title. This great honour was mostly reserved for governing princes. With such marriages they were considered brothers-in-law of the emperor and thus possessed the privilege of bearing the title *tabunang*. In the allocation of these titles, a fixed property was connected with the level of the title.

Another privilege connected with the title of prince was the allocation of personal *khamjilaga* (subordinates), the number of whom corresponded to the level of the title. These were released from state and military service. The emperor decreed the relevant laws some time before the Dolonur conference when he was granting privileges to the Inner Mongolian princes. The number of personal *khamjilaga* of a prince was calculated according to the number of men. The Mongolian nobility were allotted such subordinates in the following order: *ching vang* – 60 men; *jung vang* – 50 men; *beil* – 40 men; *beis* – 35; *güng* – 30 men (*Lifanyuan zeli*, bk 23); *tabunang* of various classes – 20 to 40 men (*BNMAU-yn tüükh* 1968: 181). This meant, for example, that a *ching vang* having 60 men had in fact 200 to 400 people, since each *khamjilaga* had a family that also belonged to the prince.

Another important privilege of the Mongolian princes was the right granted by the emperor to exact taxes once a year from the population of the *khoshuu*. This tax obligation was given legal form in the codex of 1789. After the Dolonur conference, hereditability of a ruling prince's title became more apparent. Under Emperor Qianlong (1736–95), the titles of ruling princes were accorded the status of hereditability. This decree applied to the majority of governing princes of Khalkha Mongolia in the year 1781. For the confirmation of the hereditability of titles, military service was of decisive importance. As regards succession, one should differentiate between governing and non-governing princes. The son of a governing prince inherited, in addition to his father's title of nobility, the fief and the title belonging to it, while the son of a non-governing prince only inherited the title of nobility. The position of non-governing princes thus differed both politically and economically from that of governing princes.

All non-governing nobles bore the title of a *taij*, but Manchu legislators differentiated between *taij* of direct Genghisic descent and *taij* of, for example, descendants of the brothers of Genghis Khaan.

The membership of a *taij* to the one or the other group defined his position in the Manchurian administration system to a decisive degree.

According to Manchurian law, only a *taij* of Genghisic descent could become governing princes, heads of the assembly of princes, *chuulgan*s, or assistant marshals of the *aimag*, and only they were awarded high nobility titles by the emperor. If they remained *taij*, then they were by law *taij* of first, second or third class. The *taij* from the lower, non-Genghisic nobility, who as a rule were descendants of the nobility who served Genghis Khaan, were normally *taij* of fourth class. The *taij* of first class possessed 15 men or *khamjilaga*s; the *taij* of second class 12 men; the *taij* of third class 8 men; and *taij* of fourth class 4 men (*Lifanyuan zeli*, bk 23). There were totally impoverished *taij* who did not even own a mount (Gongor 1970: 290), which in Mongolian nomadic conditions was a dire situation indeed. Within the *khoshuu*, the *taij*s and their subjects formed the so-called *otog* or the subordinated unit within an *otog – bag*, which enjoyed an autonomous status with respect to the *sum*. This was especially manifested by the fact that subjects of the *taij* did not have to perform administrative services.

Due to the above-mentioned hereditability mechanism, which the Lifanyuan established for nobles of Outer Mongolia, the number of *taij*s increased dramatically in the eighteenth century. Their membership of the ruling class thus correspondingly fell. Increasingly Genghisic *taij*s also served in lower *khoshuu* offices, however the number of *taij*s quickly overtook the actual number of *khoshuu* offices.

The situation of the *taij* in the eighteenth century was marked by a process of impoverishment. Non-Genghisic *taij*s in some *khoshuu* did not live any better than common livestock keepers. To an ever-increasing degree, the lower nobility also lost their subjects and personal *khamjilaga*s. Nonetheless, in this period there occurred no decline of the living standards of the *taij* who had no possessions to the level of common livestock keepers. Small privileges ensured by the Genghisic high-ranking nobility and the emperor rendered the lower nobility, who had no possessions, into a social group that belonged politically to the ruling strata and economically to the common livestock keepers.

The position of the livestock keepers

After the establishment of Manchurian rule, fundamental changes arose in the dependency relationship between livestock keepers and nobility in Mongolia. Regarding this problem, we shall limit our attention to the situation in Khalkha Mongolia, particularly in the eighteenth century. At the start of the eighteenth century, the emperor allotted personal *khamjilaga*s from the *khoshuu* population to the governing princes and *taij*s. This measure can be dated in the case of Khalkha Mongolia to 1705 which is the year when the word *khamjilaga* is first mentioned in Mongolian and Manchurian documents. In documents written before 1705, only the term *dagaldakh er* (attendants or escorts) and the general term *albat* or *albat ard* (person obliged to render service and pay tax) appear in this respect. The emergence of the *khamjilaga*s practically meant the division of the *khoshuu* population into two groups: 1) *khamjilaga*s and *khamjilaga ard* on the one hand, who rendered service and paid tax only to the lord allotted to them and were released from all state service, for example military service, and 2) *albat*s on the other hand, who were available for all Manchurian state or, if one identifies the emperor with the state, imperial services.

The *khamjilaga*s formed the majority of livestock keepers. They and their families were each in possession of a small household and a set number of livestock. According to some documents, their livestock numbered about 75 and was sufficient to provide the family with meat and dairy produce.

The *albat*s were subjects of both the emperor and the governing princes who, as high-ranking state officials, had the right to claim them for their *khoshuu*s. The *albat*s had to render services and pay taxes. For example they had to engage in military, border security and relay post services; to participate in hunts for the state meat supply; to labour on plantations for the army; to work in the *khoshuu* and *aimag* representations (*jisaa*) in the four cities; to tend the state or imperial livestock; and to defray administration costs. The *albat* comprised a group called *sum er* or *sum ard* (those belonging to a *sum*) which had emerged at the time of the establishment of the *khoshuu* and *sum* system in the year 1691 and which was available exclusively for military service. Later on, it was also responsible for other state services such as for the relay post, etc. In later files the terms *albat ard* and *sum ard* are used in similar ways, sometimes with the differentiation *ulsyn albat* (subjects of the state) and *eznii albat* (subjects of the emperor).

With the division of subjects into *khamjilaga ard* and *albat* or *sum ard*, it was at first in the best interests of many livestock keepers to go over to an *albat* or *sum* in order to avoid paying taxes to the princes. However, since the state services came to be more and more cumbersome, the reverse began to apply. In addition, it was in the best interests of the Mongolian princes to acquire *khamjilaga*s who were competent. As a result, the better livestock keepers gradually became *khamjilaga*s or were acquired by princes in exchange for poor livestock keepers, so that it came to pass that only poor livestock keepers remained in the state service. By means of the codex of 1789 the *sum ard* and *khamjilaga ard* were newly registered and crossings over between the two were strictly controlled. In this law it was also prescribed that *sum*s and *khamjilaga*s who crossed *khoshuu* borders with their livestock and without the knowledge of their lord were to forfeit their entire livestock to the *khoshuu* prince into whose territory they had entered. Severe punishment awaited them on their return to their original *khoshuu*.

Substantial evidence of the personal dependence of livestock keepers on the lords and their officialdom lies in the restriction of the rights of this 'class'. Manchurian legislation for Mongolia as well as the *Khalkha Jirum* excluded from the outset an administration of justice in favour of livestock keepers, and thus bore a 'class character'. This class character of the established law is reflected in particular in the differing punishments prescribed for members of the nobility and livestock keepers. While members of the nobility as a rule were confronted with material punishments – mostly fines of at least nine animals[5] – livestock keepers received severe punishments such as flogging (as a consequence of which the offender often died), death penalty (decapitation, throttling, dismemberment), 'enslavement' and deportation of the offender's family to the Chinese provinces Henan and Shandong as forced labour. A significant example of the unequal allotment of punishment can be seen in the punishment for murder stipulated in the codex of 1789 (Alinge 1934: 149). While it was customary in Europe to sell or give away serfs, Manchurian legislation for Mongolia forbade the sale and giving away of *khamjilaga*s and *albat*s from the *khoshuu* population if such persons had been registered (ibid.). This measure was taken so as to ensure a sufficient quantity of soldiers from the *khoshuu*.

Under conditions of socage, the *khamjilaga*s and *albat*s were confronted with a difficult political and socio-economic situation. The Manchu emperor allowed the Mongolian nobility to demand from the *khamjilaga*s and *albat*s services and taxes in the form of labour and produce. These services and taxes were legally prescribed in the codex of 1789, as indeed were their amounts. However, generous interpretation of the law often entailed these amounts being exceeded, since taxes in the form of produce were exacted for a whole array of beneficiaries: the livelihood of the governing princes and their families; the officials of the *khoshuu* and *aimag* administration, regular or irregular 'presents' for the emperor; presents and bribes for the marshals and Manchurian officials who often travelled to Mongolia; 'holy gifts' for the religious head of Mongolia *rJe-bcun dam-pa khutagt* of the capital Khüree as well as for other grand dignitaries, *khutagt* and *khuvilgaan*; journeys of the princes to Peking and Lhasa; military expenditure; payment of governing princes' debts, etc. The Manchu did not prescribe taxes or regular contributions for Khalkha Mongolia, but they demanded many services closely connected with the administrative use of the country and its people for military purposes. These services clarify the close relation between the military administration and the socio-economic situation of the *albats* who alone were responsible for their execution, and can essentially be divided into two groups:

- services rendered to the emperor, which were designated as 'high service' and which could be regular or sporadic,

- services directly connected with the maintenance of the administrative system.

Both of these groups were composed of many separate services. These Manchurian state services contributed to the rapid impoverishment of the Khalkha Mongolian population.

In addition to the *sum ard* and *khamjilaga ard*, there were several small groups *darkhan, bool, sul albat, khermel* and *inji*. These are often mentioned in the statute books such as *Khalkha Jirum* and official files.

The *darkhan* were in principle descendants of the group that emerged in the thirteenth century and later, whose members had been awarded special rights by the Khaan, such as freedom from service and taxes. In Manchurian legislature there are no references to *darkhan* awards, but there are cases of Mongolian princes following ancient tradition and awarding *darkhan* rights to certain persons, mainly relatives, in order, for example, to release them from payment of taxes (Zamcarano 1934: 188). With the awarding of *darkhan* rights, a certificate was handed over, in which it was stated whether the right was restricted to a single generation or was heritable.

The persons named *bool* in the seventeenth–nineteenth centuries were partly the remainder of the *bool* from the period of the Mongolian Empire. The *bools* helped throughout the generations in the princes' households. In later times, the group was formed from children of poor Mongolian families who could not support and thus sold them. In official files, *bool* women are referred to as *shivigchin*. 'At least until the communist period, *bool* were found in the Mongol areas near the Great Wall but not in nomad areas' (Jagchid and Heyr 1979: 289).

Persons belonging to a *sum* who were under or over the age of recruitment are called *sul albat* in legal files.

As *Khalkha Jirum* reports, there were livestock keepers and livestock keeping families, called *khavchuur*, who, mainly in order to avoid service and tax, ran away from their prince or territory to another *khoshuu* (Zamcarano 1959: 24, 31). During the intensification of Manchurian-Chinese oppression, the numbers of refugees increased. Out of these emerged the vagabonds known throughout the country as *khermel*, whose affairs had to be regulated by a vagabond chancellery in the capital Khüree.

Because the practice of giving servants as dowry continued until the beginning of the twentieth century in Mongolia, such dowry servants came to form a social group. A large number of dowry servants were exempt from service and tax. For this reason, the Manchurian statute books prescribed the number of *inji*s that a prince's daughter might have according to her social standing. For example, the married daughter of a prince of the rank *ching vang* could have 8 maidservants and 5 accompanying families; the married daughter of a prince of the rank *jung vang* could have 7 maidservants and 4 families; the married daughter of a prince of the rank *beil* could have 6 maidservants and 3 families; the married daughter of a prince of the rank *beis* could have 5 maidservants and 2 families and the married daughter of a prince of the rank *tushee güng* could have 3 maidservants and 2 families (*Lifanyuan zeli*, bk 25).

It can be concluded from the above that social differentiation in the pre-Manchurian period was shaped by familial and ethnic-social factors and had no economically determined character. With the politico-administrative and economic policy of Manchuria-China, social changes of a much more marked nature than ever before occurred in Mongolia, and out of these developed economically determined dependency relations in addition to the existing personal relations.

CRITICISM OF 'FEUDAL CLASS RELATIONS' IN MONGOLIA

One of the aspects of the theme of 'Mongolian feudalism' is the problem of the putative formation of a feudal and feudal-dependent class in Mongolia during the thirteenth century. In the works of B. Vladimircov,

I. Zladkin, Sh. Nacagdorj, N. Ishjamc and D. Gongor, in which the 'class structure' of Mongolian nomadic society is analysed, the development of this 'class structure' in Mongolia is divided into the following three periods:

1. *The period up to the formation of the Mongolian Empire at the start of the thirteenth century.* In this period, differences in wealth between tribal members emerged and the tribal structure began to crumble, essentially resulting in the formation of the class of feudal lords on the one hand and the class of serfs on the other.

2. *The period from about the thirteenth century to the seventeenth century.* The difference between these two classes deepened and accordingly the religious and secular feudal lords' oppression of their subjects intensified, resulting in an intensification of the class struggle.

3. *The period from the eighteenth century to the twentieth century.* Although there are no characteristics of a new era, researchers consider this period separately from the viewpoint of the development of class relations.

We believe that such an evaluation of the development of the 'class structure' of Mongolian nomadic society is based on the assumption of the theoretical concept of the universally historical feudal society. One should, however, be careful in applying the term 'class structure' in its true sense to Mongolian nomadic society.

In research works that focus on 'Mongolian feudalism', it is concluded in reference to the thirteenth century that in addition to the feudal class that comprised the Khaan, his family, princes of various ranks, attendants, privileged nobles, military commanders and wealthy aristocracy, there developed the class of serfs from common livestock keepers and servants. There is no doubt that in the sources social obligations of certain persons are referred to. There are, however, two problems in defining these groups as classes in the true sense of the word.

First it has to be clarified whether such terminology really refers to social standing and differences in obligations and wealth and defines fixed social groups. As we have mentioned, people were categorised principally by their familial and ethno-social backgrounds. Dependency relations were determined not by economic but by personal factors.

It must also be clarified whether social differences during this period were actually initiated by the process of social production, which in the end determines the formation of the entire social system, and whether they represented a process of the formation of a group of exploiters and a group of exploited. Under the conditions of nomadic livestock keeping, production was not socially organised. This means that common nomads were not producers in a socially organised production system but were small producers in a natural economy organised in the framework of the household. The economic dependency relations were in fact very weak.

These two problems are relevant not only in the thirteenth century but also in the period up to the Manchurian conquest in the seventeenth century. As we have mentioned above, it can be inferred from the records that the character of the social strata hardly changed before the seventeenth century and that there were no social changes which could have led to the formation of feudal classes.

In this connection it is worth mentioning some points that characterise the peasants and the nobles within the feudal means of production in pre-industrial Europe.

Peasants

In factual possession of the means of production and integrated into the local village form of co-operation, peasants in principle produce independently and are oriented towards the goal of directly consuming the annual yield whose fluctuations they attempt to balance by intensifying and extending their labour or vice versa. Long-term effects that stimulate production are caused more by external factors in the peasant production sphere: pressure of appropriation and marketing possibilities.

Their internal economic differentiation is determined by the type and quantity of the decisive means of production, the cultivated land, yet is limited from above by the labour capacity of their household community and from below by the availability of land, predominately the rights to use common land. If there are no such rights, the rural producer loses his peasant 'quality': he is economically dependent and cannot found a family.

From the peasant's perspective, the means by which surplus is appropriated represent variations of the general form of restriction of freedom. The basic elements are:

- limited freedom of movement (boundedness to the land);
- limited power to dispose of land (agreement of the lord to sell or bequeath);

- restriction of choice of marriage partner (assent to marry);
- enlistment for socage;
- limited availability of personal (familial) labour and of equipment;
- fee for the use of the latter, the setting up and operation of which remains the right of the lord;
- handing over of the annual yield as well as the stock of goods at the end of the fief period.

The general principle of all these forms is the long-term binding of the peasant economy to the lords so that the continued appropriation of surplus is ensured.

In order to further ensure this continuity, the peasants are cut off from the military apparatus and the most important organs of administration of justice.

Owing to the feudal pressure of rent, peasant resistance to the same and fluctuating economies, the peasants' legal and economic situations are in constant conflict.

Nobility

The collective status of the European feudal nobility is in principle characterised by:

- profit from peasant and demesne agriculture, from mining and quarrying, from manual labour production, from circulation of goods, wares and money and from rents;
- monopoly of weapons and execution of 'just' force;
- jurisdictional authority;
- authority over dispensation of religious care;
- 'innate' free standing;
- ostentatious consumption;
- corresponding forms of socialisation.

If one were to compare the above points with the traits of social differentiation in Mongolia, one would clearly see a basic difference. In Mongolian nomadic society of the period under consideration this differentiation was determined predominantly by the tradition of the nomadic way of life, for example by familial and ethnic factors and the military structure, and – to a lesser extent – by economic factors. In pre-industrial Europe social class structure was determined by ownership of the means of production and of land as well as by the organisation and division of labour. Therefore it is wrong to conclude that economically determined conditions for a feudal and a feudally dependent class existed in Mongolia, which would 'confirm' a development of feudal class relations in the country.

While social differentiation in the pre-Manchurian period was characterised by familial and ethno-social factors and was not of an economically determined nature, social changes, more marked than ever before, occurred in Mongolia with the politico-administrative and economic policies of Manchuria-China, as a consequence of which economically determined dependency relations within the population developed in addition to existing personal dependency relations. Owing to a complete social differentiation within the monastic system, with which we shall deal in the next chapter, the process of social differentiation in the entire society was deepened and accelerated. It can be maintained that from this period onwards, due to the effects of external factors, feudal conditions and social classes (which can be designated as feudal classes) began to form within Mongolian nomadic society which had hitherto developed basically by virtue of its own internal mechanism. The highly developed form of these feudal conditions and social classes can be especially seen in the transition period of the nineteenth–twentieth centuries.

5. The Effect of Lamaism on Traditional Mongolian Nomadic Society

The Spread of Lamaism in Mongolia

The changes that occurred in Mongolia in the course of its history were shaped not only by factors from the secular sphere but also to a large extent by its religion, e.i. Lamaism, the specific form of Buddhism. Because Shamanism, the traditional and indigenous religion of the country, was from the start a reflection of nomadic life and thus represented a spiritual world adapted to nomadism, it did not bring about changes to the nomadic way of life in the course of Central Asian history.

The spread of Lamaism in Mongolia, however, had an effect not only on spiritual life but also on economic, social and political organisations and on Mongolian life in general. We believe that the development of Lamaism as an external factor led to substantial changes in the course of traditional nomadic society, which since ancient times had proceeded naturally.

The dissemination of Lamaism amongst Mongolian nomads was not an easy process since nomadic society was a stable system of economy and corresponding forms of social organisation and thus was resistant to outside influence. The dissemination and attempts at the same extended over a period of centuries, and can be considered as occurring in two waves:

1. from the beginning of the thirteenth century until about the middle of the sixteenth century,

2. further dissemination after the end of the sixteenth century.

Genghis Khaan made many attempts to become acquainted with Buddhism. For example, he invited the Buddhist scholar, Lama Guntanba from Tibet; he lived and taught in Kara-Korum until the rule of Ogadai Khaan. There are also reports in the Tibetan chronicle of the nineteenth century, *Debter rGya-mcho*, that Genghis Khaan met with an influential monk of the Sa-skya school of Tibetan Buddhism, Sina, in north Tibet. The Khaan was inspired by his knowledge and engaged him for religious services in the royal court. With the support of Godan, Genghis Khaan's grandson Sina constructed the temple Sina-Sandub-Lin. The head of this temple, Sheirab-Eshei, later arranged the significant meeting of Sa-skya Pandita and P'ags-pa blama with the leading Mongolian princes (Dugarov 1983: 13).

After Genghis Khaan, the Khaans of the Mongolian Empire were tolerant towards foreign religions and even granted privileges to Buddhist monks. Because a successful governance of conquered peoples could only be achieved by acceptance of their religions, Buddhism was politically recognised for populations within Buddhist spheres of influence. The first significant contact between Mongolian princes and Tibetan religious dignitaries was made by Godan (d. 1252), the second son of Ogadai Khaan, in the period of the Grand Khaan Güyüg in 1247. With this, Buddhism gained a certain influence. When in 1578 Altan Khaan (1507–83) and the third Dalai Lama (1543–88) exchanged gifts and titles, Khutugtai Secen Khung *taij* (1540–86), the nephew of Altan Khaan, made the following speech:

> By command of the divine princes of heaven, our ancestor, the renowned Genghis Khaan, conquered by the five colours of his own people and the four related peoples of his rule. His two grandsons, the reincarnated one of Buddhist perfection, Bodhisattva Godan Khan, and the ruler of the world Khublai Secen Khaan placed the founder of the depths of all knowledge Sa-skya Pandita[1] and the religious light of breathing beings, the king of the teaching Phags-pa lama[2] at the pinnacle of spiritual administration and, following their example, summoned the faithful princes of the Mongol Lamas of the Sa-skyas and made breathing beings as happy as possible by just management of the administration (Schulemann 1958: 208–9).

The subsequent rule of Münkhe Khaan witnessed the ascendance of the Buddhist religion to primal position. For example, during the period of his rule there was a series of debates between the learned men of Taoism and of Buddhism, in which the latter triumphed (Thiel 1962).

However, Mongols did not detach themselves from traditional Shamanism. The reports of European travellers of this period such as W. Rubruck, G. Carpini, Marco Polo, etc., show that Mongols, from common livestock keepers to the Khaan, had faith in their shamans. From the various legends concerning the history of Mongolian Shamanism it can be seen that shamans strongly opposed the spread of Buddhism in Mongolia (Badamkhatan 1956: 226–27, 234). During the rule of Khublai Khaan, Buddhism was especially supported owing to the political interests of those governing Buddhist populations; consequently Buddhist monks were granted privileges. Khublai Khaan decreed that if anybody were to touch a Tibetan lama or a pupil of a lama, his hand would be cut off; if anybody insulted a Tibetan lama or a pupil of a lama by word, his tongue would be pulled out (Dalai 1992: 164). Succeeding Mongolian Grand Khaans of the Yüan dynasty always had Tibetan lamas as advisers in their courts, not only Sa-skya-pas and Karma-pas[3] but also followers of the ancient rNimma-pa school[4]. In particular, the friendship of Khublai Khaan with the nephew and successor of Sa-skya Pandita, Phags-pa Lama, laid the foundation for 'state-religious' development (Kaschewsky 1986: 89).

They created the concept of the Two Systems (*khoyor yosun*) and used it to develop not only a theory of harmonious relations between organised religion and the state but also a teaching of harmonious relations between the religious and the secular spheres in general (Sagaster 1976).

This teaching, however, found no real expression in the first wave of Buddhism in Mongolia. In spite of support from many sides for Buddhism and its important role in the political arena, Shamanism was not neglected. In the religious sacrificial ceremonies that were celebrated several times a year in the cities of Dadu and Shandu, Mongolian shamans participated, carried on their cult and conjured up their spirits (*Yuanshi*, vol. 77).

With the end of the Yüan dynasty in 1368 and the resulting collapse of the political unity of the Mongols, Buddhism had no chance of survival. The Mongols could indeed obtain scant motivation from the bordering areas of Buddhist spheres of influence, for example Amdo[5], but this had no effect in the face of the political disunity of the people. Buddhism only remained as a sort of guarantor of political rule for some princes, for example those of the West Mongols, in particular Batula Chingsan, his son Togan *taij*, and especially Togan's son Esen *taij*. The Karma-pa school and not the Sa-skya-pa school, however, was here dominant – perhaps this was to ensure the goodwill of the early Ming emperors Hongwu (ruled 1368–87) and Yongle (ruled 1404–25), who were favourable towards Tibetan Buddhism (Moses 1977: 84).

In all, in the thirteenth and fourteenth centuries the new religion Buddhism left its mark only on the environs of the imperial court in Kara-Korum and later in Dadu, as well as on urban estates. The religious life of the general population was not lastingly influenced by Buddhism, and Shamanism remained the traditional religion (Banzarov 1955: 97). After the collapse of the Yüan Empire, Shamanism was even restored to its earlier status. Thus in the first period of its dissemination, Buddhism did not gain sufficient influence so as to alter visibly the traditional structure of society. At first its effect was limited to the royal palace and the high-ranking nobility.

Reports concerning Buddhism re-emerge in Mongolia only after about the second half of the sixteenth century, but now in its form of Lamaism. This time its influence in the country was incomparably stronger and more lasting than during its first dissemination. Throughout the first half of the fourteenth century, Tibetan Buddhism was in deep crisis on account of internal disputes amongst monks, an exclusive concentration on the cult of Tantric divinities, poor discipline in monasteries and the dominating role of magic. The Tibetan monk rJe-rin-po-tsche Blo-bzang grags-pa bTsong-kha-pa (1357–1419) reformed Buddhist teaching and its Tibetan institutions and founded in 1409 his Lamaist sect dGe-lugs-pa, which was called the 'Yellow Cap Sect' or the 'School of Virtue'. He thus achieved his aim of harmoniously uniting the branch of Buddhism based on monastic discipline and philosophy with the branch of Tantric ritual. When the Mongols were converted to Buddhism for the second time, the Lamaistic 'Yellow Cap Sect' had already attained a pre-eminent position in Tibetan Buddhism.

The second spreading of Buddhism was substantially accelerated by the efforts of individual princes such as Altan Khaan (1507–82) of Tümed, and Abtai Sain Khan (1554–88) and Khutugtai Secen Khung *taij* (1540–86) of Ordos. An event of greatest significance for the intensified dissemination of Lamaism in Mongolia was the meeting of Altan Khaan with the chief lama of Tibet, Sodnomjamc (1542–1588), in the year 1578, during which Altan Khaan professed his Lamaist faith and declared it the state religion. Sodnomjamc promptly conferred upon him the title of one of 'the world rulers who turn a thousand golden wheels' and thus acknowledged his secular power. Altan Khaan, for his part, granted Sodnomjamc the title of a Vajirdara Dalai Lama (thunderbolt-wielding priest of the ocean)[6]. Tibetan Buddhism in its Lamaist form was then able to find renewed energy in Mongolia.

Although political interests of Mongolian princes endangered the renewed emergence of Buddhism and proselytising was initially an affair exclusively of princely houses, there is no justification for inferring a conscious action from outside to pacify and weaken the 'bellicose' Mongols. Patriotic Mongolian princes saw in Buddhism a sort of ideological prerequisite for the political and ethnic unification of the country. For example, the Lamaist religion in Mongolia had a definite influence on new notions of a 'pan-Mongolian union', which the South Mongolian Cakhar prince Ligden Khaan (1604–34) attempted to realise. The same also applies to Khalkha Mongolia in the following period. The great step of one of the Khalkha khans, Tüsheet Khan Gombodorji, of declaring his son Zanabajar (1635–1723) the religious ruler of Mongolia, was supported by all seven *khoshuu*s of Khalkha Mongolia and was confirmed by the Dalai Lama of Tibet who gave him the name *rJe-bcun dam-pa* (holy venerable ruler). This was the first 'Living Buddha' of Mongolia. This first *rJe-bcun dam-pa* was soon honoured as a holy man Öndör Gege'en (Öndör Gege'en Zanabajar). Later a line of succession of his earlier incarnations was compiled: this began with a pupil of the Buddha, Sakyamuni, and ended temporarily with his immediate 'predecessor', the great Tibetan lama and historian Taranatha (b. 1575) (Bawden 1968: 53–57, 68–80). The appointment of Öndör Gege'en to ruler of the Lamaist religion in Khalkha Mongolia was a veritable touchstone for Manchurian policy, which wavered between thoughts of a military conquest and of a peaceful subjugation of Khalkha Mongolia via its religion. At the high point of the military conflict between the West Mongolian prince Galdan (1632–97) and the princes of Khalkha Mongolia, the latter decided to surrender to the Manchu emperor.

In addition, measures were taken on the Manchurian side which favoured Lamaism. When the Manchu came to power in China

(1644) and then turned their attention towards Mongolia, the 'yellow religion' suffered no harm. Emperor Kangxi (1662–1722) built the monastery of Dolonur in 1700–1706 and many other monasteries far into the West Mongolian Alashan region, and from 1718–20 published a new de-luxe edition of the Mongolian *Ganjur*.[7] In the periods of rule of the Manchu emperors Yongzheng (1723–35) and Qianlong (1736–95), large monasteries such as Amurbayasgalant (1727) and Dambadarja (1750) were built in Khalkha Mongolia. Emperor Qianlong, the grandson of Kangxi, was a patron of the religion. During his rule in 1742–1749, *Danjur*,[8] a collection of commentaries, as well as the second part of the *Ganjur* were translated. The most important Buddhist canon was thus now completely available in the Mongolian language.

The Monastery Settlement as a New Phenomenon

In order to be in a position to understand the effect of Lamaism upon nomadic society, one must first separately analyse the institutions of the Lamaist religion, such as its monasteries, its economy and its monastic social differentiation, which from many sides influenced the society which had hitherto evolved by its own natural dynamics.

It was only at the end of the sixteenth century, with the second wave of Buddhist proselytisation by members of the dGe-lugs-pa sect, that a period of great activity began, especially regarding the construction of monasteries and temples whose economic and socio-political influence affected the nature of settlement in Mongolia all over.

The Buddhist monastery stood from the start in stark contrast to the nomadic way of life. It was here more a question of settlements attached to monasteries than settledness itself. Although nomadic society as an economically and socio-politically stable system had been resistant to external influences and in theory could not assimilate Buddhism within its mobile way of life, the contrary proved to be true in the end. While there had been no considerable permanent settlements, except the capital Kara-Korum, before the spread of Buddhism, monastery settlements now began rapidly to be built everywhere. Initially, but only for a short time, Mongols were content with mobile tent temples and *yurt* monasteries which were suited to their nomadic lifestyle. In the course of time, however, these became stationary.

The causes of this stationing of Lamaism in Mongolia are as follows:

First, Buddhism, or Lamaism, is a monastic religion and its history is predominantly one of monastic communities. Stationary activity in the Buddhist religion was originally determined by the fact that monks had to live in a community. Under the conditions and rules of monastic life, measures were necessary in order to maintain discipline, punish transgressors and possibly expel them from the monastery. Therefore the killing of a living being, a lack of chastity, theft and boasting of supernatural abilities resulted in exclusion from the community. There were 253 prohibitions in all, the observance of which was supervised by the entire monastic community. Moreover, from the start, monastic life was recommended to and imagined by the people as an object of religious adoration, as the sole life-penetrating, supernatural and at the same time most perfect field of activity with the aim of attaining supernatural reward. In general this is true even today.

Second, Buddhism was and still is no simple religious form, as was Shamanism. When it reached Mongolia in its Tibetan form of Lamaism, it was already more than 1,500 years old. It incorporated the many spiritual and practical achievements of oriental society. Thus the dissemination of Lamaism in Mongolia brought with it a complex cult and ritual system, extensive teachings and sacred buildings. All these were intricately connected with one another:

1. the extensive collections of canonical texts, tracts and non-canonical literature, and with these the printing works;

2. the need for permanent sites for studying texts, for instructing lama pupils, for holding religio-philosophical debates, for sacred rites and ceremonies and for assemblies of various sorts;

3. the numerous iconographic objects, cult images, masks and musical instruments required for rituals and the many other furbishments of monasteries.

Religious centres of such a nature did not accord with the conditions of nomadism and could only be maintained as permanent establishments. One might perhaps enquire why permanent monasteries were built and why *yurt*s on an enlarged scale could not have fulfilled this function. First, Buddhist ritual and monastic architecture formed a unity. This means that the style of temple most suited to Lamaism in Mongolia was that of the Chinese and Tibetans. Second, simple nomadic *yurt*s and tents did not functionally accord with the needs of a permanent site. The mobility of religious sites was gradually phased out.

- After the establishment of monastic ownership of *nutug*s, nomadic *yurt* monasteries became increasingly more settled and a process of settlement was introduced in the religious centres of Khalkha Mongolia. The ownership of *nutug*s by the Lamaist religion and the *khutagt*s and *khuvilgaan*s (possession of *shavi* livestock keepers with their animals and of pasture land, etc.) emerged in about the middle of the seventeenth century. One of the forces behind this development was the active support of the princes who frequently declared their children or the children of near relatives as reincarnations of a *khutagt* or a high-ranking lama and thereby presented them with a share of their possessions. For example, with the appointment of Öndör Gege'en as the first *rJe-bcun dam-pa khutagt* in Khalkha Mongolia, the princes presented him with 32 *ail*s as *shavi*s.

- It is true, as most scholars write, that the initially mobile temples grew with the rapidly increasing number of monks and in the end had to become stationary. Monasteries under the conditions of Mongolian nomadic society were not only the religious but also the sole spiritual-cultural centres. Thus the number of permanently residing Lamas quickly grew. There is unfortunately no information about the number of Lamas in the seventeenth and eighteenth centuries. According to a list dating from the 1930s, there were still 90,000 Lamas in Mongolia, which, in comparison with the size of the population, is a huge number. A census in 1918 revealed that there were 542,504 people living in the four *aimag*s of Khalkha Mongolia including the Khövsgöl and Khovd regions (Maiskii 1921: 16). For the monks it was more difficult to conduct their activities in the framework of a nomadic lifestyle. For faithful nomads, on the other hand, it was easier to make use of permanent centres.

It can be conjectured that, in addition to the above internal reasons, there was also an external, subjective influence on the settling of Lamaist monasteries. In the building of a monastery it was necessary to create a worthy and impressive site of worship for the sake of one or more revered personages, for example 'Erdeni zuu', one of the first monasteries in Khalkha Mongolia, which was built in 1586 near Kara-Korum. In addition, many temples were built by dignitaries who sought to appear more beneficent. Under the direction of Öndör Gege'en, at least 16 monasteries (Maidar 1972: 52) were founded and built up to the end of the seventeenth century.

Moreover, the Manchu emperors supported the building of monasteries in Khalkha Mongolia and had many built throughout the entire Mongolian region. The emperors Kangxi (1662–1722), Yongzheng (1723–35) and also Qianlong (1736–95) not only built 'imperial' monasteries in Mongolia, they also provided for the livelihood of the lamas; however, to finance this they obliged surrounding *khoshuu* areas to pay regular taxes.

In all, there were large monasteries, which formed a city settlement (*khüree*), average sized and smaller monasteries, hermitages (*khyid*) and rural settlements which were not always lived in (*süm-e, khural*). The largest and most renowned monasteries were mostly sites of worship of reincarnated high-ranking Lamaist dignitaries, *khutagt*s and *khuvilgaan*s, as well as imperial monasteries in certain provinces and regions. D. Cedev writes that in 1796 there were 114 religious centres in Mongolia (Cedev 1964: 7). In the course of time the number of monasteries of various sizes constantly increased. In 1937 there were in all 771 monasteries (*BNMAU-yn tüükh* 1984: 442) in the Khalkha Mongolian region. According to other sources, the total number of religious centres at this time was 941, of which 937 were Buddhist monasteries, one was a Roman Catholic church, one was a mosque in the capital Khüree and two were mosques in today's Bayan-Ölgii (Rinchen 1979: 24–44).

Monastic Economy

Jas (jis) *and* sang

The most important prerequisite for the establishment of the monastic economy was the extensive support provided by the nobility who handed over pasture land, livestock and subjects. Only on the basis of this was it possible for the monastic economic institution *jas* to develop. Monastic economic organisations differed from secular ones in their size and their concentrated form of operation. The emergence of the *jas* was connected with monastic economic forms becoming more and more varied. The first *jas* were founded in the second half of the seventeenth century: the *jas* of the capital Khüree in 1656 (Damdin, ch. 5, 25) and the *jas* of Zasagt Khan *Aimag* in 1684. Each monastery gradually established its own *jas* economy from donations and gifts from the faithful. Reports about the increase in the number of herds and economic procedures adopted are scarce from the end of the seventeenth century to the end of the eighteenth century. Detailed official files that date from the end of the eighteenth century show that at this time a process of development occurred, which was characterised by the founding of numerous new *khoshuu*s of the Zasagt Khan, Tüsheet Khan, Secen Khan and Sain Noyan Khan *Aimag*s, and resulted in an increase in wealth of the *jas* and in the *jas* becoming an independent institution. This economic growth resulted in turn in an extension of the Buddhist sphere of influence. This means that the acquired wealth was used not only for financing religious concerns but also for promoting a multifaceted, economically independent policy in competition with secular economic organisations, as the contacts with the merchants *daamal, zaisan, nyarav* and *baga nyarav* or *tuslagch* demonstrate.

The largest monasteries, and their *jas*, belonged to the religious head *rJe-bcun dam-pa*. The huge number of *khar-shavi*s and lamas as well as the extensive possession of herds and pasture land of *rJe-bcun dam-pa*, which were distinguished from the possessions of other religious grand dignitaries by the names *ikh shavi* and *bogdyn shavi*, necessitated the creation of a general religious administration. The chancellery *erdene shanzavyn yam* was founded by decree of the Manchu emperor in 1723 as the highest administrative organ of the *ikh shavi* and its authority was later extended. For example, in 1822 it was the administrative equal of the *chuulgan* chancellery. The *ikh shavi* became in the nineteenth century a unit economically comparable to the four *aimag*s.

It can be inferred from official files from the end of the eighteenth century that another economic form emerged within the monasteries of some *khutagt*s and *khuvilgaan*s, i.e. the *sang* which became independent economic entities. At the end of the eighteenth century and particularly in the nineteenth century, the number of herds belonging to the *jas* and *sang* continued to increase. This growth in the monastic economy can be attributed to the following:

- Freedom from taxes for the *jas* and *sang* favoured the economic development of monasteries.

- Due to the growing influence of Lamaism amongst the population, livestock donations became more and more significant.

- The faithful tended the herds of monasteries and high-ranking monks and worked without payment, as a divine sacrifice so to speak.

- The economic policy of *jas* and *sang* officials contributed substantially to the consolidation of monastic economy.

As a consequence, at the end of the nineteenth century, the number of herds belonging to the *jas* and *sang* was greater than that belonging to the secular nobility. For example, the livestock of the *jas* and *sang* from the Jung-Vang *khoshuu* of the Secen Khan *Aimag* comprised in 1890 some 85% of the entire *khoshuu*'s livestock (*Secen Khan*... 1897).

The Manchu took absolutely no measures to solve the problem of *khoshuu* pasture land required by the *shavi*s for livestock belonging to the Lamas. After 1772 an assembly of Mongolian princes confirmed the right of the *shavi*s to use pasture land in all four Khalkha *aimag*s.

Forms of exploitation in the monastic economy

As subjects dependent on the monasteries and monks, the *shavi*s had to render labour and produce to the monasteries and their *khutagt*s and *khuvilgaan*s. The services which the *khar-shavi* had to carry out for their *khutagt*s and *khuvilgaan*s were varied. They tended the animals, worked in the various areas of livestock economy and served in the lamas' households. Because most monasteries consisted of tent temples and *yurt*s until the start of the eighteenth century, the *shavi*s were obliged to carry out chores pertaining to removal. This last service gradually faded out as monasteries became settled.

The most important service was the tending of animals. This can be classified into two forms:

1. Compulsory tending: in the chronicles this form is mentioned frequently from the end of the eighteenth century (Purevjav 1978: 146). This is because up till then, the number of livestock kept by the monasteries and monks was not great and there were enough live-stock keepers who voluntarily performed this task. In the course of the eighteenth century the number of Lamas grew dramatically; these, being occupied with ritual and ceremony, had practically no involvement in the running of the *jas* and *sang*. Thus the number of *khar-shavi*, livestock keepers belonging to monasteries or dignitaries, who voluntarily tended *jas* and *sang* herds, fell. As a result the monastic administration compelled non-lama *shavi*s and livestock keepers to tend *jas* and *sang* livestock.

2. Towards the end of the eighteenth century, the *jas* and *sang*s began to introduce payment for tending their livestock. This was an econo-mic mechanism, which was hitherto unknown in

Mongolia. Because this payment was very low, tenders were allowed freely to use animal produce. It is worth mentioning that from the end of the nineteenth century, a new tax regulation was enforced, according to which tax was due on semi-finished products per animal.

The obligation of the *shavi*s to render produce was, as we have already mentioned, one of the most important forms of exploitation by the monastic economy. In the sources it is written that this obligation was introduced in about the second half of the eighteenth century (Purevjav 1978: 193–94). Although there are no references to the extent of rendering produce in Manchurian legislation, it was approximately the same as in the secular sphere (ibid., 193). Rendering of produce existed in the form of animal products such as milk, dairy produce, meat, fat, wool, hides, etc., or in the form of fuel, household articles and clothing or in the form of draft animals, agricultural produce, etc.

In addition to the regular rendering of produce, other dues were exacted in special cases. According to official files, these dues also applied to non-*shavi*s.

Another incipient form of tax – payment in the form of money within the sphere of the monastic economy – is encountered in official files from the end of the eighteenth century. This form became more frequent in the course of the nineteenth century.

Money-lending

A source of wealth throughout the monastic economy, which did not exist in the economy of traditional nomadic society, was money-lending, carried out by the monasteries in competition with Chinese money-lenders. In the wake of changes in Manchurian immigration policy, Chinese money-lenders started to come to Khalkha Mongolia in the second half of the eighteenth century (Ochir and Dashnyam 1988).

It might well be conjectured that money-lending assumed a significant form in the monastic economy, for which there is some documentary evidence. This shows that the *rJe-bcun dam-pa* and the high-ranking monks condemned such practices. Because there is little information concerning money-lending in the eighteenth century, no conclusions can be reached as to the extent which it attained. On the other hand, there are ample official files from the nineteenth century which deal with money-lending in the monastic economy of Khalkha Mongolia. This indicates that money-lending continued to increase in the nineteenth century.

Monastic Social Differentiation

Originally there were no statements in Buddhist teaching which permitted a social differentiation amongst monks. In the course of the spread of Buddhism in India, China and Tibet, however, socio-economic secular influences on Buddhism increased, with the result that secular forms of social differentiation appeared in monastic life. When Buddhism began to spread in Mongolia in the thirteenth and fourteenth centuries, it was already the arena of the religio-political and economic struggle between the Sa-skya-pa and Gar-ma-pa schools in Tibet. This had as a consequence the emergence of a highly branched hierarchy and social differentiation. When bTson-kha-pa, as we have already mentioned, founded in 1409 the dGe-lugs-pa (yellow cap sect) with the aim of freeing Buddhism from its internal disputes, social inequality continued to deepen. Because the dissemination of Buddhism in Mongolia in the period of the thirteenth and fourteenth centuries did not extend much further than the environs of the imperial court and the higher-ranking princes, the internal strata of Buddhism were unimportant in Mongolia. It was only after the second half of the seventeenth century that social differentiation within monastic life appeared rapidly in Khalkha Mongolia in connection with the explosive spread of Lamaism. It had a definite influence on the transformation of the structure of the entire nomadic society.

High-ranking monks

High-ranking monks were as a rule community members of aristocratic background, such as *rJe-bcun dam-pa khutagt*, *khutagt*s with and without seal,[9] the grand *toyin lama*s[10] and the *khuvilgaan*s. Apart from their differing degrees of holiness, these high-ranking dignitaries as a rule held the office and the honours of chief monks of monasteries which, in the majority of cases, they had founded. As such they had the monastery property at their complete disposal. Although the *rJe-bcun dam-pa* was the head of Buddhism in Khalkha Mongolia, the *khutagt*s and *khuvilgaan*s were only partially subordinated to him.

The other groups of monks of high standing were the lamas working in the monastic administrative apparatus, such as the *khamb* (abbot), the *corji* (director of the monastery management), the *dalama* (throne lama), the *umzad* (choir leader or main reciter), the *geskü̈i* (chief supervisor), etc. There are references in legal writings that even in the first half of the seventeenth century, a large number of *corji, umzad, gesgüi* and lama teachers were of noble birth. Although these offices were allocated not according to background but according to age and competence, there are references that higher offices were attained more and more frequently by means of bribery (Sumbe Khambo 12–13).

The lower social strata: khar-shavi *and* lam- *(or* lama-*)* shavi

The lower social strata of monasticism consisted of subjects or *khar-shavi*s, and monks or *lam-shavi*s, belonging personally to the high-ranking lamas. Initially a small group of *ail*s belonged as subjects only to the monastery Erdeni zuu. In the course of time the number of *khar-shavi*s increased, and they came to be categorised as *shavi*s of the *rJe-bcun dam-pa* or as *jas otog*s or, in the case of smaller units, as *bag*s (Perlee 1978: 83–85). According to statistics from 1918, the *rJe-bcun dam-pa khutagt* had altogether 198 *otog*s and *bag*s. Most of these were not independent territorial-administrative units; rather they represented ownership of pasture land, livestock and subjects within the *khoshuu*. The difference between a *khar-shavi* and a secular subject was only formal. The only difference worth mentioning lay in the fact that *khamjilaga* subjects were inherited by secular princes while *khar-shavi*s, being subjects of reincarnated *khutagt* and *khuvilgaan*, were not inherited (Nacagdorj 1978: 211). This means that the economic situation of *khar-shavi*s did not differ at all from that of secular subjects.

In the pre-Manchurian period, there was also the peculiarity that the *shavi*s did not have their own territory. Because they were not directly drawn into service for the monastic economy, they remained in their former homelands, as a result of which a difficult problem arose. On the one hand they were no longer subordinated to the rule of their former princes; on the other hand, they used pasture land within his territory. Thus there arose frequently struggles for pasture land in smaller princedoms. Another problem arose due to the dramatic increase in the number of *lam-shavi*s and *khar-shavi*s. This development occurred on account of the possibility of escaping dependence upon the princes, since a *lam-shavi* or a *khar-shavi* was exempt from certain duties, for example military service.

With the Manchurian conquest of Khalkha Mongolia, little changed at first in the religious situation in the country. In 1657 the Manchu passed a law that limited the number of lamas in each *khoshuu* to 40. This law was later enforced throughout Khalkha Mongolia, yet they continued with their policy of tolerance towards the religion. Furthermore, the religious institution was granted gifts and several monasteries were founded. The law limiting the number of lamas in a *khoshuu* was liberally interpreted, as a consequence of which the number of *lam-shavi*s and *khar-shavi*s continued to grow. For example, in 1825 *rJe-bcun dam-pa* alone had 111,466 *lam-shavi*s and *khar-shavi*s (Cedev 1964: 26), while the number had been 17,000 in 1710 (*BNMAU-yn tüükh* 1968: 182). The total population figure, which would make these statistics more meaningful, is unfortunately not known. The census conducted in 1918 reported that there were 476,504 inhabitants in the four *aimag*s, and 542,504 inhabitants if one includes the West and North Mongolian peoples in the Khovd and Khövsgöl regions. If one considers that the *shavi* regions of the *rJe-bcun dam-pa* did not at this time extend far beyond the territories of the four *aimag*s, the total number of *lam-shavi*s and *khar-shavi*s could well have amounted to between a fifth and a quarter of the population.

CONCLUSIONS

Until about the middle of the sixteenth century the religious life of the population had not been lastingly influenced by Buddhism. In this period only the environs of the imperial court were marked by it. After about the second half of the sixteenth century, the main period of dissemination of Buddhism began. Initially this was accelerated by the efforts of individual princes who saw in Buddhism a sort of ideological prerequisite for the political and ethnic reunification of the Mongols.

After the Manchurian conquest, the Manchu emperor took many measures in Mongolia that favoured Lamaism. This was because the Manchu recognised at an early stage the effect of the Buddhist religion, which could well pacify the 'bellicose Mongols'. As a result of the 'second conversion' of the Mongols, Lamaism exerted a substantial influence on all social spheres of the country.

As a consequence, various phenomena arose which had an effect on the evolution of Mongolian nomadic society. The building of monasteries was a factor of settledness in contrast to the traditional Mongolian mobile way of life. In comparison to secular economic organisations, monastic economic organisations were characterised by their size and the concentrated form of operation. Exploitation, labour, and the rendering of produce and money resulted in the monastic economy (in comparison to the secular economy) achieving a more organised and fixed character. Another source of wealth that was widespread in the monastic economy and that did not exist in the economy of traditional nomadic society, was money-lending. With a complete social differentiation within monastic life, the process of social differentiation in the entire society was deepened and accelerated.

6. The Dynamics of the Development of Mongolian Nomadic Society

It is first necessary to clarify the framework in which nomadic society should be considered and exactly what the term 'nomadic society' should encompass. We shall appraise nomadic society in its natural-ecological and socio-political framework. Nomadism as 'socio-ecological mode of culture of the nomads', as the German scholar of nomadic studies F. Scholz formulates it (1995: 24–32), should not be taken to mean a form of survival for part of the population or a rudimentary economic form, but a system of society. In other words, the system of nomadic society has an internal structure and functions arising from this structure: if the stability of the structure and functions is lost owing to either internal change or external influences, the system no longer exists as nomadic society.

In order to understand the dynamics of the development of nomadism amongst the Mongols, two aspects need to be investigated: the constituents of the nomadic society system; the evolution of nomadic society.

Constituents of the Nomadic Social System

Nomadic livestock keeping as basis of nomadism

As we have already seen in Chapter 2, the natural-ecological conditions in the Central Asian highlands compelled the peoples to keep livestock in order to ensure their own survival. Not only does this economic form represent a complete adaptation to the special natural conditions: it is in fact the only possible economic form that can make use of these conditions. The natural barrenness of the land, its topography and expansive distances demand an optimally adapted and lasting means of use. Suitable and repeated migrations of herds between natural pastures as well as an appropriate herd-pasture management serve this purpose. By means of 'nomadism' the peoples of this region resolved the dilemma of an effective usage of pasture land to satisfy the food requirements of their animals and the seasonal variations in this pasture land. Nomadic livestock keeping, or nomadism, can only be maintained within a definite socio-political framework.

This close connection between livestock keeping and nomadism shows that one must suitably differentiate between, on the one hand, peoples who have to live a nomadic life in order to keep their herds and, on the other, peoples who on account of geographic conditions conduct livestock keeping in a settled form. In this connection it is worth citing what E. E. Vardiman remarks on Near Eastern nomadism:

> With the rearing of cattle, which require care and good feed, migratory life stopped. Livestock keepers were forced to acquire land on which they could cultivate feed to supply to large animals during the dry season. The beginning of cattle breeding was also the beginning of agriculture ... Cattle breeding marked the point of time when all ancient peoples of a higher level of culture became settled (Vardiman 1990: 78, 80).

Feed and water reserves, which differ from season to season or episodically but which are however always scarce, restrict in the end the size of herds, and thus determine the size of the cooperative group of keepers. An increase in the number of members of such a group or a general population increase can only be countered by sharing resources, seeking out new pasture land, migrating and leaving the nomadic territory.

Family structure as an appropriate form of social organisation

A culture geared towards mobility can only survive with an appropriate organisation of society. This manifests itself in social forms such as tribes, semi-tribes and extended families which are founded acephalously or patrilinearly. Kh. Perlee, doyen of ancient Mongolian research, noted during his investigations into tribal seal impressions the interesting phenom-enon that the nomadic peoples of Central Asia who left their territory, gradually gave up their tribal structure as they adopted a settled way of life (Perlee 1976: 36). This demonstrates the close connection between economic conditions and tribal organisation. Tribal coherence is an ideal condition for internal as well as intertribal solidarity, resistance to enemies, mutually beneficial partnerships, usage of pasture land and long migrations. These conditions do not arise from external actions; rather, they are determined by economic conditions.

This original amalgamation on the tribal level gave rise amongst the Mongols to such forms as *khüree*, *khoroo*, *ail* and *khot-ail*. Administrative regulation was also carried out throughout Mongolian history under the remit of family relations. Although the traditional form changed in the course of time into a form of defence and administrative unit, its fundamental and direct connection to nomadic livestock keeping continued over a definite period of time. We know that legislation such as the 'Mongol-Oirat Regulations of 1640', *Khalkha Jirum*, etc., was based on tribal organisation and tribal life. For example, there are many references in the 'Mongol-Oirat Regulations of 1640' which show clearly that during this period family relations remained strong within society. It is also believed that the way of life continued to be based on tribal and family membership even from the second half of the eighteenth century up to the realisation of Manchurian administrative policy, which led in particular to the containment of nomadism.

To view nomadic livestock keeping in relation with tribal organisation does not mean negating its development potential. If one were to adopt this viewpoint, one might well imagine tribal organisation to be an inferior stage in human history.

The above-sketched constituents of Mongolian nomadic society imply that nomadism emerges when a family-related group, in order to ensure its survival, can only make use of a barren natural-ecological land potential by migrating with herds of animals. It ceases to be nomadic when this potential changes or is no longer available or viable with this social grouping.

Military conflict as an attributive functional character of nomadic life
Why were the nomads of Central Asia aggressive?

A substantial functional component of the nomadic social system was 'bellicosity' or 'pillage', as it is frequently characterised in non-Mongolian sources and research works. 'In the highlands, apart from livestock keeping ... the peaceful nomadic life and the roving and fickle life of their pillages are to be distinguished' (Hegel 1986: 131). The history of Inner Asia is often characterised by conflicts between nomadic tribes, the ousting of nomadic empires and the wars of legendary rulers such as Genghis Khaan, and particularly by invasions of nomadic conquerors and the defences of settled agriculturists. The important question 'why?' is, however, rarely answered.

The reason for this phenomenon lies basically in the interaction between nature and society. Pastoral economy depends completely on the natural pasture which, in turn, is vulnerable to ecological changes. Nomads were able to safeguard their survival of relatively short periodic droughts by means of their mobile way of life. They left drought-stricken regions within their seasonal migration cycle until conditions there normalised and they travelled hundreds of kilometres to foreign pasture land where, however, they might not have been peacefully received. Thus the reason why nomadic tribes often engaged in conflicts with one another was the struggle for pasture land reserves. In times of long-term or global drought, however, they were obliged to attack settled peoples. Results of studies into the correlation of these two factors convincingly show that large-scale invasions of Central Asian nomads into northern China mostly ensued after years of deteriorating climatic-ecological conditions in the nomadic regions of Inner Asia. In this respect the cause of the 'bellicosity' is to be sought in the core of extensive nomadic livestock keeping, where the fundamental difference between settled and nomadic peoples lies.

Production in nomadic livestock keeping requires no technology and the division of labour demands merely an elementary, easily exchangeable specialisation, so the need for technological development, a constantly deepening division of labour and a resulting increase in production are foreign to nomadism. Hardly in a single sector was the economy in a position to satisfy the varied requirements of the people, and thus attacking other, especially settled, civilisations was the main means of developing trade relations and/or of obtaining necessary products as tribute. One cannot or does not want to subsist solely from animal produce. The most important requirements of the nomads were metal, with which they forged their weapons, grain, tea, numerous articles of luxury and textiles. Apart from hunting, which is no more efficient than livestock keeping, no non-pastoral activity could serve the nomads as a secondary economic basis to ensure their survival, especially in times of crisis. The nomads always had to satisfy some of their needs by trade with settled societies to the south.

Reciprocally, settled civilisation could find a use for the nomads' own products: commerce was regarded as mutually beneficial. The relationship between the steppe and the sown should not be envisaged as one of constant hostility, marked by a predatory urge on the one side and a fearful defensiveness on the other. In the time of peace, however uneasy, it was more a relationship of mutual dependence, though Chinese products were more central to the nomads' needs than any-thing from the steppes was to the Chinese (Morgan 1990: 33–34).

For the Mongols, just as for the pre-Mongolian Central Asian nomads, it was essentially a matter of appropriating goods produced by a settled economy, which could not be produced in the nomadic economy. This state could well be described as 'aggressive'. In contrast, for example, feudal and absolute rulers in Europe conducted many wars not for the sake of their survival, but with the aim of conquering regions of other feudal states in order to expand their personal power. It is necessary to check whether there are other differences between the 'bellicosity' of feudal princes and kings and the 'desire for conquest' of nomadic peoples, and whether these differences vanished in the period of conquests after the establishment of the Mongolian Empire. In this respect it would be superficial and simplistic to assume that the 'aggressiveness' arose on its own accord. Ruling over foreign countries and peoples was not the actual aim of Mongolian invasions. The wars which developed from the above-described causes were conducted under several especially favourable conditions with an enormous momentum and thus in terms of success far exceeded the feats of preceding nomadic peoples.

War-favouring conditions of the Mongols

The work of V. S. Taskin (1984: 36), which investigates sources connected with the history of the peoples belonging to the group Dunhu[1], demonstrates that in the history of the Central Asian nomadic empires the military function was of especially great significance. In the period of the Xiongnu dynasty (3th–2th centuries B.C.), the power of a prince was manifested in the number of his subjects, the size of his region being of little importance. Of great significance, however, was the ability to muster large numbers of warriors (Fan 1958: 76). Of all the services that Mongolian nomads had to render to their masters (e.g. beating during hunts, the relay post), the single most important was military service. In the period of the Mongolian Empire, the requirements and structure of the military-political organisation in some areas were of a far greater extent than those of previous nomadic empires in Central Asia. If, for example, in the period of the Kidan Empire in the tenth century men between the ages of 15 and 50 were enlisted as warriors (Tog-to 1958: ch. 34, 2b), then the military regimen of the Mongols, with its recruitment of men between the ages of 15 and 70, can be viewed as far more intensive (Sun Lian 1958: 98, 2a).

There are several factors explaining the invasions and successes of the Mongols in the thirteenth century: the situation of global development of the Mongols and their settled neighbours such as the Chinese state; the change in climatic-ecological conditions; their mobile way of life; their stratagem; and Shamanism.

The repeating cycle of development had more or less left its mark in the history of the peoples of the region. The temporal correlation of the cycle's concentration and dispersion phases amongst the nomads and their settled neighbours to the south and west, such as the Chinese and the Arabs, created a favourable situation for the war-waging nomads. Research into civilisations shows that, while the Chinese culture was in its decentralisation phases, the nomads were often, but not always, in their centralisation phases.

Geographical conditions played a role in many respects in the waging of war and in the huge military successes of the Mongols. As we have mentioned above, there are data in ancient Chinese chronicles which refer to decreases in temperature and to constant natural catastrophes in the nomadic homeland of today's Mongolia. A drop in air temperature, winter thunderstorms and duststorms can be demonstrated as occurring in a correlated manner in the course of the previous 1,500 years.

For example, the Chinese researcher Zhu deduced changes in air temperature mainly from phenological considerations (Zhu 1973). Although the sources of Zhu's data are diverse, ranging from ancient poems, private travel diaries, local chronicles, agricultural texts and official chronicles, his temperature curve has been judged credible by a number of researchers such as Wang. Wang inferred from ancient Chinese chronicles that for some 202 years in the period from 250 B.C.

to A.D. 1900 winter thunderstorm events occurred in the northern part of China (Wang 1980). He hypothesised that a colder and stronger Siberian high resulted in a strong, fast-moving cold front which caused a rapid uplift of warm air ahead of it and thus induced more frequent winter thunderstorms.

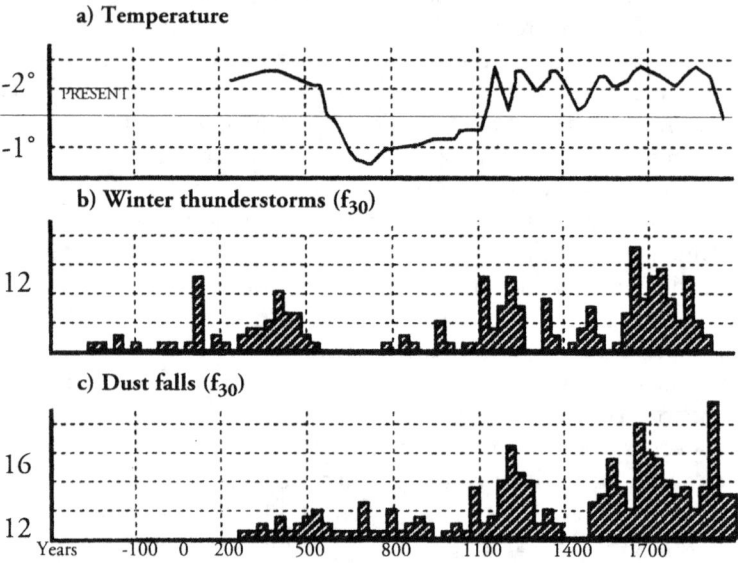

Figure 5: a) Changes in temperature, b) frequency of winter thunderstorms in intervals of 30 years (f_{30}) and c) changes in frequency of dust falls in intervals of 30 years (f_{30}) (Fang and Liu 1992)

Duststorms also reflect the change of aridity in the nomadic homelands in some way. The Chinese researcher Zhang has reconstructed time series of duststorms in Northern China in the period 470 B.C. to A.D. 1790 based on historical records in local and other chronicles. He studied the sources of the dust and its relationship to climatic change (Zhang 1984), and concluded that the dust originated from the deserts of northwestern China and Inner Mongolia where the nomadic peoples lived. He suggested that a high frequency of duststorms was associated with a stronger Siberian high, which caused a steeper pressure gradient and stronger and in principle drier winter monsoons over Eastern Asia (see Fig. 5). These facts accord not only temporally with one another but also with other information from Chinese chronicles such as large-scale migrations of nomads southwards, changes in migration, and settlement borders between nomads and Chinese and military attacks of nomads on regions to the south (see Figure 6).

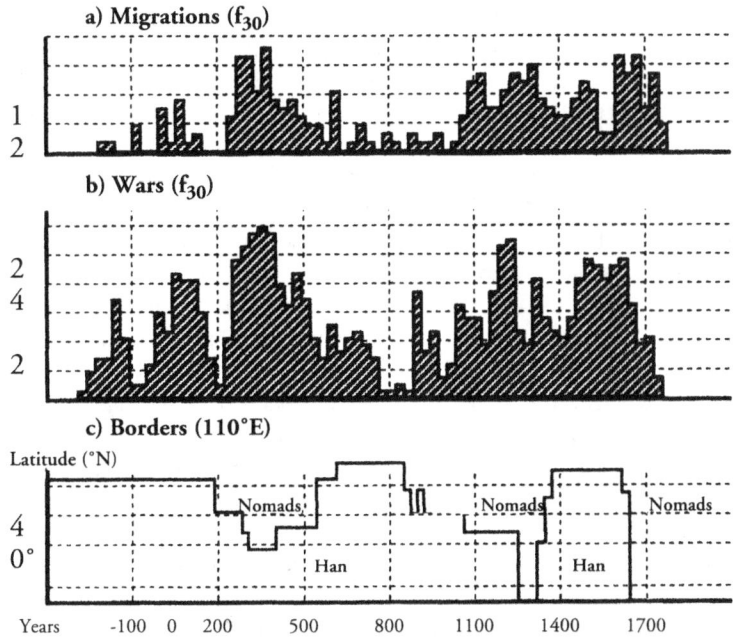

Figure 6: Correlation between number of years and a) direct migration records in intervals of 30 years (f_{30}), b) frequency of war (f_{30}) and c) changes in administrative borders between Han and nomad powers along longitude 110°E (Fang and Liu 1992)

Chinese researchers have also found in Chinese dynastic chronicles 276 years in the period 190 B.C. to A.D. 1880 which have direct records of the migrations of nomadic tribes from their homelands, with fewest direct migration records 650–1050. Furthermore, they found a total of 802 years in the period 250 B.C. to A.D. 1820 which have records of conflicts, of which the periods 280–500, 1100–1350 and 1600–1800 witnessed a China torn by war (Fang and Liu 1992: 154–56).

In addition, there are no special geographical hindrances for the southern invasions of Central Asian nomads. Such invasions were of decisive significance in the history of the development of the Chinese state. This is seen, for example, from the prevalence of explanations, on the basis of exogenous theory, of the origins and the further dynamic development of the Chinese state via the influence of external powers. Chinese culture 'differs from all other higher cultures by its relationship with the nomad problem. In no other place in the world was a so highly developed culture incessantly confronted with so expansive nomad regions and so numerous nomadic peoples' (Herzog 1988: 199). For example, Egypt was to a large degree protected by virtue of its geographical location. The deserts which surround it to the east and to the west made large-scale nomadic invasions impossible from the outset. It was able to cope with repeated attacks from Nubian and Libyan peoples (who were not in a real sense nomads) and had difficulties only with nomadic tribes from the Syrian and Arabian deserts. All this, however, had no definite influence upon its development. Mesopotamia, on the other hand, was on account of its natural conditions practically indefensible against nomadic invasions. The line of defence was too long and the country, apart from periods of short duration, was never under a centralised control, with the result that a unified defence strategy was not possible. Thus there were always attacks, predominantly from Semitic tribes, which the population was able to fend off only with its almost inexhaustible capacity for integration. Other regions, for example, Bactria and East Persia, bordered on extensive nomadic zones; however the cultural differences between the settled and nomadic peoples were not very great.

The nomadic livestock keeping lifestyle demands more flexibility, versatility, independence and initiative than the agricultural lifestyle. Such characteristics were advantageous in war. The mobile way of life facilitated the proliferation of enduring pillage campaigns.

The nature of nomadic society on the steppe was such that to speak of the Mongol army is really no more than to speak of the Mongol people in one of its natural aspects. For the whole of life was a process of military training. The same techniques that were necessary for survival in a herding and hunting environment were, with little adaption, those used in warfare (Morgan 1990: 84).

Hunting served as a sporting activity and was thus a good preparation for warfare. In addition, the nomads' expertise with horses and their physical ability to endure long rides was for them a considerable advantage over settled peoples. Their being accustomed to keeping their households to a minimum was also a plus in waging war, and their use of light but practical clothing and of preserved food, such as dried meat and desiccated milk, during rides of months' duration was also of major importance. Due to the extreme continental climatic conditions, the nomads of Central Asia possessed special mental and physical characteristics which helped them endure or adapt to new natural regions – a necessity which followed from migrations between high- and low-lying locations and constant change of abode.

The ruse of war (or stratagem), passed down from generation to gener-ation by the nomads of Central Asia, is of course one of the main factors for their military successes. Much has been written in the chronicles about the military techniques of the Mongols. They employed strategies such as the concerted attack; sham retreat, in which they withdrew up to distances of 12 days' march; giving the impression that their numbers were greater via their quantity of horses, scare tactics and lighting fires at night at numerous sites (SHM, §193); hails of arrows; etc. (Carpini, ch. 6, §§3, 4, in Shagdarsüren 1988). In addition, the knowledge which several influential persons had of settled peoples was also significant for the military successes. For example, Sübedei (d. 1248), one of the greatest of Genghis Khaan's generals, had amassed immense knowledge about the minutest details of the West, even down to the family connections of the rulers of Russia and Western Europe, while European opponents knew next to nothing about the Mongols. Also Yelü Chucai (1189–1243),[2] Genghis Khaan's secretary and later director of the central chancellery and administrative head of North China under Ogadai Khaan, was well versed in Chinese culture.

Another factor contributing to the military success was Shamanism, the religion of Mongolian nomads. Historical investigations and research have long suffered from a tendency to disregard moral, mental and spiritual forces as movers of history. Instead, the focus has been on measurable and economic factors. Shamanism played indeed a role as spiritual guide of the Mongols and had an effect on their success. In Shamanism, the sky is the central cult object as general protector against misfortune. The fanatic belief in the 'eternally blue sky' (Mong. *münkh khökh tengger*) and in shamans was in fact the motivation behind the mobilisation of all warriors' powers. Before large-scale campaigns, they turned to the sky (Banzarov 1955: 54–62). As the SHM reports, Genghis Khaan once placed his belt over his throat, turned towards the sky and prayed (SHM, §103). Somewhat more detailed reports concerning the influence of Shamanism date from the periods of Ogadai Khaan, Guyug Khaan and Münkhe

Khaan. The shamans were prophets of all activities and events. The SHM reports an extreme example: when Ogadai Khaan was stricken by a severe illness in 1231, shamans consulted the oracle and declared that someone from the Khaan's family had to be sacrificed in order to appease the evil spirits. Prince Tului, Genghis Khaan's youngest son, thus sacrificed his life (SHM, §272). Rubruck reports: 'As the Khaan himself admitted, the seers play for him the role of priests, and that which they command is carried out without delay' (Rubruck 1925: 141). 'Without their prophecy nobody musters an army or conducts war ...' (ibid., 142).

On the basis of the above, it is necessary, when dealing with Mongolian history, to take into consideration the close connection between natural and geographical conditions, the livestock economy, the nomadic way of life, the organisation of tribes and families and military activity. A system moulded by such relations existed in Central Asia in principle from the period of the Xiongnu dynasty up to the end of the seventeenth century. After this, it gradually disappeared, mainly on account of external effects. If one regards this evolution, which took place over a long time frame, from a merely political viewpoint, one would believe that there were many temporal breaks since tribes amalgamated, developed and dissolved. However the essence of the general social structure was preserved.

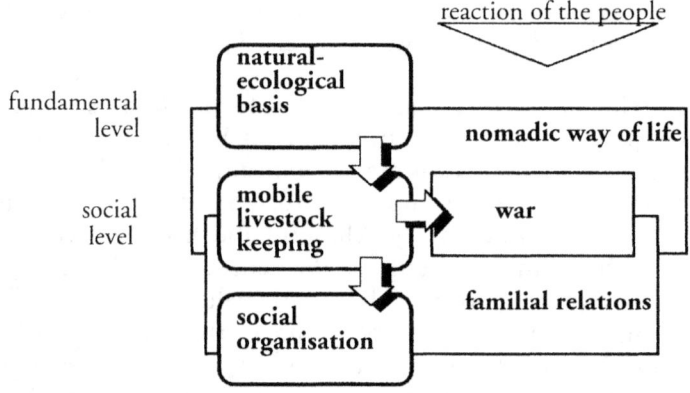

Figure 7: Model of the social system of the nomads of Central Asia

EVOLUTION OF NOMADIC SOCIETY

When one investigates the historical development of Mongolian nomadic society, one often finds in research works the tendency to divide into periods. Such a tendency has become a stereotyped habit, especially in historical investigations that adopt a Marxist viewpoint as a generally accepted methodological approach. For example, the stages of social development in Central Asia have been described in works concerning the history of Mongolia as follows: the nomadic empires up to the Mongolian period in the thirteenth century represent the emergent phase of feudalism or early feudalism; the Mongolian state represents the complete formation of feudal conditions; and the period after the fourteenth and fifteenth centuries represents the continued decline of feudalism. Thus the error arises that the progressive stages of development, which are typical for peoples involved in intensive economic forms, are also typical for nomadic peoples.

A thorough evaluation of the evolution of Mongolian nomadic society can only be made in close connection with pre-Mongolian Central Asian nomadism, with the development of nomadism in other regions of the arid belt of the ancient world and in general with the global forms of development of peoples of the world.

It can be concluded from the development of nomadism amongst Central Asian peoples after the first nomadic empire of the Huns (Xiongnu) that, in evaluating the evolution of Mongolian nomadic society from the twelfth to the seventeenth centuries, the problem of division into periods should not be placed in the foreground. Rather, this entire period should be regarded as a continuation of a process which started with pre-Mongolian nomadism. It is characterised by continuation, maintenance and repetition, although in another temporal dimension. Every moment in the course of history incorporates the unity of the aspects of tradition, i.e. repetition and in-novation, and the relation of these two aspects to each other depends basically on the intensity of production of the respective economic forms of the peoples. The traditional factor was especially strong in the history of the peoples of Central Asia on account of extensive nomadic livestock keeping. In this connection G. E. Markov writes:

> Scholars who try to demonstrate rapid processes of economic and other development amongst nomadic peoples, forget that the nomadic economy is extensive. And because it is extensive, it is little capable of perfection. If the livestock keeping economy were to assume an intensive character, it would cease being nomadic,

and all traditional institutions of the nomads would thus collapse and their way of life would fully change. (Markov 1981: 15)

We believe that it is no exaggeration to maintain that apart from Chinese trade, livestock keeping as carried out by nomads for centuries offers the only means of food supply for today's nomads after the fall of the socialist regime.

It is no coincidence that Chinese sources which report on pre-Mongolian nomadic peoples of Central Asia, frequently refer to the 'uniformity' (Taskin 1984: 36) of successive nomadic empires. Although it is without doubt that each empire developed and progressed in comparison to its predecessor, not only did the general character remain essentially the same, but this state also continued without substantial change even after the twelfth century. O. Lattimore was one of the first to analyse this problem in detail and to dispute the views of Soviet historians (e.g. Vladimircov) in the 1930s. He wrote:

> To assume for instance that the imperial centralisation achieved by Genghis Khaan was something entirely new is to distort the earlier history of the succession of steppe peoples to which the Mongols belonged. The truth is that the dispersion and disorder of the Mongols and related peoples just before the time of Genghis Khaan was a repetition of previous periods of the same kind; while the success of Genghis in uniting the nomads created an empire greater than previous nomad empires, but not different from them in kind. (Lattimore 1962: 252)

Some scholars are even of the opinion that this process lasted until the beginning of the twentieth century. For example V. Veit writes that 'the spirally upward and cyclic coursing evolution of Mongolian livestock keeping nomads ... continued until 1911' (Veit 1986: 180).

The norms for evaluating the development of culture and economy consist in general of the degree to which dependence upon nature decreases and social and economic differentiation, control of the basics of production and productivity increase (White 1969). Societies whose development does not accord with these norms are classified as backward or stagnant. In this respect the intensity of development or the means of development of the nomadic societies of Central Asia must be evaluated in comparison with the general process of mankind's development.

The transition from food gathering to food production and thus to definition of territories, the so-called 'neolithic revolution' (Childe 1964), led – in dependence on initial ecological conditions and intercultural situations – to the formation of three types of archaic society:

- peasant cultures, which were organised in differentiated horticultural villages, for example the Donau peasant cultures;
- nomadic livestock keeping tribes (including those temporarily settled), for example the Scythians, the Nu and the peoples of Central Asia;
- the 'rural artisan states' with the first forms of functionally differentiated political roles, for example the early Sumerian cities.

The most successful development is represented by the rural artisan states: D. R. Ribeiro cites these as Uruk (4000–3000 B.C.), Harappa (2500 B.C.), Xia, Yangshao (2000 B.C.), Crete (1700 B.C.), Athens (550 B.C.), Rome (350 B.C.), Uxmal (A.D. 300), and Ghana (A.D. 800) (Ribeiro 1970). It is the form from which higher civilisations developed. The Babylonian, Indian, Chinese, Hellenistic, Roman and ancient American empires are products of these processes of development which have their origin in rural artisan states.

The peasant cultures were – insofar as they were in political range of expanding cities – incorporated into these civilisations: in India, Egypt and the ancient American high cultures they were still able to maintain their independence. In Greece and Rome, on the other hand, these primitive societies disappeared in the wake of forms of private ownership.

The historical role of the nomads in this connection appears to be such that nomads intruded from outside into the intensive process of civilisation: thus they were either assimilated, as were for example the Dorians, the Mongols, the Teutons, the Vandals and the Goths, or driven back into their original territories and thus to their own level of development, like for example the Arabs in today's Saudi Arabia, and the Mongols and Manchu in Central Asia.

In the civilisation of the nomads with all its varieties 'no evolutional sequence or stages of development as a consequence of technological revolution, social processes and/or endogenous increase in production and division of labour can be observed' (Scholz 1995: 28) in comparison with the above-mentioned forms of development. Political events, upon which speculative explanations of the stages of development in nomadic societies are mostly based, do not represent watersheds in development at a general social level. Nomadic societies remain untouched in their traditional form, for which nomadic livestock keeping is the basis, until that time when they are forced to submit to substantial external influences.

In conclusion, the evolution of traditional Mongolian nomadic livestock keeping society in the twelfth–eighteenth centuries as the unmediated continuation of previous nomadic societies of Central Asia appears, in respect to the forms of development of mankind in general, as an upward spiralling and cyclic coursing process, changing qualitatively but extremely slowly. The factors that give rise to these repeating cycles can be summarised as follows:

• *mobile livestock keeping*, as the main economic activity, cyclically determined, completely dependent upon nature and organised into individual households, with little active and creative expenditure of labour in comparison with agricultural and artisan production;

• *nomadic tribes*, as a social form functionally adapted to mobile live-stock keeping;

• *centralisation*, from patriarchal clan to a politico-military and tri-bally determined nomadic empire with familial rights to the Khaan title, followed by relapse into small nomadic tribes.

Concluding Remarks

Mobile livestock keeping as the basis of traditional Mongolian nomadic society represents an optimal adaptation to the particular natural-ecological conditions in the Central Asian highlands and is indeed the only possible economic form under such conditions. Economic activity based on spatial mobility can only endure under an appropriate social organisation. The essence of the organisation of Mongolian nomadic society, as of all nomadic cultures, is manifested in social forms such as tribes, semi-tribes and extended families which are acephalously or patrilinearly founded. These determine its political and social structure. The functions arising from its internal structure were originally oriented towards its external social framework and guaranteed within this system the nomads' existence.

If one compares nomadic society with other peoples whose social structures are not economically based on nomadic livestock keeping (for example the peasant societies of the Mediterranean region), one sees differences in the entire economic system as a result of specific ownership conditions, in the state regime, in social differentiation, as well as in the area of material and intellectual culture. For this reason it is wrong to evaluate the development of Mongolian nomadic society according to theoretical models or evolutionary norms derived from the evaluation of settled peoples with an agricultural means of production.

Traditional Mongolian nomadic society was substantially changed by the Manchurian conquest and Manchurian policies. The changes encompassed not only the political but also the economic and social spheres. Moreover, the spread of Buddhism in Mongolia, which occurred at about the same period, had an effect not only on spiritual life but also on economic, social and political organisation and on all areas of nomadic culture.

If changes arising from external factors take place in the internal socio-political framework within which nomadism has hitherto existed as an optimal form of survival and thus been able to endure, then the internal functions of the society can no longer be carried out satisfactorily within the new framework. The modified internal structure of society presupposes to an ever-increasing degree the externally influenced functions, and thus nomadic society is transformed. Such a transformation means one of two things: a constant process of impoverishment amongst nomads, leading to the eventual disappearance of nomadism (which was almost the consequence of Manchurian-Chinese rule at the turn of the the nineteenth century) or a rudimentary form of nomadism, maintained only by great effort in order to ensure the survival of the majority of the population and to integrate other eco-nomic spheres of the country.

The latter continue to be dependent on nomadic livestock keeping, as was the case with the socialist collective economy in Mongolia.

Effective economic spheres arose out of the urbanisation and industrialisation measures undertaken during the socialist period in Mongolia, and a heterogeneous economic structure has been created which consists of the traditional nomadic livestock economy as well as agricultural and industrial occupations. The collectivisation of the livestock keeping economy, which was based on the nationalisation of livestock, was an attempt to unite nomadic livestock keeping and the industrial sphere into a single complex. With the introduction of democracy and free market economy, the economic system in Mongolia, which is incorporated into a centrally administered state and into international economic relations with the former Soviet Union and other countries of the Council for Mutual Economic Assistance, has collapsed. As a result, state support for the livestock keeping economy has ceased. The livestock of the collectives, which formed the collectives' economic basis, has been totally privatised. The organisation of livestock keeping, of use of pasture land and of sales of animal produce has collapsed, and infrastructural administration is non-existent. As a novelty of history, livestock keepers have been left totally isolated. The state is not in a position to unite private livestock keeping and other economic activities into a single complex, and does not pay sufficient attention to the problem. If one considers that more than 20% of the country's gross national product arises from the livestock keeping economy and that more than 40% of the population are directly engaged in livestock keeping, and that these numbers can only be reduced gradually over a long period of time, one realises that neglect of this area represents a very serious problem for the economy of the country and for the people.

NOTES

CHAPTER 1

1. See Perlee and Sükhbaatar 1976; Bira et al. 1980; Chuluun 1988: 5–18; Batbayar 1988: 49–59.

2. 'History of the Yuan Dynasty' (*Yuanshi*): This important source was translated into Mongolian in 1917–22 by the Mongolian scholar Chimed Demchigdorji (1863–1932) who bore the nickname Dandaa. In 1914 he left his home in the Kharchin-Koshuu of the Zostyn-Chuulgan region for Khüree, the capital of Outer Mongolia. The 'History' was subsequently also translated in 1923–28 by C. Zamcarano by commission of the minister for foreign affairs. The two translated copies of the manuscript (which comprises 210 volumes) are located in the State Library of Mongolia in Ulaanbaatar. The version used as original is not considered the best which is a product of a comparative revision of many versions (*Bo-na-ben*, Shanghai 1958) dating from the period of the emperor of the Ming dynasty, Hung-wo (1368–87). The translation of this work in Europe was begun in the nineteenth century. N. Ya. Bichurin translated the first four volumes into Russian (*Istoriya pervykh chetyrekh khanov iz doma Chingisovy*, St. Petersburg, 1829). At the start of the twentieth century volumes 93, 94, 102, 107 and 108 were translated into French and German (Hambis, L., *Le chapitre CVII du Yuan she*, Leiden, 1945, *Le chapitre CVIII du Yuan she*, Leiden, 1954; Krause, F. E. A., *Cingis Han, Die Geschichte seines Lebens nach den chinesischen Reichsannalen*, Heidelberg 1922).

3. Here it is necessary to differentiate between 'khan' and 'khaan'. In many books dealing with the history of the Mongols these two words are used synonymously. If one follows the meaning of the words in Mongolian chronicles, it becomes clear that Khaan was the title of the king of a state while Khan later designated the ruler of a region and its population.

4. The identity of the author of this work is still a matter of dispute; P. Pelliot, N. Z. Munkuev, P. Olbricht and E. Pinks, P. Hauer, etc., believe it to be Chao Hong, the author of *Meng Da beilu*. Some researchers maintain, however, that Meng Hong (1195–1244), general of the Song state, is the author.

5. Tabris (Täbris) is a place dating from the fourth millennium B.C., and was the capital of various Mongolian khaans after the thirteenth century. Today it is the capital of the Iranian province East Azerbaijan.

6. Dolo'on Boldag: according to the opinion of some researchers the location named 'Kelürenu ködö'e aralun dolo'an boldaq-a' (SHM, §§136, 282) is today's Mount Dolood-uul E 108° 48', N 47° 4' (Report on the Joint Investigation ... *GURVAN GOL* ... 1994: 30).

7. Shilgincig is assumed to be the area about today's 'Avragyn-gol' River E 109° 8', N 47° 1'.

8. Köde'ü aral-a. This name is mentioned three times in the SHM: §136 'Kelürenu ködö'e aralun dolo'an boldaq-a'; §269 'Kelürenu köde'ü aral-a'; §282 'Kelürenu ködö'e aralun dolo'an boldaq-a'. The location of the Köde'ü on the Kelürenu is mentioned not only in the SHM but also in the *Yuanshi* (vol. 2: 1a): In 1229 Ogadai was enthroned at a diet held 'in the region of Qudiao alan (Köde'ü aral) of the Qie-lülian River (Kelüren = Kerülen)'. The text adds that the enthronement took place at Kutiewu alan li (Köde'ü aral: an island in countryside), which is a needless duplication of the former name arising from the hasty compilation of the *Yuanshi*. According to Pelliot, the commissioned translators of Qianlong misunderstood in the first passage the word *qu* as meaning 'bend', so that the diet was believed to be held at 'Diao alan' on the 'bend' (*qu*) of the Kerülen River; this fictitious 'bend of the river' occurs more than once in later Chinese sources (*Shengwu qinzheng lu,* Wang Guowei's note, 65a) and of course cannot be taken into account for the identification of the place (Pelliot 1959: 322). It is a fact, however, that to the east of the Tula, the Kerülen River, which in its upper course flows southwest, makes a big curve to the south, then to the southeast, and finally follows a north–northeastern course. In Yanai's opinion, 'Köde'ü aral' was an island at the confluence of the Sengkür River (now called Cenkheriin-gol) and Kerülen (Yanai 1930: 594, 672). Popov relates in more detail. The Cenkher is an intermittent stream which runs from north to south inside the bend of the Kerülen and flows into the Kerülen. There are several 'sand islands' (*sha-chou*) in the upper course of the Kerülen (Popov 1895: 399–400); moreover *aral* may mean not only an 'island' but an entire region determined by the confluence of two rivers. In 1990, a monument commemorating the 750th anniversary of the composition of the SHM was erected at this location (E 108° 50', N 47° 2').

9. Lifanyuan (Chin.) was the special ministry (Mong. 'Yeke jurgan' or 'Monggol jurgan': great ministry or ministry for Mongolia) of the Manchurian government for ruling the Mongolian regions. The Manchu, who after the conquest of Inner Mongolia and many other territories had the difficult task of governing the subjected regions and their populations, created the Ministry for Governing the Outer Provinces in 1638. The ministry ruled all conquered peoples beyond the Great Wall by commission of the emperor.

10. Mong. *Jarlig-bar togtogagsan gadagadu Monggol Qotong ayimag-un wang güngüd-un iletkel shastir*: mostly abbreviated as *Iletkhel Shastir*. See Sanchirov 1976.

11. 'Middle epoch'. By this term we mean the period of Mongolian history from the thirteenth century to the middle of the eighteenth century. In some

research works the term 'Mongolian Middle Ages' is used. We believe that it is questionable to apply this term, which arises from the peculiarities of European history, to the history of non-European states. Results of research into the Middle Ages show that this period was marked by a spatial and a temporal component – it was a European period, and indeed the period of the beginning of Europe. It comprises the foundation of Europe, its inner differentiation and the varied tensions which arose from the composition and opposition of its respective forces.

12. See Nacagdorj 1963, 1978; Shirendev 1971; Dalai 1973, 1983; Ishjamc 1976; Bira 1977; Gongor 1978.

13. Münkhe Khaan (1208–59) was the eldest son of Tului, Mongolian Grand Khaan 1251–59. With Münkhe Khaan, whose election was effected by the efforts of Batu Khaan and his brother Berke, the Grand Khanate and direct inheritance of Genghis Khaan was transferred from the clan line of Ogadai to that of Tului.

14. In this period, the first scientific societies for oriental studies were founded in France, England and Germany, and the first specialised journals for Oriental Studies were published.

15. See, for example, Varg 1925; Kantorovich 1926; Kyuner 1927; Papayan 1930.

16. See, for example, Günter and Schrot 1963; Semenov 1966; Danilov 1968: 30; Gurevitsch 1968; Tökei 1966; Eichhorn and Küttler 1989: 77–78.

17. See, for example, Rathmann 1971: 137–54; Büttner 1971: 116–36; Töpfer 1985: 117–56, 169–97; Werner 1985: 71–87.

18. The term Europe is itself a historical product with time-specific constituents; we can only describe it here approximately as a region that comprises the countries of Central Europe, the British Isles and the Italian and Iberian peninsulas, and Scandinavia.

Chapter 2

1. *Nutug* or *nuntug*: a home, domicile (Schmidt 1835; Boberg 1959: 372); pasture, nomad grounds, native place, domicile, homeland, territory, country, area, locality (Lessing 1960).

2. See SHM, §§1, 72, 74, 89, 96, 114, 118, 119, 135, 137, 138, 149, 214, 249, 265, 278, 279; Poppe 1941: frag. XXIII, 28, frag. XXIX, 33.

3. *Etügen* and *yurt*: see SHM, §§113, 190, 201, 245, 254; Rashid ad-Din 1952: vol. 1, bk 1: 136.

4. Nine animals (Mong. *yes*): nine animals – consisting of four large animals (cattle or horses) and five sheep – was the customary unit of fining. In cases where the fine was to be more explicitly defined, it was stated which types of animal were to be included, e.g. nine animals including an adult camel, etc. Variations of this fine in the criminal law section of the Codex of 1789 entailed exacting multiples of the nine animal fine. According to the codex this fine consisted of '2 horses, 2 adult bulls, 2 cows, 2 three-year-old bulls and 1 two-

year-old bull. The five-animal fine means 1 adult bull, 1 cow, 1 three-year-old bull and 2 two-year-old bulls. For the benefit of the authority of enforcement, 1 three-year-old bull must be given up in each case' (Alinge 1934: 155).

5. Five hunting reserves were located in the territory of the *khoshuu* and were in the vicinity of the capital Urga (Khüree). The others were located near Ulistai, Bürkhi, Gurvan-baidrig, Bulnai, Tuul-Gol and Galttai.

6. The relay lines in Mongolia extended in the following directions:
- the military relay line towards Altai (Mong. *Altai zamyn buukhia örtöö*): there were 20 stations for which 280 families were economically responsible. In the year 1728 this line was established with altogether 64 stations between the Chinese gate station of the Great Wall, Chuulalt-Khaalgan (E 115°, N 41°), and the city Uliastai of Outer Mongolia. Fifty-six of these stations were located in Inner and Outer Mongolia. The livestock-keeping families allotted to 36 of these stations came from the *kharchin* province of Inner Mongolia, and for the other 20 stations, livestock-keeping families from Outer Mongolia were responsible. They were known by the name '36 *kharchin* stations' (Mong. *kharchin örtöö*) and '20 Outer Mongolian stations' (Mong. *khalkha örtöö*);
- from Khüree northwards to the city Khiagt: there were eleven stations for which 70 families were economically responsible;
- from Khüree southwards to Sair-Us station: 14 stations;
- from Khovd to Uliastai: 14 stations;
- from Uliastai northwards to the Zinzileg region: 9 stations for which 54 families were economically responsible;
- from Uliastai southwards to the Bar-khöl region: 14 stations;
- from Khovd northwestwards to the Sogog-us region: there were 8 stations for which 44 families were economically responsible;
- from Khovd to the Güencin region: 8 stations. (Korostovetz 1926, map: Outer Mongolia (Khalkha))

The number of managing families of each station was on average 10, and each family had at its disposal more than 50 horses, 10 camels and 100 sheep. In some stations, however, the number of families and animals was extremely high. For example 162 families alone managed the 5 stations between Khar-Nuden and Sargalzuut on the Altai line, and each station had between 4,000 and 8,500 animals (*BNMAU-yn tüükh* 1968: 202).

7. See Note 14 of this Chapter.

8. See Note 11 of Chapter 3.

9. *Khalkha Jirum* (*Qalq-a Jirum*): The compendium of laws known by the name *Khalkha Jirum* arose on the basis of Mongolian common law which had formed through the centuries. It consisted of 24 legal edicts from the years 1709, 1718, 1722, 1724, 1726, 1728, 1729, 1736, 1745, 1746, 1754 and 1770, which were discussed and decided upon at assemblies of the khans ruling the four *aimag*s of Khalkha Mongolia (Outer Mongolia), and other influential princes.

10. Dolon Nuur (or Dolonur) is the name of the location E 116°, N 42°. 'Dolugan Nagur un Chigulgan' (conference at the location of Lake Dolugan

Notes

Nagur). This conference, with which the official and legally defined subjection of the Khalkha princes began, took place in 1691 at a location near Dolugan Nagur. The conference of Dolugan Nagur represents an important political watershed in Mongolian history. It marked the conclusion of the second stage of the conquest of Mongolia by the Manchu and the beginning of Manchurian-Chinese rule in Khalkha Mongolia. During this conference, Emperor Kang-hsi (1662–1722) appointed 34 members of the Genghisic nobility as governing princes (Mong. *zasag noyad*) and enfeoffed each of them with a *banner*. This measure signified the introduction of the Manchurian *banner* system into Khalkha Mongolia.

11. *Ail*: *yurt* (Turkish), livestock keeping family, *yurt* site, nomadic livestock keeping farm.

12. *Khot-ail* has in general been translated as fenced enclosure, stalls, collection of *yurt*s, village, etc. The best explanations of the term can be found in Pallas (1776: 142–43) for the Kalmucks; Radloff (1892: 462) for the Kazakhs; Vreeland (1957) for the Mongols of Mongolia in the twentieth century; Mostaert (1956: 279–89) for the Ordos region. For the sixteenth century, the report of Siao-ta-heng should be pointed out (Serruys ed. 1945). For the thirteenth century, see also Carpini (1182–1252) and Rubruck (1220–93) and the Meng-ta-Bei-lu (in Munkuev 1975: chs 8, 12). For further details, see Potanin (1879–83).

13. 'Mongol-Oirat Regulations of 1640': the threatening growth of Manchurian power compelled the princes of Outer Mongolia (Khalkha Mongolia) and the Oirats of West Mongolia to take energetic steps towards an internal stabilisation and an outward directed defence. At the instigation of the Oirat prince Baatar Khan, princes from 40 Outer Mongolian and four Oirat realms of ten thousand assembled in 1640. One of the results of this assembly was the written record of a large series of norms which were collected in the legal code *Caazyn bichig* or 'Mongol-Oirat Regulations'.

14. *Otog* and *aimag*: these words underwent appreciable changes of meaning in the course of time. From the seventeenth century onwards, *aimag* became the designation for the territorial-administrative main unit of Mongolia. *Otog* had at this time the same meaning as the term *khoshuu*. Later it became a designation for the pasture land and subject property of high-ranking monks. For further details, see Chapter 3.

15. *Khoshuu*: the territorial-administrative unit in Mongolia in the period 1691–1932. Although the term *khoshuu* had been used much earlier, since the middle of the sixteenth century, it did not at that time have the meaning of a strongly controlled territorial-administrative unit. For further details, see Chapter 3.

Chapter 3

1. *Onggod* (spirits). Shamans evoked or appeased their own ancestors who had become *onggod* after their deaths. As a rule shamans received their calling from the *onggod*. The *onggod* were mostly local ancestral or tutelary spirits of which

images were made: wooden figures or felt dolls which were hung up or embroidered into material.

2. The tribe Khiad Borjigin, the main tribe of the Mongolian tribal unit from which Genghis Khaan originated, had, for example,
- offering with white falcons, *Cagan shongkhor shuvuun takhilga*,
- a black *Süld* genius, *Khar süld*: this black *süld* (or *tug*) was the standard of war and was carried in front of the troops in times of war to support the victory, to give intrepidity to the warriors, and to terrify the enemy. After the victorious war an important prisoner was sacrificed to the *khar süld*.
- a nine-pointed white *banner, Yösön khölt* (or *khökhölt*) *cagaan tug*: this white *tug* or *süld* was the symbol of the well-being and welfare of the clan and its descent as well as that of the White's or noble lineage of the clan or chieftainship.

3. To the Gurvan Merget (three Mergets) belonged Uruyid Merget, Khaad Merget and Uvas Merget. To the Dörvön Oirat (four Oirat) belonged Coros, Dörvöd, Khoid and Khoshuud. To the Kereyit belonged the *obog*s such as Kereyid, Jirkin, Qonqayit, Sakayit, Tumaut, Albat and Kirkün. Of which *obog* Onggut consisted is unknown. To the Yesen Tartar (nine Tartars) belonged Barkhuyi, Kamas, Neyici, Teryiat, Tutukulti, Koyin, Alsi, Ayirut and Buyirut. To the Khamag Mongol belonged 16 Darlikin *Aimag*s and 19 Nirun (Nirugun) *Aimag*s.

4. The name Mongol appears for the first time in the annals of the Chinese Tang dynasty (602–901), in which the people were called Shiwei Mengwu 'tribe Mongu', later Men-gu-li.

5. Khotul Khaan: the SHM reports that in the second half of the eleventh century, a Mongolian ruling line of succession began with Khaidu Khaan, the first ruler of the Mongols, and was continued by Khabul Khaan, Ambagai Khaan (d. 1161) and the fourth ruler Khotul Khaan.

6. Batumünkhe Dayan Secen Khaan (1464–1543) was Grand Khaan in the years 1470–1543). Between 1483 and 1488 he was able to conquer the Oirat in several campaigns and to seize from them the rule over all Mongolian peoples. However, towards the end of his reign, Mongolia declined once again.

7. The main tribal unions such as Khalkha, Cakhar and Uriankhan formed the left-hand wing of Mongolia and were claimed by Bodi-Alag Khaan (1504–47), the grandson of Batumünkhe Dayan Khaan. Khalkha consisted of 12 tribes in all: seven *otog*s of the northern Khalkha (Jalair, Besud, Iljigin (Erchigin), Gorlos, Khukhuid, Khatikhin and an Uriankhan *otog*) were under the direct rule of Geresenz, the eleventh son of Batumünkhe, and five *otog*s of southern Khalkha (*bagarin*, Jarud, Khonkharid, Bayagud and Uchirad) were under the rule of Alchi-Bolod, the fifth son of Batumünkhe. The territories of the seven *otog*s of northern Khalkha later increased and were divided into 13 *otog*s. To Cakhar, which was under the personal rule of Bodi-Alag Khaan, belonged Abaga, Abaganar, Muumyangan (these last two were ruled by the tenth son of Batumünkhe, Ger-Bolod), Aokhan, Dörvön khüükhed (ruled by the sixth son of Batumünkhe, Ochir-Bolod), Keshigten, Naiman, Onginuud (ruled by the seventh son of Batumünkhe, Ara-Bolod), Khuuchid, Sönid, Uzumchin and Urad.

NOTES

8. The main tribal unions Arvan khoyor Tümed (twelve *tümed*s), Ordos and Yunsheebuu, Asud, Kharchin formed the right wing of Mongolia and were ruled by the third son of Batumünkhe, Barsu-Bolod (d. 1532), as *jinon*. The 12 Tümeds were ruled by Arsu-Bolod, the fourth son of Batumünkhe. Ordos was under the direct rule of Barsu-Bolod; and the tribes Yunsheebuu, Asud and Kharchin were ruled by the ninth son of Batumünkhe, Chin *taij*.

9. Dolonur or Dolon Nuur: see Chapter 2, note 10.

10. *Shavi*: The subjects of the high-ranking monks are designated in Mongolian sources by the term *shavi*. *Shavi* comprised the lama *shavi* (lama pupils) and the *khar-shavi* (common, non-lama *shavi*).

11. *rJe-bcun dam-pa*: Bogd Gege'en (holy enlightener) *rJe-bcun dam-pa khutagt*: in Mongolian history, eight *rJe-bcun dam-pa* have been reincarnations of Mayidar *khutagt* (1592–1635), of whom the first two came from Mongolia and the other six, owing to the Manchurian policy of eliminating the threat of Mongolian dignitaries and princes becoming independent, from Tibet:

    1. *rJe-bcun dam-pa* (1635–1723), reincarnation in 1649;

    2. *rJe-bcun dam-pa* (1724–57), reincarnation in 1737;

    3. *rJe-bcun dam-pa* (1758–73), reincarnation in 1763;

    4. *rJe-bcun dam-pa* (b. 1776);

    5. *rJe-bcun dam-pa* (b. 1815), reincarnation in 1820;

    6. *rJe-bcun dam-pa*, 1842;

    7. *rJe-bcun dam-pa* (b. 1849), reincarnation in 1855. (Bawden, 1961, 41–90)

    8. *rJe-bcun dam-pa* (1869–1924), reincarnation in 1874. (Idshinno-rov and Cerendorj 1990)

12. The term 'Inner Mongolia' appears in chronicles and documents with the incorporation of South Mongolia into the Manchu Empire.

13. Khovd (Qobdu): the settlement of Khovd is very old. Some sources report that the *yurt* palace of Galdan (Boshigtu Khaan) (1632–1697) was located in this region. In 1717–18 the Manchurian grand dignitary Furdan (1683–1753) established a supply base for his troops there. Because Khovd had always been an agricultural area and offered good climatic and soil conditions, Manchurian troops took control of the agricultural plantations by imperial decree in 1716.

14. *Jisaa* is a Manchurian word which means shift. Because representatives of the *aimag*s and *khoshuu*s had to render service in shifts of 3–6 months, the use of the word became common.

CHAPTER 4

1. There are differing interpretations: 'people of free standing' (Palladii Kafarov), 'common warriors, soldiers' (Vladimircov), 'common people' (Haenisch), 'free men' (Damdinsuren; Ardjab), '*Zorigdaan khün* (independent person)' (Kozin), 'rich people' (Gongor), etc.

2. For more about Mongolian Shamanism, see Banzarov 1955: 44–100; Rinchin 1955: 8–16, 1981: 94–112; Dalai 1959; Heissig 1970: 305, 1992, 1996: 249–58. Cybikov 1981: 169–75; Purev 1998.

3. According to the SHM and *Altan tobchi*, Alan-go'a had two sons by her husband Dobun-mergen. After him she had 'from a heavenly being' three more sons, one of whom was Bodonchar-mungkhug.

4. Khabich-bagatur was one of Genghis Khaan's ancestors. He was the son of Bodonchar-mungkhug, one of the five sons of Alan-go'a. According to Rashid ad-Din, a son of Bodonchar was Bukha who was also called the Khabich-bagatur or Barim-Siriyetü-Khabich-bagatur.

5. See Chapter 2, note 4.

Chapter 5

1. Sa-skya Pandita Kun-dga' rgyal-mchan (1182–1251) was one of the five highest masters and the sixth Sa-skya patriarch of Tibetan Buddhism. He was known for his mastery of the ten spheres of knowledge of Buddhism and of ancient Mongolian script.

2. Phags-pa Lama (1235–80): inventor of the quadrate script used by the Mongols for a short period; nephew and successor of Sa-skya Pandita (1182–1251).

3. Sa-skya-pa: Sa-skya was a Tibetan grand monastery founded in 1073 in the vicinity of Lhasa; Sa-skya-pa is the name of a hierarchy and one of the four schools or orders of Tibetan Buddhism.

4. rNimma-pa school: one of the four schools or orders of Tibetan Buddhism: Lamaist school connected with Padmasambhava.

5. Amdo is a place in northeastern Tibet which comprises the region of the upper Huanghe River. It is divided by the river into a northern and a southern part: the northern part was formerly called Ashi and is known today by the name Khökhe-Nuur. Here, Mongols have lived since ancient times together with Tibetan tribes.

6. After this second proselytisation of the Mongols, the Mongolian term 'Dalai Lam' was used for the Tibetan chief lama (Tibet. *rGya-mts'o bLama*). The Tibetan title of this chief lama was earlier *rGyamts'o* (ocean) and is often appended to the Mongolian title.

7. *Ganjur* or *Kanjur* (Tibet. *bKa-'gyur*: the translated word of Buddha). This canonical Lamaist collection of writings in 108 volumes, with six parts and 1,055 separate text passages, was translated from Sanskrit into Tibetan and then in turn into Mongolian. The number of volumes is generally 108 but varies according to different editions.

8. *Danjur* or *Tanjur* (Tibet. *bsTan-gyur*: the translated teaching of Buddha). The second part of the *Ganjur* contains commentaries as well as treatises on science and magic. This canonical Lamaist collection of writings is a translation of ancient Indian commentaries to the Buddha's teaching and runs into 225 volumes with slight variations between different editions.

9. *Khutagt*s with seal: the higher-ranking *khutagt*s could own land according to the law just like the secular princes. At the start of the twentieth century there were altogether 11 (13?): Yeguzer *khutagt* of the Secen Khan *Aimag* (seal

awarded 1846), Jalkhanz *khutagt* of the Zasagt Khan *Aimag* (seal awarded 1824), Yalguusan *khutagt* of the Zasagt Khan *Aimag* (seal awarded 1821), Nomon-Khan *khutagt* of the Zasagt Khan *Aimag* (seal awarded 1853), Zaya-Bandit *khutagt* of the Sain Noyan Khan *Aimag* (seal awarded 1737), Erdene-Bandit *khutagt* of the Sain Noyan Khan *Aimag* (seal awarded 1737), Nar-Banchin *khutagt* of the Sain Noyan Khan *Aimag* (seal awarded 1772), Erdene-Mergen-Noyan *khutagt* of the Sain Noyan Khan *Aimag* (seal awarded 1826), Chin-Sujigt-Nomon-Khan *khutagt* of the Sain Noyan Khan *Aimag* (seal awarded 1751), Naran *khutagt* of the Sain Noyan Khan *Aimag* (seal awarded 1897) and Khamba-Nomon-Khan *khutagt* of the Sain Noyan Khan *Aimag* (seal awarded 1807).

There were about 50 *khutagts* without seal in the four *aimag*s of Outer Mongolia.

10. *Toin-Lama*: the lamas whose fathers or ancestors had been influential or governing princes.

CHAPTER 6

1. Dunhu: ancient, Mongolian-speaking tribal grouping to which the nine tribes Uhuan', Syambi, Cifu, Tufu, Shivey, Kumosi, Kidan', Tuyuyhun' and Zuan'zuan' belonged.

2. He was an official of the former northern Chinese Jin or Jurchen dynasty, which existed from 1115 to 1234 and fell with the conquest of the Mongols.

LIST OF PEOPLE, PLACES AND TERMS

ail	1) family; 2) livestock keeping family
aimag	1) small nomadic group; 2) biggest territorial-administrative unit. See also Chapter 2, note 14
airag (*kumis*)	fermented mare's milk
akh	leader of family group of *khot ail*
akhlagch	leader of *khot ail*
albat	state serfs in the pre-socialist period
Altan Khaan	founder of the Tümed khanate (1507–83)
altan urug	golden family or golden tribe of *borjigin* (tribe)
Ambagai	third Khan of Mongol tribes (d. 1160)
arad	common herders or common people
aravt	1) group of ten: a group of nomad families from which ten warriors could be mobilised; 2) group of ten families: an administrative unit
Arig-Bukh	Khublai Khaan's brother (d. 1266)
bag	smallest administrative unit within a *khoshuu* in the pre-socialist period; 2) smallest administrative unit within a *sum* in the socialist and post-socialist period
Batumünkhe	Bat(u)münkh Dayan (Secen) Khaan, king of the Mongolian state (1464–1543). See also Chapter 3, note 6
bilcheer	pasturage
Bodi-Alag	King of the Mongolian empire (b. 1504)
böge, böö	shaman
bool	serf, slave

LIST OF PEOPLE, PLACES AND TERMS

Borjigin	*khiad-borjigin*: name of the Mongolian ancestral tribe founded by Bodonchar whose eleventh-generation descendant was Genghis Khaan
Boshigtu	see Galdan
buuc	*ötög-buuc*: winter-spring site of nomads
cherbi	noble rank
Chingim	Khublai Khaan's youngest son (d. 1285)
chinsan	high-ranking official title
Dadu	capital of the Yuan Dynasty (1271–1368); today's Beijing
darkhan	title of people who performed outstandingly in battle and were rewarded with special rights by the Khaan
Dolonur (Dolon Nuur)	located at 42°N, 116°E, site of the 'Dolugan Nagur un Chigulgan' (conference at Lake Dolugan Nagur) in 1691, from which the official and legally defined subjection of the Khalkha princes began.
Galdan (Boshigtu)	West Mongolian ruler (1632–97)
Gamal	Khublai Khaan's third son (1258–1303)
gazar	old Mongolian length unit, equivalent to the Chinese length unit *li*, used in the 17th–19th centuries (one *gazar* = 576 m)
Genghis Khaan	founder of the Mongolian empire (1161–1227)
güng	noble rank, higher than a *vang*
Huns (Xiongnu)	nomad empire of Huns in Central Asia (3rd–2nd centuries BC)
Ikh Yasag	Great Yasa, Mongolian statute book of Genghis Khaan, which was used from the start of the 13th century.
jas	monastic economic institution
jisaa	representations of *khoshuu*s in their administratively affiliated *aimag* centres, also representations of *aimag*s in the cities of Uliastai, Khovd, Khüree and Khiagt. See also Chapter 3, note 14
rJe-bcun dam-pa	*rJe-bcun dam-pa khutagt* (Mong: Bogd Gege'en: holy enlightener), the Lamaistic religious head in Khalkha Mongolia (1650–1924) and the head of state and religion (1911–1921). In history of Mongolia eight *rJe-bcun dam-pa* have been found as reincarnations of the Tibetan Lama Mayidar *khutagt* (1592–1635). See also Chapter 3, note 11
Kara-Korum	capital of Mongolian empire (established in 1220)

Mongolian Nomadic Society

Kereit	name of a tribe
Khaan	a king of the Mongolian empire and/or state
Khabul Khan	leader of a federation of Mongolian tribes; Genghis Khaan's great-grandfather
Khaidu	Ogadai's grandson (1235–1301)
Khaidu Khan	ruler of a federation of Mongolian tribes (b. 1035)
Khalkha Mongolia	Outer Mongolia: northern part of Mongolia which remained independent until 1691; the conquest of southern parts of Mongolia by Manchus took place in 1632
khamjilaga	serfs of nobles in the pre-socialist period
Khamag Mongol	confederation of Mongolian tribes before the foundation of the Mongolian empire in 1206
Khan	ruler of tribes or federation of tribes, or of a region and its population
khar-shavi	livestock keepers belonging to monasteries or to dignitaries
khoshuu	territorial-administrative unit within an *aimag* in Mongolia in the period 1691–1932. See also Chapter 2, note 15
khot-ail	cooperation between livestock-keeping families and a traditional unit of socio-economic organisation at the local level. See also Chapter 2, no. 12
Khotul	fourth Khan of Mongolian tribes, Khabul Khan's son. See also Chapter 3, note 5
Khublai Khaan	Genghis Khaan's grandson, founder of Yuan Dynasty (1215–94)
khurildai	quasi-political assembly
khutagt	higher-ranking lamas
khuvilgaan	reincarnated high-ranking lamas
kumis	see *airag*
lama	Buddhist monk
lama-shavis	monks belonging personally to the high-ranking lamas
li	Chinese unit of length: one *li* = 576 m
Lifanyuan	special ministry of the Qing government for ruling the Mongolian regions (established in 1638). See also Chapter 1, note 9
Lifanyuan zeli	Manchurian-Chinese code from the year 1789; a Statute Book, established by the Highest Command, of the Ministry of the Government of the Outer Provinces
Ligden (Khaan)	last Khaan of Mongolian state (1592–1634)

Münkhe Khaan	Khaan of the Mongolian empire (1208–59). See also Chapter 1, note 13
myangan (pl. *myangat*)	group of thousand – main military-administrative unit in Mongolia in the 13th century; a tribe or a federation of tribes from which a thousand warriors could be mobilised.
negdel	agricultural cooperative in the period 1930s–1990
nutug	family territory; herder's customary pastures
obog (or *omog*)	tribe or clan
Ogadai	Khaan of Mongolian empire, Genghis Khaan's third son (1186–1241)
Oirat	West Mongolian tribe
Ölziit-Tömör	Khaan of the Mongolian empire, Chingim's eldest son (1265–1308)
omog	see *obog*
Öndör Gege'en	Öndör Gege'en Zanabajar: 'Living Buddha' of Mongolia, the first *rJe-bcun dam-pa* (1635–1723)
örtöö	relay line and relay station, and/or length unit: one *örtöö* = about 30 km
otog	small nomadic group: bigger than *aimag* (1). See also Chapter 2, note 14
ötög (or *ötög-buuc*)	see *buuc*
otor	form of individual migration of nomads in order to make use of feed reserves in distant pastures, while the family remains at a site with the rest of the animals
Outer Mongolia	see Khalkha Mongolia
Qing	Manchurian-Chinese dynasty (1644–1911)
Sain Noian Khan	noble title of the leader of Sain Noian Khan *Aimag*
sang	independent economic entities of some *khutagt*s and *khuvilgaan*s
Secen Khan	noble title of the leader of Secen Khan *Aimag*
shavi	regions (property and subjects) in *aimag*s belonging to higher Buddhist dignitaries *khutagt*s
SHM	'Secret History of the Mongols', Mongolian chronicle from the 13th century most probably written in 1241. (Some scholars, however, suspect that the chronicle was written in 1227 and extended later on to cover the events until 1264.)
sum	territorial-administrative unit within *aimag*
taij	lowest noble title
Togoon-Tömör	last Khaan of the Yuan Dynasty (1320–70)

Tului	Genghis Khaan's youngest son (1190–1232)
Tümed	name of tribe
tümen	group of ten thousand; federation of tribes from which ten thousand warriors could be mobilised.
Tüsheet Khan	noble title of the leader of Tüsheet Khan *Aimag*
vang	noble rank: higher than a *taij*
Xiongnu	the Huns
Yelü Chucai	former Jin official who was appointed as director of a central chancellery in Kara-Korum in autumn 1231 by Ogadai Khaan
Yesun-Tömör	Khaan of the Mongolian empire (1276–1328)
Yuan Dynasty	Mongolian empire founded by Khublai Khaan (1271–1368) in today's Mongolian and Chinese territories
Yuanshi	'History of the Yuan Dynasty', written in 1369/70
Zasagt Khan	noble title of the leader of Zasagt Khan *Aimag*
zuut	group of hundred; group of nomad families from which hundred warriors could be mobilised

REFERENCES

Abott, J., 1900, *Genghis Khan*, New York.
Alinge, C., 1934, *Mongolische Gesetze*, Leipzig.
Amar, A., 1934, *Monggol-un teuke* [History of Mongolia], Ulaanbaatar.
Ardajab, E., 1986, *Monggol-un nigucha tobchiyan* [The Secret History of the Mongols], Khökhe khota.
Badamkhatan, S., 1965, *Khövsgöliin darkhad yastan* [Darkhat People of the Khubsgul Region], Ulaanbaatar.
Badargult töru-yin 24 düger on-du Yeke Küriyen-u Cogchin bolon Dashichoyimbol, Güngachoyilin, Jüd, Jirukhayi, Lamrim zerke 9 dacang-un jisa-uud-un mal-g bayichagagsan dangsa [Census of Livestock owned by nine Temples of the Capital Cogchin, Dashichoyimbol, Güngachoyilin, Jüd, Jirukhayi, Lamrim in the 24th year of the Manchurian Emperor Guan'-shiu (1898)] (Manuscript: Central Archives of History in Ulaanbaatar, F.A. 98, HN. 111).
Bagana, B., *Khyatan naryn asuudal* [Questions on Kitan People] (Manuscript: Manuscript Collection of the Institute of History of the Mongolian Academy of Sciences).
Banzarov, D., 1955, 'Chernaya vera, ili shamanstvo u mongolov' [The Black Faith, or Shamanism among the Mongols]. In G. D. Sanjeev, and G. N. Rumyancev (eds), *Sobranie sochinenii* [Works], Moscow, pp. 48–100.
Barkmann, U., 1986, 'Die militärisch-feudale Administration der Manjuren in der Qalq-a-Mongolei des 18. Jahrhunderts-ein Werkzeug der manjurischen Fremdherrschaft in der Qalq-a-Mongolei', Diss. Humboldt-Univ., Berlin.
——, 1991, 'Einige Bemerkungen zum Problem des Eides in der "Geheime Geschichte der Mongolen"', *Central Asiatic Journal*, vol. 35, Wiesbaden.
Barthold, V. V., 1966, *Sochineniya* [Works], vol. 2, Moscow.
Batbayar, Z., 1988, 'Feodalyn türüü üeiin mongolyn tüükhiin zarim asuudlyg BNKhAU-yn tüükhchid kherhen tusgaj baigaa n'' [Reflection of Historians of the People's Republic of China on Problems of Earlier

History of Mongolian Feudalism]. In Ch. Dalai and D. Dunger-Yaichil (eds), *Khyatad Japon dakh' mongol sudlalyn toimoos* [Survey of Mongolian Studies in China and in Japan], Ulaanbaatar.

Bat-Ochir, L., 1986, *Ard angi: butec, öörchlölt, khorshoojilt* [Class of Livestock Keepers: Structure, Change and Cooperation], Ulaanbaatar.

Batuvachir (Shadar), C., 1927, *Monggol-un erte eduge-yin ulamjilagsan bichig* [Records of Ancient and Present Mongolia], Ulaanbaatar.

Bawden, C. R., 1961, 'The Jebtsundamba Khutukhtus of Urga. Text, Translation and Notes'. In *Asiatische Forschungen,* vol. 9, Wiesbaden.

——, 1968, *The Modern History of Mongolia*, London.

Bazargür, D., B. Chinbat, and S. Shiirev-Ad'ya, 1989, *Bügd Nairamdakh Mongol Ard Ulsyn malchdyn nüüdel* [Migration of Livestock Keepers of the Mongolian People's Republic], Ulaanbaatar.

Benedetto, L. F., 1928, *Marco Polo, Il Milione*, Florenz; L. Hambis (transl.), *Marco Polo, La description du monde,* Paris 1955; T. A. Knust (ed.), *Marco Polo, Von Venedig nach China. Die größte Reise des 13. Jahrhunderts,* Tübingen 1982.

Berber, F., 1973, *Das Staatsideal im Wandel der Weltgeschichte,* München.

Berezin, I. N., 1858–88, *Sbornik letopisei. Istoriya Mongolov sochinenie Rashid'-Eddina* [Collection of Histories. History of the Mongols by Rashid ad-Din]. In Trudy Vostochnago Otdeleniya Imperatorskago Arkheologicheskago Obshchestva [Works of Department of Oriental Study of the Royal Archaeological Society], vols V, VII, XIII, nos 1–4 (1858, 1861, 1868, 1888), St Petersburg.

Bernshtam, A. N., 1951, *Ocherki istorii Gunnov* [History of Xiongnu], Leningrad.

Bichurin, N. Ya., 1828, *Zapiski o Mongolii sochinennie monakhom Iakinfom* [Reports on Mongols by Monk Iakinf], vol. 1, St Petersburg.

——, 1950, *Sobranie Svedenii o narodakh srednei azii v drevnie vremena* [Collection of Information about Peoples of Central Asia in Ancient Times], vol. 1, Moscow–Leningrad.

Bira, Sh., 1977, *BNMAU-yn tüükh, soyol, tüükh bichlegiin asuudald* [Questions on History, Culture, and Historiography of the Mongolian People's Republic], Ulaanbaatar.

——, N. Ishjamc and Sh. Sandag, 1980, *Maoistskaya falsfikaciya istorii MNR i istoricheskaya pravda* [Maoist falsification of History of the Mongolian People's Republic and Historical Reality], Ulaanbaatar.

BNMAU-yn tüükh, nen ertnees XVII zuun [History of the Mongolian People's Republic: From the Earliest Times to the Seventeenth Century], 1966, vol. 1, Ulaanbaatar.

BNMAU-yn tüükh, 1604–1917 [History of the Mongolian People's Republic: 1604–1917], 1968, vol. 2, Ulaanbaatar.

BNMAU-yn tüükh [History of the Mongolian People's Republic], 1984, Ulaanbaatar.

REFERENCES

Bobek, H., 1959, 'Die Hauptstufen der Gesellschafts- und Wirtschaftsentfaltung in geographischer Sicht', *Die Erde*, vol. 90, no. 3, Berlin.

Boberg, F., 1959, *Mongolian–English Dictionary*, Copenhagen.

Boesch, H., 1977, *Weltwirtschaftsgeographie*, Braunschweig.

Bogolepov, M. and M. Sobolev, 1911, *Ocherki russko–mongol'skoi torgovli* [Trade between Russia and Mongolia], Tomsk.

Bold, B.-O., 1988, 'Mongolyn nüüdliin mal aj akhuin üildverlel dekh üildverleliin kheregseliin büreldekhüüniig sudlakh arga züin asuudald' [On Methodological Problems for Study of Structure of the Means of Pastoral Production], *Shinjlekh Ukhaany Akademiin Medee* [Report of Academy of Sciences], no. 4, Ulaanbaatar.

——, 1990, 'Sumbe Khambo Ishibaljoryn "dpag-bsam ljon-bzang" büteel dakh' tüükhiin filosofiin asuudal' [Aspects of the Philosophy of History in the Book *'dpag-bsam ljon-bzang'* by Sumbe Khambo Ishibaljor]. In *Mongolyn filosof setgelgeenii tüükhees* [On History of Mongolian Philosophy], Ulaanbaatar.

——, 1992a, ' "Mongolyn feodalizmyn" shalguuryn tukhai asuudlaar margakh n' ' [Contribution to a Discussion about the Criterion of the 'Mongolian Feudalism'], *Bodrol Byasalgal*, no. 2, Ulaanbaatar.

——, 1992b, 'Formaciin onolyn tukhai nekhen ögüülekh n' ' [Again on Marx's Theory of Socio-Economic Formations], *Bodrol Byasalgal*, no. 5, Ulaanbaatar.

——, 1996, 'Socio-economic Segmentation – "Khot-ail" in Nomadic Livestock Keeping of Mongolia', *Nomadic Peoples*, no. 39.

——, 1997, 'The coordination of territorial-administrative divisions with pastoral areas – an important prerequisite for the effective use of pasture land', *Mongolian Studies*, vol. 20, Bloomington.

——, 1998a, 'The Quantity of Livestock Owned by the Mongols in the Thirteenth Century', *Journal of the Royal Asiatic Society*, vol. 8, Part 2, London.

——, 1998b, 'New Discovery of Petroglyphs in the Mongolian Gobi', *NIASnytt, Nordic Newsletter of Asian Studies*, no. 1, Copenhagen.

——, 1998c, 'The Range of Legal Conditions Concerning Pasture Land Use in Mongolia from the Thirteenth to the Nineteenth Certuries', *Asien, Afrika, Lateinamerika*, vol. 26.

— and F.-V. Müller, 1996, Zur Relevanz neuer Regelungen für die Weidelandnutzung in der Mongolei, *Die Erde*, no. 127, Berlin.

Boyle, J. A. (transl.), 1958, *The History of the World-Conqueror by 'Ala-ad-din 'Ata-Malik Juvaini*, vols 1–2, Manchester.

Brentjes, B., 1988, *Die Ahnen Dschingis Chans*, Berlin.

Bridgeman, H. A., 1983, 'Could Climatic Change Have Had an Influence on the Polynesian Migrations?', *Palaeogeography, Palaeoclimatology, Palaeoecology*, no. 41, pp. 193–206.

Bryson, R. A. and T. J. Murray, 1977, *Climates of Hunger, Mankind and the World's Changing Weather*, London.

Buell, P. D., 1981, 'Steppe Perspectives on the Medieval History of China: Modern Mongol Scholarship on the Liao, Chin and Yüan Periods', *Zentralasiatische Studien*, no. 15, Wiesbaden.

Büttner, T., 1971, *Geschichte Afrikas. Von den Anfängen bis zur Gegenwart*, Berlin.

Butzer, K. W., 1983, 'Human Response to Environmental Change in the Perspective of Further, Global Climate', *Quaternary Research*, no. 19, pp. 279–92.

Buyanchigulgan, B., 1934, *Aji akhui-iin temdeklel* [Notes on Economy], Ulaanbaatar.

——, *Mongol-un tariyalan-un teuke* [History of Mongolian Agriculture], (Manuscript: Manuscript Collection of the Central Archives of History in Ulaanbaatar).

Cahun, L. (David Léon), 1877, *La bannière bleue: aventures d'un musulman, d'un chrétien et d'un paien à l'époque des croisades et la conquête mongole*, Paris.

——, 1896, *Introduction à l'histoire de l'Asie: Turcs et Mongols des origines à 1405*, Paris.

Cedev, D., 1964, *Ikh shav'* [Economic Institution of rJe-bcun dam-pa – Ikh shav'], Ulaanbaatar.

Cerenpuncag, Sh., 1971, *Temeen sürgiin ashig shim* [Productivity of Camels], Ulaanbaatar.

Chen Yuanqin, 1935, *Mu yan czi* [Notes on Cattle Breeding], Shanghai.

Childe, G. V., 1964, *What Happened in History*, London.

Chuluun, O., 1988, 'BNKhAU dakh' mongol sudlalyn toim' [Mongolian Studies in the People's Republic of China]. In Ch. Dalai and D. Dunger-Yaichil (eds), *Khyatad Japon dakh' mongol sudlalyn toimoos* [Survey of Mongolian Studies in China and in Japan], Ulaanbaatar.

Cin' Yui-fu, 1957, *Zhong-guo shi-syue shih* [History of Chinese Historiography], Shanghai.

Colmon, S., 1987, 'Mongolyn feodalizmyn khögzliin khev shinjiin asuudal' [Question of Development Form of Mongolian Feudalism]. In Sh. Nacagdorj (ed.), *Mongolyn feodalizmyn niitleg onclogiin zarim asuudal* [Some Questions on Generality and Particularity of the Mongolian Feudalism], Ulaanbaatar.

Coulbourn, R. (ed.), 1956, *Feudalism in History*, Princeton.

Curtin, J., 1908, *The Mongols: A History*, with a Foreword by Theodore Roosevelt, Boston.

Cybikov, G. C., 1981, 'O central'nom Tibete, Mongolii i Buryatii' [About Central Tibet, Mongolia and Buryat]. In *G. C. Cybikov, Izbrannye Trudy v dvukh tomakh* [Selected Works in two Volumes], Novosibirsk.

Dahlin, B. H., 1983, 'Climate and Prehistory of the Yucatan Peninsula', *An Interdisciplinary, International, Journal Devoted to the Description, Causes and Implications of Climatic Change*, no. 5, pp. 245–63.

REFERENCES

Dalai, Ch., 1959, *Mongolyn böögiin mörgöliin tovch tüükh* [Short History of Mongolian Shamanism], Ulaanbaatar.

——, 1973, *Yüan gürnii üeiin Mongol* [Mongolia during the Yuan Dynasty], Ulaanbaatar.

——, 1983, *Mongoliya XIII–XIV vv,* [Mongolia in the 13th–14th Centuries], Moscow.

——, 1992, *Mongolyn tüükh (1260–1388)* [History of Mongolia (1260–1388)], Ulaanbaatar.

Damdin, Z., *Altan debter* [Golden Book], (Manuscript (transl. from Tibetan): Manuscript Collection of the Institute of History of the Mongolian Academy of Sciences).

Damdinsuren, C., 1957a, 'Khüü ba khüükhen gedeg ügiin uchir' [About the Contents of the Words *Khüü* and *Khüükhen*]. *Mongol khel bichgiin tukhai* [On Mongolian Philology], Ulaanbaatar.

——, (ed.), 1957b, *Mongolyn nuuc tovchoo* [The Secret History of the Mongols], Ulaanbaatar.

Danilov, L. V., 1968, *Problemy istorii dokapitalisticheskykh obshchestv* [Problems of History of Pre-Capitalist Societies], vol. 1, Moscow.

Dawson, C. (ed.), 1955, *The Mongol Mission: Narratives and Letters of the Franciscan Missionaries in Mongolia and China in the 13th and 14th centuries,* New York.

Demchigdorji (Dandaa), C., *Shin-e zasag-un gol yosun* [Principles of New Government], (Manuscript, vols 1–2: State Public Library in Ulaanbaatar).

Dendeb, L., 1934, *Monggol-un tobchi teuke* [Short History of Mongolia], Ulaanbaatar.

Derevyanko, A. P. and D. Dorj, 1992, 'Neolithic Tribes Nothern Parts of Central Asia'. In A. H. Dani and V. M. Masson (eds), *History of Civilizations of Central Asia,* vol. 1, *The Dawn of Civilization: Earliest Times to 700 BC,* Paris.

Dorjsüren, C., 1961, *Umard khünnü* [North Xiongnu], Ulaanbaatar.

Douglas, R. K., 1877, *The Life of Genghis Khan,* London.

Drevnetyurkskii slovar' [Old Turkish Dictionary], 1969, Leningrad.

Dugarov, R. N., 1983, *'Debter-Chzamco' – istochnik po istorii mongolov Kuku-nora* [*Debter-Chzamco* – a Source-book for Study of History of Mongols in the Kuku-nor Region], Novosibirsk.

Dylykov, S. D. (ed.), 1981, *Ikh Caaz 'Velikoe ulojenie'* [The Great Code], Moscow.

Eder, K., 1973, 'Komplexsität, Evolution und Geschichte'. In F. Macieyewski (ed.), *Theorie der Gesellschaft oder Sozialtechnologie,* Frankfurt/M.

Eder, K., 1980, *Die Entstehung der staatlich organisierten Gesellschaften,* Frankfurt/M.

Eichhorn, W. and W. Küttler, 1989, *... daß Vernunft in der Geschichte sei,* Berlin.

Erdmann, F., 1962, *Temudschin der Unerschütterliche*, Leipzig.

Erkim toyin-u ayimag-un sürüg-un tengri tetkeksen-ü 62 dugar on-du bayichagagsan dangsa [Census of Livestock Owned by the Municipal District Erkim Toin Aimag of the Capital in the 62nd year (1797) of the Manchurian Emperor Ch'ien-lung (1736–97)], (Manuscript: Central Archives of History in Ulaanbaatar: F. M. 113, HN. 1, 1797).

Fan E., Hou. (ed.), 1958, *Han-shih* [History of Han], Peking.

Fang, Jin-qi, 1990, 'The Impact of Climatic Change on the Abandonment of Some Historical Agro-Cities in Arid Northwestern China', *Journal of Nanjing University* (Geography Edition, 1990), pp. 63–72, Nanjing.

—— and Liu Guo, 1992, 'Relationship between Climatic Change and the Nomadic Southward Migrations in Eastern Asia during Historical times', *An Interdisciplinary, International Journal Devoted to the Description, Causes and Implications of Climatic Change*, vol. 22, no. 2.

Fedorov-Davydov, A., 1976, 'Obshchestvennii stroi kochevnikov v sredne-vekovuyu epokhu' [Societal System of Nomads in the Middle Ages], *Voprosy Istorii* [Questions of History], no. 8, Moscow.

Flor, F., 1930, 'Haustiere und Hirtenkulturen; kulturgeschichtliche Entwicklungsumrisse'. *Wiener Beiträge zur Kulturgeschichte und Linguistik*, I, 1–238.

Gaadamba, Sh., 1990, *Monggol-un nigucha tobchiyan* [The Secret History of the Mongols], Ulaanbaatar.

Gaubil, A., 1739, *Histoire de Gentchiscan et toute la dynastie des Mongols, ses successeurs conquérants de la Chine*, Paris.

Gendendaram, Z., 1992, 'Chingisiin ikh yasa bolon aildvaruud' [Genghis's Great Yasa Code and His Maxims], *Bodrol Byasalgal*, no. 5, Ulaanbaatar.

Gerbillon, F., 1779, *La Grande Tartarie*, Paris.

Gilmour, J., 1883, *Among the Mongols*, London/New York.

——, 1886, *Adventures in Mongolia*, London.

Gol'man, M. I., 1988, *Izuchenie istorii Mongolii na zapade, (XIII–sredina XX v.)* [Study of Mongolia in the West (17th–mid-20th Centuries], Moscow.

Golstunskii, K. F., 1880, *Mongolo-Oiratskie zakony 1640 goda (dopolnitel'nye ukazy Galdan khuntaijiya i zakony sostavlennie dlya voljskikh Kalmykov pri kalmyckom khane Donduk-Dashi)* [Mongol-Oirat Regulations of 1640 (Supplementary Decrees by Galdan Khuntaij and Rules for Volga-Kalmyks Compiled during the Reign of Kalmyk Leader Donduk-Dashi Khan)], St Petersburg.

Gombojab, [n.d.] 1960, *Ganga-yin uruskhal (Istoriya Zolotogo roda vladiki Chingisa). Sochinenie pod nazvaniem 'Techenie Ganga'* [The *Gang-yin Uruskhal* Chronicle (History of the Golden Tribe of Genghis Khaan). A Book named 'Stream of Ganga'], edited by L. S. Puchkovskii, Moscow.

Gongor, D., 1964, *Khovdyn khuraanguj tüükh* [Short History of the Khovd Province], Ulaanbaatar.

References

——, 1970, *Khalkha tovchoon* [History of Outer Mongolia], vol. 1, Ulaanbaatar.

——, 1978, *Khalkha tovchoon* [History of Outer Mongolia], vol. 2, Ulaanbaatar.

Guignes, J. de., *Histoire générale des Huns, des Turcs, des Mongols et des autres Tartares occidentaux avant et depuis Jésus Christ jusqu'à présent*, vols 1–2 (1756), vol. 3 (1757), vol. 4 (1758), vol. 5 (1824), Paris.

Gumilev, L. N., 1960, *Gunnu* [Xiongnu], Moscow.

——, 1989, *Etnogenez i biosfera zemli* [Ethnogenesis and Biosphere of the Earth], Leningrad.

—— and A. I. Kurkchi, 1992, *Khar domog* [Black Legend], Ulaanbaatar.

Günter, R. and G. Schrot, 1963, 'Bemerkungen zur Gesetzmäßigkeit in der auf Sklaverei beruhenden Gesellschaftliche', *Wissenschaftliche Zeitschrift der Karl-Marx Universität*, no. 1, Leipzig.

Gurevich, A. Ya., 1968, 'K diskussii o dokapitalisticheskykh obshchestvennykh formaciyakh: formaciya i uklad' [On Discussion of Pre-Capitalist Social Formations: Formation and Social Form], *Voprosy Istorii* [Questions of History], no. 2, Moscow.

Guvaini, [n.d.] 1958, *The History of the World-Conqueror by 'Ala-ad-din 'Ata-Malik Juvaini*, translated by J. A. Boyl, vols 1–2, Manchester. (New edition by D. Morgan, 1997.)

Guzgani, [n.d.] 1864, *The Tabaqát-i Násiri of Aboo 'Omar Minháj al-Dín 'Othmán ibn Siráj al-Dín al-Jawzjani*: Edited by W. Nassau Lees, and Mawlawis Khadim Hosain, and 'Abd al-Hai, Calcutta.

Haenisch, E., 1948, *Die Geheime Geschichte der Mongolen*, Leipzig.

——, 1980, '... Men-ta pei-lu und Hei-ta Shih-lüeh'. *Asiatische Forschungen*, vol. 56, Wiesbaden.

Hahn, E., 1891, 'Waren die Menschen der Urzeit zwischen der Jägerstufe und der Stufe des Ackerbaus Nomaden?', *Das Ausland. Wochenschrift für Erd- und Völkerkunde*, vol. 64, no. 25.

Hedley, J., 1910, *Tramps in Dark Mongolia*, London.

Hegel, G. W. F., 1986, *Vorlesungen über die Geschichte der Philosophie*. Edited by E. Moldenhauer and K. M. Michel, vol. 12, Frankfurt/M.

Heissig, W., 1953, 'Neyici-Toyin. Das Leben eines lamaistischen Mönches', *Sinologica*, vol. 3.

——, 1959, *Die Familien- und Kirchengeschichtsschreibung der Mongolen*. *Asiatische Forschungen*, vol. 5, Wiesbaden.

——, 1964, *Ein Volk sucht seine Geschichte*, Vienna–Düsseldorf.

——, 1968, *Mongolistik an deutschen Universitäten*, Wiesbaden.

——, 1970, 'Der Schamanismus der Mongolen'. *Religion der Menschheit*, vol. 20, Stuttgart.

——, 1992, *Schamanen und Geisterbeschwörerin der östlichen Mongolei*, Wiesbaden.

——, 1996, 'Recent East Mongolian shamanic traditions'. *Religion and Society*, no. 36 (Shamanism and Northern Ecology), Berlin/New York, pp. 249–58.
Herzog, R., 1988, *Staaten der Frühzeit*, München.
Hövermann, J. and H. Süssenberger, 1986, 'Zur Klimageschichte Hoch- und Ostasiens', *Berliner Geographische Studien*, vol. 20, pp. 173–86.
Huc, R. E. and J. Gabet, 1928, *Travels in Tartary: Thibet and China 1844–46*, vols 1–2, London.
Huntington, E., 1907, *The Pulse of Asia*, Boston.
——, 1914, 'The Solar Hypothesis of Climatic Change', *Geological Society of America. Bulletin*, no. 25, pp. 477–590.
——, [1915], 1927, *Civilization and Climate*, New Haven.
——, 1935, 'Climate Pulsation'. In *Geografiska annaler, Hyllningsskrift tillägnad Sven Hedin på hans 70-årsdag den 19 februari 1935*, no. 17, Stockholm.
Hyacinth, I., 1828, *Zapiski o Mongolii* [Notes on Mongolia], St Petersburg.
Idshinnorov, S. and G. Cerendorj, 1990, 'Javzandamba-agvaanluvsan-choijin-nyama-danzanvanchig-balsambuu (1869–1924)' [The Eighth Religious Head Zavzandamba-Agvaanluvsan-Choijin-Nyama-Danzanvanchig-Balsambuu (1969–1924)], *Ünen* (newspaper), 16.6.1990, no. 143 (17673).
Injannashi, V., 1961, *Köke sudar* [Blue History], Khökhe khota.
Irinchin, I., 1980, '10–12 dugar zagun-u monggol niigem dakhi bogol' [On Slaves in the Mongolian Society of the 10th–12th Centuries], *Uver Mongol-un Yeke Surgagul-un Erdem Shinjilgen-u Setigül* [Journal of Inner Mongolian University], no. 3, Khökhe khota.
Ishibaljir, Sumbe Khambo, *mKham-po Aerte-ni pandi-tar grags-pa'i sryod tshul brjod-pa sgra-dzin beud len zhes-bya-ba bzhugs-so* [Autobiography of Sumbe Khambo Ishibaljir], pp. 12b–13b, (Tibet. Manuscript: Library of the Monastery Gangdan Tegchinlin in Ulaanbaatar).
Ishjamc, N., 1956, 'Khünnügiin udam ugsaa niigemlegiin baiguulal' [Origin of Xiongnu and Their Societal Organisation], *Sinjlekh Ukhaany Khüreelengiin Erdem Shinjilgeenii Büteel* [Journal of Institute of Sciences], vol. 12, no. 2, Ulaanbaatar.
——, 1976, *Mongold negdsen tör baiguulagdaj feodalizm bürelden togtson n'* [Establishment of the Mongolian United State and Formation of Feudalism], Ulaanbaatar.
Istoriya Mongol'skoi Narodnoi Respubliki [History of the Mongolian People's Republic], 1954, Moscow.
Istoriya Mongol'skoi Narodnoi Respubliki [History of the Mongolian People's Republic], 1967, Moscow.
Jagchid, S. and C. R. Bawden, 1965, 'Some Notes on the Horse-Policy of the Yuan Dynasty', *Central Asiatic Journal*, vol. 10, Wiesbaden.
—— and P. Hyer, 1979, *Mongolia's culture and society*, Colorado.

REFERENCES

Jagvaral, N., 1974, *Aratstvo i aratskoe khozyaistvo* [Livestock Keepers and Livestock Keeping Economy], Ulaanbaatar.
Jimbadorji, 1834–37, *Bolor tol'* [The *Bolor tol'* Chronicle], vols 1–12.
Kantorovich, A. Ya., 1926, 'Sistema obshchestvennykh otnoshenii Kitaya dokapitalisticheskoi epokhi' [The System of Societal Relationship of Pre-Capitalist China], *Novyi Vostok* [New East], no. 15, Moscow.
Kaschewsky, 1986, 'Die Religion der Mongolen'. In M. Weiers (ed.), *Die Mongolen. Beiträge zu ihrer Geschichte und Kultur*, Darmstadt.
Kazakevich, V. A., 1934, 'Nekotorie voprosy istorii mongolii v svete Arkheologii' [Some Archaeological Questions Concerning the Mongolian History], *Sovremennaya mongoliya* [Contemporary Mongolia], no. 4, Irkutsk.
Khobdu ayimag-un süme keyid-un teuke [History of Buddhist Temples in Khovd Aimag], (Manuscript: Central Archives of History in Ulaanbaatar, Collection: Religion).
Klaus, D., 1980, *Natürliche und anthropogene Klimaänderungen und ihre Auswirkungen auf den wirtschaftenden Menschen*, München.
Kohl-Estivend, I., 1915, *Otricatelnie Faktory mongol'skogo skotovodstva* [Negative Factors of the Mongolian Pastoral Economy], Harbin.
Kononov, A. N. (ed.), 1986, *Mongolica. Pamyati akademika Boris Yakovlevicha Vladimircova 1884–1931* [Mongolica. In Memory of Academician Boris Yakovlevich Vladimircov 1884–1931], Moscow.
Koppers, W., 1932, 'Könnten Jägervölker Tierzüchter werden?', *Biologia Generalis*, vol. VII, 1, 179–86.
Korostovetz, I. J., 1926, *Von Chinggis Khan zur Sowietrepublik*, Berlin.
Kovolevskii, O. M., 1844–49, *Dictionnaire Mongol–Russe–Français*, vols 1–3, Kazan.
Krader, L., 1966, *Peoples of Central Asia*, Indiana University, Bloomington.
Kreißig, H., 1981, 'Antike Produktionsweise-Eigentumsverhältnisse'. *Handbuch. Wirtschaftsgeschichte*, vol. 1, Berlin.
Krüger, H., 1964, *Allgemeine Staatslehre*, München.
Kuchenbuch, L. (ed.), 1977, *Feudalismus-Materialien zur Theorie und Geschichte*, Frankfurt/M.
Kuhle, M., 1991, 'Die Vergletscherung Tibets und ihre Bedeutung für die Geschichte des nordhemisphärischen Inlandeises'. In B. Frenzel (ed.), *Klimageschichtliche Probleme der letzten 130,000 Jahre*, Paläoklimaforschung, vol. 1, Stuttgart–New York.
Küner, N. V., 1927, *Ocherki noveishchei politicheskoi istorii Kitaya* [Modern Political History of China], Habarovsk/Vladivostok.
Kurzrock, R. (ed.), 1981, *Mittelalterforschung, Forschung und Information*, Schriftreihe der Rias-Funkuniversität, Berlin.
Lamb, H. H., 1982, *Climate, History and the Modern World*, London.

Lattimore, O., 1962, *Studies in Frontier History. Collected Papers 1928–58*, Paris.
Legrand, J., 1976, *L'administration dans la domination Sino-Mandchoue en Mongolie Qalq-a, Version mongole du Lifan Yuan Zeli*. Mémoires de l'Institute des Hautes Etudes Chinoises, vol. II, Paris.
Lenk, A., 1974, *Die Gezeiten der Geschichte. Wie das Klima unsere Vergangenheit, Gegenwart und Zukunft beeinflußt*, Düsseldorf/Vienna.
Lessing, D. F., 1960, *Mongolian-English Dictionary*, Los Angeles.
Lifanyuan zeli: Jarlig-bar togtogagson gadagad monggol-un törü-ig jasakh yabudal-un yamun-u khauli juyile-iin bichig [Statute Book, established by all highest Command, of the Ministry of the Government of the Outer Mongolian Provinces], 1908 (Central Archives of History in Ulaanbaatar, 'Manchurian Collection').
Lin Kun and N. Z. Munkuev, 1960, 'Kratkie svedenie o chernykh tatarakh P'eng Ta-ya i Sü T'ing' [Short History of Black Tatars by P'eng Ta-ya and Sü T'ing], *Problemy vostokovedeniya* AN SSSR [Problems of Oriental Study of Academy of Sciences of the Soviet Union], no. 5, Leningrad.
Lloyd, Ch., 1991, 'The Methodologies of Social History: A Critical Survey and Defense of Structurism'. *History and Theory*, vol. XXX, no. 2, Wesleyan University.
Luvsandanzan, 1990, *Altan tobchi* [The *Altan tobchi* Chronicle]. Edited by C. Shagdar, Ulaanbaatar.
Mad'jar, L. I., 1928, *Ekonomika sel'skogo khozyaistvo v Kitae* [Agricultural Economy of China], Moscow.
Magsarjab, A. (Magsar Khurca), *Monggol ulus-un shin-e teuke* [Modern History of Mongolia], (Manuscript: State Public Library in Ulaanbaatar).
Maidar, D., 1972, *Mongolyn arkhitektur ba khot baiguulalt* [Mongolian Architecture and Urban Development in Mongolia], Ulaanbaatar.
Mailla, G. M., 1777–85, *Histoire générale de la Chine aux annales de cet empire*, vols 1–12, Paris.
Maiskii, I. M., 1921, *Sovremennaya Mongoliya* [Contemporary Mongolia], Irkutsk.
——, 1960, *Mongoliya na kanune revolyucii* [Mongolia on the Threshold of Revolution], Moscow.
Markov, G. E., 1976, *Kochevniki azii: Struktura khozyaistva i obshchestvennaya organizaciya* [Asian Nomads: Economic Structure and Societal Organisation], Moscow.
——, 1981, 'Ausbeutungs- und Abhängigkeitsverhältnisse bei den Nomaden Asiens'. In R. Krusche (ed.), *Die Nomaden in der Geschichte und Gegenwart*, Berlin.
Marx, K., 1961, 'Zur Kritik der Politischen Ökonomie (Vorwort)'. *Marx Engels Werke*, vol. 13, Berlin.
Mengu-u-mu-tschzi; *Mên-gu yu-mu czi*, see P. S. Popov, 1895.

REFERENCES

Minis, A., 1968, *MAKhN-aas feodal angiin uls tör ediin zasgiin noyorkholyg ustgakhyn tölöö yavuulsan temcel* [Policy of Mongolian People's Revolutionary Party for Liquidation of Political and Economical Power of Feudal Class], Ulaanbaatar.

Mongol ba töv aziin tüükhend kholbogdokh khoyor khovor survalj bichig [Two Old Chronicles Concerning the History of Mongolia and Central Asia], 1974, Ulaanbaatar.

Mongol-Oirat Regulations of 1640, see: Golstunskii, 1880; Alinge, 1934; Riasanovsky, 1965; Dylykov, 1981.

Morgan, D., 1990, *The Mongols*, Oxford.

Moses, L. W., 1977, *The Political Role of Mongol Buddhism*, Bloomington.

Mostaert, A., 1953, 'Sur quelques passages de l'Histoire Secrète des Mongols', *Harvard Journal of Asiatic Studies*, vol. XVIII.

Müller-Mertens, E., 1966, 'Zur Feudalenentwicklung im Okzident und zur Definition der Feudalverhältnisse', *Zeitschrift für Geschichtswissenschaft*, vol. XIV.

Munkuev, N. Z., 1970, 'Zametki o drevnykh mongolakh' [Notes on the Ancient Mongols]. In L. V. Matveeva (ed.), *Tataro-Mongoly v Azii i Evrope* [Tartar-Mongols in Asia and in Europe], Moscow.

———, (ed.), 1975, *Men-da Bei-lu. Polnoe opisanie Mongolo-Tatar* [Complete Description of the Mongol-Tartars'. Men-ta bei-lu], Moscow.

Nacagdorj, Sh., 1958, *Iz istorii aratskogo dvizeniya vo vneshnei mongolii* [Some Aspects of History of the Movement of Herding People in Outer Mongolia], Moscow.

———, 1963, *Khalkhyn tüükh* [History of Outer Mongolia], Ulaanbaatar.

———, 1978, *Mongolyn feodalizmyn ündsen zamnal* [Ways of Mongolian Feudalism], Ulaanbaatar.

———, (ed.), 1987, *Mongolyn feodalizmyn niitleg onclogiin zarim asuudal* [Some Questions on Generality and Particularity of the Mongolian Feudalism], Ulaanbaatar.

Nasanbaljir, C. (ed.), 1960, 'Sagan Secen, *Erdeniin tobchi*' [The *Erdeniin tobchi* Chronicle by Sagan Secen], Ulaanbaatar.

———, (ed.), 1960, Galdan (Khung) *taiji*, *Erdeni-yin erke* [The *Erdeni-yin erke* Chronicle by Galdan taiji], Ulaanbaatar.

———, (ed.), 1961, *Khalkh Jirum* [The *Khalkh Jirum* Code], Ulaanbaatar.

Navaannamjil, G., 1947, *Avtonomt-un üi-e-yin Monggol-un teuke* [History of the Autonomous Outer Mongolia], (Manuscript: Manuscript Collection of the Institute of History of the Mongolian Academy of Sciences).

Niedenzu, H., 1982, *Die Entstehung von herrschaftlich organisierten Gesellschaft*, Frankfurt/M.

Nikiforov, V. N., 1975, *Vostok i vsemirnaya istoriya* [The East and World History], Moscow.

Nominkhanov, Z. D., 1975, *Materialy k izucheniyu istorii kalmyckogo yazyka* [Materials for Study of History of Kalmyk Language], Moscow.

Novgorodova, E. A., 1989, *Drevnyaya Mongoliya (Nekotorye problemy khronologii i etnokul'turnoi istorii)* [Ancient Mongolia (Problems of Chronology and of Ethnocultural History)], Moscow.

Ochir, A. and G. Dashnyam (eds), 1988, *Ar Mongol dakh' Khyatadyn khudaldaa möngö khüülel (1751–1911)* [Chinese Trade and Moneylending in Outer Mongolia (1751–1911)], Ulaanbaatar.

Okladnikov, A. P. and A. P. Derevyanko, 1970, 'Tamsag-Bulagskaya neoliticheskaya kul'tura Vostochnoi Mongolii' [Tamsag-Bulag's Neolithic Culture in the Eastern Mongolia]. *Materialy po istorii i filologii Central'noi Azii* [Materials for Study of Philology and History of Central Asia], vol. 5, pp. 3–20.

Olbricht, P. and E. Pink, 1980, 'Men-ta Pei-lu und Hei-ta Shih-lüeh. Chinesische Gesandtenberichte über die frühen Mongolen 1221 und 1237. Übersetzt und kommentiert nach Vorarbeiten von E. Haenisch und Yao Ts'ung-wu. Eingeleitet von W. Banck'. *Asiatische Forschungen*, vol. 56, Wiesbaden.

Onuki, M., 1990, *Nüüdliin mal aj akhuin niigmiin orchin üe* [Mongolian Nomadic Society in the Present], edited by D. Dashpurev, Osaka.

Orkhon, D., 1992, 'Mongolyn negdsen töriin üüsliin züi togtolyn tukhai' [On Foundation of Unified Mongolian State], *Bodrol Byasalgal*, 1992, no. 2, Ulaanbaatar.

Otremba, E., 1969, *Der Wirtschaftsraum – seine geographischen Grundlagen und Probleme*, vol. 1, Stuttgart.

Pallas, P. S., 1776, *Sammlungen historischer Nachrichten über die mongolischen Völkerschaften*, St Petersburg; new edition: 1980, Graz, vols 1–2.

Papayan, G. K., 1930, *'Zin' tan'. Agrarnyi stroi drevnogo Kitaya'* [*Zin' tan'*. Agricultural System of Ancient China], Moscow.

Pelliot, P., 1959, *Notes on Marco Polo*, Paris.

——, 1960, *Notes critiques d'histoire kalmouke*, Paris.

—— and L. Hambis, 1951, *Histoire des campagnes de Gengis Khan. Cheng-Wou Ts'in-Tcheng Lou*, Leiden.

Pepper, J., 1927, 'Evropeisko-amerikanskii imperializm i kitaiskaya revolyuciya' [European and American Imperialism, and Chinese Revolution], *Pravda* 1.5.1927.

Perlee, Kh., 1956, *Mongolyn tüükhiin ur'd medegdeegüi zarim on cagiin medee* [Informations Concerning Hitherto Unknown Dates of Mongolian History], Ulaanbaatar.

——, 1959, *Kyatan nar, tednii mongolchuudtai kholbogdson n'* [The Khitans and Their Relationship with Mongols], Ulaanbaatar.

——, (ed.), 1960, *Jamba, Asragch nertiin tüükh* [The *Asragch nertiin tüükh* Chronicle by Jamba], Ulaanbaatar.

——, 1961, *Mongol ard ulsyn ert dund, üeiin khot suur'nii tovchoon* [History of Urbanization in Mongolia in the Ancient Times and in the Middle Epoch], Ulaanbaatar.

References

——, 1976, *Mongol tümnii garlyg tamgaar khaij sudlakh n'* [Study of Origin of Mongols by Means of Seal Symbols], Ulaanbaatar.

—— and G. Sükhbaatar, 1976, 'Maogiinkhan mongolyn tüükhiig guivuulsaar baigaagiin ünen uchir' [Reason for Falsification of Mongolian History by Maoist Historians], *Shinjlekh Ukhaany Akademiin Medee* [Information of Academy of Sciences], Ulaanbaatar.

Petech, L., 1966, 'Tibet'. *Handbuch der Orientalistik*, Leiden/Köln.

Phillips, E. D., 1969, *The Mongols*, London.

Pokotilov, D., 1893, *Istoriya vostochnykh mongolov v period dinastii Min 1368–1634, po kitaiskim istochnikam* [History of Western Mongolia in the Period of Min Dynasty 1368–1634], St Petersburg.

Popov, P. S., 1895, *Mên-gu-yu-mu-czi. Zapiski o mongol'kikh kochev'yakh* [Mên-gu-yu-mu-czi: Notes on Mongolian Nomadism], Zapiski Imperatorskago Russkago Geograficheskago Obshchestva [Reports of Russian Royal Geographical Society], vol. XXIV. St Petersburg.

Poppe, N. N., 1941a, *Kvadratnaya pismennost'* [Quadratic Script], Leningrad.

——, 1941b, *Zolotoordinskaya rukopis' na Bereste* [Golden Hord's Manuscript of Berest], Moscow–Leningrad.

——, 1965, *Introduction to Altaistic Linguistics*, Wiesbaden.

Posdne'ev, A. M., 1883, *Mongolskie letopisi 'Erdeniin erki'* [The Mongolian Chronicle – *Erdeniin erki*], St Petersburg.

Potanin, G. N., 1879–83, *Ocherki Severo-Zapadnoi Mongolii, Rezul'taty puteshchestviya, ispolnennogo v 1879–1883gg.* [About Northwest Mongolia: Results of a Journey in 1879–83], vol. 4, St Petersburg.

——, 1948, *Ocherki Severo-Zapadnoi Mongolii. Rezul'taty puteshchestviya, ispolnennogo v 1876–1877gg.* [About Northwest Mongolia: Results of a Journey in 1876–77], vol. 1, Moscow.

Potapov, L. P., 1955, O sushchnosti patriarkhal'no-feodal'nykh otnoshenii u kochevykh narodov [On Nature of the Patriarchal-Feudalistic Relationship among the Nomadic Peoples], *Voprosy Istorii* [Questions of History], no. 6, Moscow/Leningrad.

Poucha, P., 1956, *Die Geheime Geschichte der Mongolen*, Praha.

Puchkovskii, L. S., 1953, 'Mongol'skaya feodal'naya istoriografiya XIII–XVII vv'. [Mongolian Feudalistic Historiography of the 13th–17th Centuries]. *Uchenye zapiski instituta vostokovedeniya* [Research Reports of Oriental Institute], vol. 6.

Pumpelly, R., 1908, *Expedition of 1904*, Carnegie Institution Publication, no. 73, vol. 1, Washington, DC.

Purev, O., 1998, *Mongol böögiin shashin* [Mongolian Shamanism], Ulaanbaatar.

Purevjav, S., 1978, *Mongol dakh' sharyn shashny khuraangui tüükh* [Short History of Yellow Sect of Buddhism in Mongolia], Ulaanbaatar.

Rachewiltz, I. de, 1971, 'The Secret History of the Mongols'. *Papers on Far Eastern History*, vol. 4, Canberra.

Radloff, W., 1892, *Das Kutagtu Bilik des Jusuf Chass-Hadschib aus Bälasagun*, part 1, St Petersburg.
Ramstedt, G. J., 1914, 'Mongolia'. *China Yearbook*.
——, 1935, *Kalmükisches Wörterbuch*, Helsinki.
——, 1978, 'Seven Journeys Eastward, 1898–1912'. *The Mongolia Society Occasional Pepers*, vol. 9, Bloomington.
Rashid ad-Din, 1946–60, *Sbornik letopisei* [Collection of Histories], vols 1 (2 bks), 2, and 3: vol. 1, bk 1, L. A. Khitagurov (transl.), 1952; vol. 1, bk 2, O. I. Smirnova (transl.), 1952; vol. 2, Yu. P. Verkhovskii (transl.), 1960; vol. 3, A. K. Arends (transl.), 1946, Moscow–Leningrad.
Rathmann, L., 1971, *Geschichte der Araber. Von den Anfängen bis zur Gegenwart*, vol. 1, Berlin.
Report on the Joint Investigation under the Mongolian and Japanese GURVAN GOL Historic Relic Probe Project (1991–1993), 1994, Mongolian Academy of Sciences and The Yomiuri Shimbun, Japan.
Riasanovsky, V. A., 1929, *Customary Law of the Mongol Tribes*, Harbin.
——, 1965, *Fundamental principles of Mongol Law*, Bloomington.
Ribeiro, D. R., 1970, *Der zivilisatorische Prozeß*, Frankfurt/M.
Rinchen, B., 1955, 'A propos du chamanisme mongol. Le culte de l'ongon Dayan degereki chez les Mongols Khotougaites du Kossogol', *Studia Orientalia. Edidit Societas Orientalis Fennica*, vol. XVIII, no. 4, II, Helsinki, pp. 8–16.
——, (ed.), 1979, *Mongol ard ulsyn ugsaatny sudlal, khel shinjleliin atlas* [Atlas of Ethnology and Linguistics of the Mongolian People's Republic], Ulaanbaatar.
——, 1981, 'White, Black and Yellow Shamans among the Mongols', *Ultimate Reality and Meaning*, vol. 4, no. 2, pp. 94–112.
Risch, F, 1930, *Johann de Plano Carpini, Geschichte der Mongolen und Reisebericht, 1245–1247*, Leipzig.
Roberts, J., 1903, *A Flight for Life and an Inside View of Mongolia*, Boston.
Rockhill, W. W., 1894, *Diary of a Journey through Mongolia and Tibet in 1891 and 1892*, Washington.
——, 1967, *The Journey of William Rubruck to the Eastern Part of the World (1253–55)*, Nedeln.
Ronge, V., 1986, 'Kunst und Kunstgewerbe bei den Mongolen'. In M. Weiers (ed.), *Die Mongolen, Beiträge zu ihrer Geschichte und Kultur*, Darmstadt.
Rubruck, W., 1925, *Der Bericht des Franziskaners Wilhelm von Rubruck über seine Reise in das Innere Asiens in den Jahren 1253–1255*, H. Herbst (transl.). Leipzig.
Rumyancev, G. N., 1958, 'Trudy B. Vladimircova po istorii Mongolov' [B. Vladimircov's Works on History of Mongols]. *Filologiya i istoriya mongol'skikh narodov* [Philology and History of Mongolian Peoples], Moscow.

References

———, 1965, 'Selengiiskie Buryaty' (proiskhojdenie i rodoplemennyi sostav) [Buryats of Selenge Region (Emergence and Tribal Structure)]. *Materialy po istorii i filologii central'noi Azii* [Materials for the Study of Central Asian History and Philology], vol. 2, Ulan-Ude.

Rygdylon, E. R., 1958, 'O mongol'skom termine ongu-bogol' [About Mongolian Term Ongu-Bogol]. In *Filologiya i istoriya mongol'skikh narodov* [Philology and History of Mongolian Peoples], Moscow.

Sachin, J., 1984, 'Tibetan Buddhism: The Mongolian Religion', *Common Voice*, vol. 1.

Sagaster, K., 1970, 'Rasipunsug und der Beginn der kritischen Geschichtsschreibung der Mongolen', *Zentralasiatische Studien*, no. 4, Wiesbaden.

———, 1976, 'Die Weiße Geschichte (Cagan teuke). Eine mongolische Quelle zur Lehre von den beiden Ordnungen. Religion und Staat in Tibet und der Mongolei'. *Asiatische Forschungen*, vol. 41, Wiesbaden.

Saiishiyal, 1987, *Chinggis khagany tobchiyan* [History of Genghis Khaan], vol. 1, Khökhe khota.

Sain-Noyon-Khan-Aimgiin Al'bom [Album of Maps of the Sain-Noyon-Khan Aimag], 1987, Ulaanbaatar.

Sanchirov, V. P., 1976, ' *"Iletkhel Shastir"* kak istochnik po istorii Oirotov (kratkie itogi predvaritel'nogo issledovaniya). Social'no-ekonomicheskie i politicheskie problemy istorii dorevolucionnoi Kalmyki ['*Iletkhel Shastir*' – Source Book of History of Oirats (Short Report of Preliminary Investigation). Socio-Economical and Political Problems of Pre-Revolutionary Kalmyk History].*Vestnik Kalmyckogo Nauchno-issledovatel'skogo Instituta YaLI* [Information of Research Institute of Kalmyk for Linguistics, Literature and History], no. 15, Seriya istoricheskaya, Elista.

Sanjeev G. D. (ed.), 1958, *Filologiya i istoriya mongol'skikh narodov* [Philology and History of Mongolian Peoples], Moscow.

Sanjmyatav, T., 1991, Ertnii mongolyn gazar tarialangiin dursgalaas [Historical Monuments Concerning Development of Agriculture in Mongolia], *Chingisiin Tug* [Genghis's Flag], no. 1, Ulaanbaatar.

Schmidt, I. J., 1835, *Mongolisch–deutsch–russisch. Wörterbuch*, St Petersburg.

Schmidt, W. P., 1951, 'Zu den Anfängen der Herdentierzucht', *Ethnologie*, 76, pp. 1–41.

Schmieder, F., 1994, *Europa und die Fremden: die Mongolen im Urteil des Abendlandes vom 13. bis in das 15. Jahrhundert*, Thorbecke.

Scholz, F., 1995, *Nomadismus. Theorie und Wandel einer sozio-ökologischen Kulturweise*, Stuttgart.

Schulemann, G., 1958, *Geschichte der Dalai Lamas*, Leipzig.

Secen-Khan-Aimgiin Al'bom [Album of Maps of the Secen-Khan Aimag], 1987, Ulaanbaatar.

Secen Khan ayimag-un ilden Jüng Vang-u khosigun-u badargult törü-yin 16 dugar on-u kümün ama ba mal-un bürütgel dangsa [Results of Population Census and of Livestock Count of Ilden Jüng Vang Khoshuu of Secen

Khan Aimag in the 16th year (1890) of the Manchurian Emperor Guan'-shiu (1875–1908)] (Manuscript: Central Archives of History in Ulaanbaatar, F.M. 27, HN, 1897).

Secret History of the Mongols, see: E. Haenisch, 1948; C. Damdinsuren, 1957b; P. Poucha, 1956.

Semenov, Yu. I., 1966, 'Sovetskie istoriki o stanovlenii klassovogo obscestva v drevnem Kitae' [Soviet Historians about Formation of Class Society in China], *Narody Afriki I Azii* [Peoples of Asia and Africa], 1966, no. 1, Moscow.

Sereeter, Ch., 1974, BNMAU-yn ardyn aj akhuin tüükhiin asuudlaas [To the History of Pastoral Economy of the Mongolian People's Republic], *Ediin Zasgiin Khüreelen: Erdem Shinjilgeenii Büteel* [Journal of the Institute of Economy], no. 7, Ulaanbaatar.

Ser-odjav, N., 1976, *Ertnii mongolyn tüükh* [Ancient History of Mongols], Ulaanbaatar.

Serruys, H. (ed.), 1945, 'Siao ta heng Pei-lou fong sou, les coutumes des esclaves septentrionaux'. *Monumenta Serica,* no. 10, pp. 117–208.

Shagdar, C. (ed.), 1990, *Luvsandanzan, Altan tobchi* [The *Altan tobchi* Chronicle by Luvsandanzan], Ulaanbaatar.

Shagdarsüren, C. (ed.), 1988, *Juobanni del' Plano Karpini. Mongolchuudyn tüükh; Gil'om de Rubruk. Dorno etgeeded zorchson min'* [Juobanni del' Plano Karpini. History of Mongols; Gil'om de Rubruk. My Journey Eastward], Ulaanbaatar.

Shakhmatov, V. F., 1964, *Kazakhskaya pastbyshchnokochevaya obshchina (Voprosy preobrazovaniya, evolyucii i razlojeniya)* [Pastoral Community among the Kazaks (Questions on Reorganisation, Evolution and Disintegration], Alma-Ata.

Sharkhüü, C. (ed.), 1975, *Khuv'sgalyn ömnökh mongol dakh' gazryn kharilcaa (Arkhivyn materialyn emkhetgel)* [Relation to the Pasture Land in Mongolia before the People's Revolution (Archive Material Collection)], Ulaanbaatar.

Shastina, N. P. (ed.), 1957, *Shara Tudji: mongol'skaya letopis' XVII veka* [Mongolian Chronicle of the Seventeenth Century – *Shara Tudji*], Moscow.

Shinekhüü, M., 1975, *Tariatyn orkhon bichgiin shine dursgal* [A New Orkhon-Inscript of the Tariat Region], Ulaanbaatar.

Shirendev, B., 1971, *Mongol ardyn khuv'sgalyn tüükh* [The History of the Mongolian People's Revolution], Ulaanbaatar.

Shitügen-ü ayimag-un jisa-yin mal-g bayichagagsan dangsa [Census of Livestock owned by the Temple of Municipal District of the Capital Shitügen-Aimag], (Manuscript: Central Archives of History in Ulaanbaatar, F.M. 121, HN. 3 1).

Simukov, A. D., 1933, 'Khotony' [The Khot-Ail Group]. *Sovremennaya Mongoliya* [Contemporary Mongolia], no. 3, Irkutsk.

REFERENCES

——, 1934, 'Mongol'skie kochevki' [Mongolian Nomadic Sites], *Sovremennaya Mongoliya* [Contemporary Mongolia], no. 4, Irkutsk.

——, 1935 and 1936, 'Materialy po kochevomu bytu naseleniya M.N.R.' [Material Concerning the Nomadic Way of Life of the People of the Mongolian People's Republic], *Sovremennaya Mongoliya* [Contemporary Mongolia], no. 6 (1935), and no. 2 (1936), Irkutsk.

Sonomdagva, C., 1961, *Manjiin zakhirgaand baisan ueiin ar mongolyn zasag zakhirgaany zokhion baiguulalt (1691–1911)* [Administrative Structure of the Outer Mongolia during the Manchurian Rule (1691–1911)], Ulaanbaatar.

Spengler, O., 1922, *Der Untergang des Abendlandes*, München.

Strakosch-Grassmann, G., 1893, *Der Einfall der Mongolen in Mitteleuropa in den Jahren 1241 und 1242*, Innsbruck.

Sükhbaatar, G., 1971, *Syambi* [Xian-pei People], Ulaanbaatar.

——, 1973, 'Khünnü naryn ugsaa garlyn khamaadlyn asuudlaas' [Question on the Ethnical Affiliation of Xiongnu People], *Tüükhiin sudlal* [Study of History], vol. 10, Ulaanbaatar.

——, 1980, *Mongolchuudyn ertnii övög* [Ancestors of Mongols], Ulaanbaatar.

——, 1992, *Mongol nirun uls (330–555)* [Mongolian Nirun Empire (330–550)], Ulaanbaatar.

Sumbe Khambo: see Ishibaljir, Sumbe Khambo.

Sun Lian, 1958, *Yuanshi* [History of Yuan Dynasty], Peking.

Sze-ma Ts'ien (or Szu-ma Ch'ien), 1963, *Shih-chi* [Historical Book], vols 1–10, Shanghai.

Taskin, V. S., 1973, *Materialy po istorii Syunnu (po kitaiskim istochnikam)* [Historical Materials of the Xiongnu according to Chinese Chronicles], vol. 2, Moscow.

——, 1984, *Materialy po istorii drevnykh kochevykh narodov gruppy)* [Historical Materials of the Ancient Nomadic Peoples of the Dunhu-Group], Moscow.

Tengri tetkeksen Khagan-u 60 on-du Jüd dacang-un sürüg-g bayichagagsan dangsa [Count Result of Livestock owned by the Temple Jüd in the 60th year (1795) of the Manchurian Emperor Ch'ien-lung (1736–96)] (Manuscript: Central Archives of History in Ulaanbaatar, F.M. 91, HN.1, 1795);

Thiel, P. J., 1962, 'Der Streit der Buddhisten und Taoisten zur Mongolenzeit'. *Monumenta Serica*, pp. 20, 1–81.

Tog-to, 1958, *Liaoshi*, Peking.

Tökei, F., 1966, *Sur le mode de production asiatique*, Budapest.

Tolybekov, S. E., 1955, 'O sushchnosti patriarkhal'no-feodal'nykh otnoshchenii u kochevykh narodov' [On the Nature of the Patriarchal-Feudalistic Relationship among the Nomadic Peoples], *Voprosii Istorii* [Questions of History], no. 1, Moscow.

——, 1971, *Kochevoe obshchestvo kazakhov XVII– nachale XX veka. Politiko-ekonomicheskii analiz* [Nomadic Society of Kazakhs of the Seventeenth to the Beginning of the Twentieth Centuries. Political and Economical Analysis], Alma-Ata.
Tömörtogoo, D., 1983, *Mal aj akhuin khödölmör* [Labour in the Livestock Keeping Economy], Ulaanbaatar.
Töpfer, B. (ed.), 1985, *Allgemeine Geschichte des Mittelalters*, Berlin.
Topolski, J., 1976, *The Methodology of History*, Warsaw.
Toynbee, A. J., 1934, *A Study of History*, vol. III, London.
Trauzettel, R., 1986, 'Die Yüan Dynastie'. In M. Weiers (ed.), *Die Mongolen, Beiträge zu ihrer Geschichte und Kultur*, Darmstadt.
Tüsheet-Khan-Aimgiin Al'bom [Album of Maps of the Tüsheet-Khan Aimag], 1987, Ulaanbaatar.
Uspenskii, V. M., 1880, *Strana Kuke-nor ili Cin-khai, s pribavleniem kratkoi istorii oiratov i mongolov* [Kuke-nor or Qinghai Province against the background of the Short History of Oirats and Mongols], Zarskoe Russkoe Geograficheskoe Obshchestvo, Otdelenie etnografiya [Russian Royal Geographical Society. Department of Ethnography], vol. VI. St Peters-burg.
Vajda, L., 1968, *Untersuchungen zur Geschichte der Hirtenkulturen*, Wiesbaden.
Vardiman, E. E., 1990 *Nomaden. Schöpfer einer neuen Kultur im Vorderen Orient*. Herrsching.
Varg, E. S., 1925, Ekonomicheskie problemy revolyucii v Kitae [Economic Problems of the Chinese Revolution], *Planovoe khozyaistvo* [Planned Economy], no. 12.
Veit, V., 1986, 'Von der Clanföderation zur Volksrepublik. Versuch der Analyse wirtschaftlicher und gesellschaftlicher Gegebenheiten eines Hirtennomadenvolkes'. In M. Weiers (ed.), *Die Mongolen, Beiträge zu ihrer Geschichte und Kultur*, Darmstadt.
Verbrugge, R., 1926, *La Mongolie: un instant autonome*, Anvers.
Vipper, P. B., 1975, 'Istoriya razvitiya rastitel'nogo pokrova severnoi mongolii v golocene' [A Development of Vegetative Covering of the Northern Mongolia in the Holocene Period], *Botanikiin Khüreelengiin Erdem Shinjilgeenii Büteel* [Journal of Botanic Institute], no. 1, Ulaanbaatar.
— Dorofeyuk, N., A. Liiva, A. Metel'ceva, and V. Sokolovskaya, 1985, 'Paleogeografiya Golocena severnoi Mongolii' [Palaeogeography of Holocene of the Northern Mongolia], *Botanikiin Khüreelengiin Erdem Shinjilgeenii Büteel* [Journal of Botanic Institute], no. 7, Ulaanbaatar.
Visdelou, C., 1779, *Histoire de Tartarie*, Paris.
Vladimircov, B. Ya., 1929, 'Po povodu drevnetyurkskogo Ötüken-yish' [Concerning the Old Turkish Word Ötüken-yish]. '*Doklady AN SSSR*'

REFERENCES

[Reports of the Academy of Sciences of Soviet Union], Serii 'B', pp. 133–36, Moscow.

——, 1934, *Obshchestvennyi stroi mongolov: mongol'skii kochevoi feodalizm* [Societal Organisation of the Mongols: Mongolian Nomadic Feudalism], Leningrad.

Volkov, V. V. and E. A. Novgorodova, 1974, 'Arkheologicheskie raboty v Mongolii' [Archaeological Works in Mongolia]. *Arkheologicheskie otkrytiya 1973 goda* [Archaeological Discovery in 1973], Moscow.

Vreeland, H. H., 1957, *Mongol Community and Kinship Structure*, New Haven.

Wainstein, S. I. and Yu. I. Semenov, 1977, 'Recenziya na 'G. E. Markov, Kochevniki azii: Struktura khozyaistva i obshchestvennaya organizaciya' [Review of G. E. Markov's book Asian Nomads: Economic Structure and Societal Organisation], *Sovetskaya etnografiya* [Soviet Ethnography], no. 5, Moscow.

Wang, Pao-kuan., 1980, 'On the Relationship between Winter Thunder and the Climatic Change in China in the Past 2200 Years'. *An Interdisciplinary, International, Journal Devoted to the Description, Causes and Implications of Climatic Change*, no. 3, pp. 37–46.

Wassaf, Kitab-i mustatab-i, 1852–53, *Steindruck in 5 Bänden nebst einem persischen Wörterverzeichnis*, Bombay.

Weber, M., 1964, 'Feudalismus und Patrimonialismus'. *Wirtschaft und Gesellschaft*, Cologne/Bonn.

Weiers, M., 1969, 'Untersuchungen zu einer historischen Grammatik des präklassischen Schriftmongolisch'. *Asiatische Forschungen*, vol. 28, Wiesbaden.

——, (ed.), 1986, *Die Mongolen. Beiträge zu ihrer Geschichte und Kultur*, Darmstadt.

Weiss, B., 1982, 'The Decline of Late Bronze Age Civilization as a Possible Response to Climatic Change', *An Interdisciplinary, International, Journal Devoted to the Description, Causes and Implications of Climatic Change*, no. 4, pp. 173–98.

Werner, E., 1985, 'Einige Charakteristika des vorder- und mittelasiatischen Feudalismus'. In E. Müller-Mertens (ed.), *Feudalismus. Entstehung und Wesen*, Berlin.

Werth, E., 1956, 'Zur Verbreitung und Entstehung des Hirtennomadentums'. *Abhandlungen und Aufsätze AD Institut für Menschen – und Menschheitskunde*, pp. 3–5, 6–9, 14–6.

White, L. A., 1969, *The Science of Culture. A Study of Man and Civilisation*, New York.

Wyngaert, A. van den, 1929, *Itinera et relationes Fratrum Minorum saeculi XII et XIV*, Sinica-Franciscana, vol. 1, Quaracchi-Firenze.

Yui-Bayan (Yui-Yuan-an'), 1958, *Chen-cy-sy-han' Juan* [History of Genghis Khaan], Shanghai.

Zamcarano, C., 1934, 'Jalovannaya gramota Secenkhana, dannaya lame Luvsanbaidubu' [Secenkhan's Formal Complaint Lodged to Monk Luvsanbaidubu]. In *Sbornik 'Sergeyu Feodorovichu Ol'denburgu k 50 letiyu nauchno-obshchestvennoi deyatel'nosti 1882–1932'* [In Honor of Sergei Feodorovich Ol'denburg for 50 Years of Scientific and Social Activities], Leningrad.

——, 1936, *Mongol'skie letopisi XVII veka* [Mongolian Annals of the Seventeenth Century], Moscow/Leningrad.

——, (transl.), 1959, *Qalq-a Jirum* [The Khalkh Jirum Code], B. Rintchen (ed.), Ulaanbaatar.

Zasagt-Khan-Aimgiin Al'bom [Album of Maps of the Zasagt-Khan Aimag], 1987, Ulaanbaatar.

Zhang, De-er, 1984, 'Synoptic-Climatic Studies of Duststorms in China since Historic Times', *Science Sinica*, Series B, no. 27, 825–36.

Zhu, Ko-Zhen., 1973, 'A Preliminary Study on the Climatic Fluctuations during the Last 5000 Years in China', *Science Sinica*, Series B, no. 16, pp. 226–56.

Zlatkin, I. Ya., 1955, 'O sushchnosti patriarkhal'no-feodalnykh otnoshenii u kochevykh narodov' [On the Nature of the Patriarchal-Feudalist Relationship among the Nomadic Peoples], *Voprosy Istorii* [Questions of History], no. 4, Moscow.

——, 1973, 'Nekotorie problemy social'no-ekonomicheskoi istorii kochevykh narodov' [Some Problems of the Socio-Economic History of the Nomadic Peoples], *Narody Azii i Afriki* [Peoples of Asia and Africa], no. 1, Moscow.

——, 1977, 'Stanovlenie krepostnichestva v srednevekovoi Mongolii' [Formation of Bondage in the Mongolian Middle Age], *Narody Azii i Afriki* [Peoples of Asia and Africa], no. 1, Moscow.

INDEX

References to major entries are in **bold typeface**.

Abtai 95, 134
agriculture 29–30, 75, **76–77**, 128
   and climate 28
   development of 27
   and feudalism 20
   and labour 63–65 *passim*
   and Manchu 44, 77
ail 58–82, 113, 137, 143, 169 n. 11, 174. *See also khot (khot-ail)*
aimag 29, 34, 39, 44–57, 68, 69, 82, 92, 94–96 *passim*, 98, 99–104 *passim*, 117, 142–144, 171 n.14, 174
akh 69, 73, 174
akhlagch 73, 117, 174
albat 122–125, 174
Altan Khaan 131, 133–134, 174
altan urug (golden family or golden tribe) 48, 84, 112, 174
Ambagai 170 n. 5, 174
arad 109,114, 174
aravt 85, 174
Arig-Bukh 90
Aukhan 82

bag 46, 59, 121, 143

banner system 97, 104, 168 n. 10, 170 n. 2
Batumünkhe Dayan Khaan 86, 93, 94, 96, **170 nn. 6**–7, 171 n. 8, 174
beil 107, 120, 125
beis 120, 125
Bodi-Alag 94, 170 n. 7, 174
böge (*böö*) 80, 109, 174
bögechi 80, 109, 112
Bold-*chinsan* 8–9
bool 109, 114–115, 124–125, 174
Borjigin 84, 112–113, 170 n. 2, 175
Buddhism 13, 34, 44, 60, 78, 131–145 *passim*. *See also* Lamaism; monasteries
Buddhist dignitaries 43, 44, **46–47**, 57
buuc 47, 75, 175

camel 30, 31–32, 36, **38–39**, 40–41, 64, 66. *See also* livestock
   as payment 167 n. 4
cattle 36, **37**, 40–41, 66, 148. *See also* livestock
   as payment 167 n. 4

cherbi 109, **110–111**, 175
ching vang 119, 125
Chingim 90, 175
China 3–6, 13–16 *passim*, 20, 35, 99, 153–154
Chinese language 4, 6, 11, 113
chinsan 91–92, 93
chuulgan 95, **97**, 103–104, 108

Dadu 90, 132, 133, 175
Dalai Lama 95, 131, 134
darkhan 96, **110**, 124, 175
Dolonur (Dolon Nuur) 96, 104, 119, 120, 135, 168 n. 10
Dunhu 151, **173 n. 1**
duststorm **35**, 151–152

economy
  in familial production form 75
  feudal 49
  nomadic 49
elchin **81**
ey-e 83

feudalism **15–19**, 20, 48, 50, 86–89, 125, 157
  nomadic 11, **21–24**
  European 49, 127

Galdan 135, 171 n. 13, 175
Gamal 90, 175
gazar 38, 45, 175
Genghis Khaan 5–9, 62, 84, 85–86, 87, 110–114 *passim*, 155, 158, 175
  and Buddhism/Lamaism 131
Genghisic lineage 48, 90, 103, 104, 117–121 *passim*, 168 n. 10. *See also altag urug*
Ghazan 8
goat 31, 32, **36–37**, 40, 41. *See also* livestock

Godan 131
golden family. *See altan urug*
'Golden Tribe'. *See altan urug*; Genghisic lineage
güng 105, 120, 175
Güyüg 131

historical source material
  Chinese 3–6
  dynastic history 4. *See also Yuan-shi*
  European 12–15
  Mongolian 9–11
  Persian 12–15
Hongwu 134
horse 30–32, 36, 37–39, 40, 41, 154, 155. *See also* livestock
  as payment 167 n. 4
  in relay stations 168 n. 6
Hun(s) 36, 61, 87, 157, 175. *See also* Xiongnu

Ikh Yasag 5, 175
ikh shavi 139
Irinchinbal 101

janjin 100, 104, 105
jas **138–140**, 143, 175
rJe-bcun dam-pa 46, 59, 102–103, 124, 134, 137, 139, 141–144 *passim*, **171 n.11**, 175
jinvang 92, 93
jisaa 101, 104, 122, **171 n. 14**, 176
jung vang 125

Kangxi 6, 77, 135, 138
Kara-Korum 8, 62, 78, 84, 90–93 *passim*, 131, 133, 135, **175**
Kereit 82, 176
Khabich 113, 172 ch. 4 n. 4

Khabul Khan 170 n. 5, 176
Khaidu 90, 172 n. 5, 176
Khalkha 77, 94, 95, **170 n. 7**
Khalkha Jirum 47, 69, 95, 116, 117, 118, 123–125 *passim*, 147, **168 n. 9**
Khalkha Mongolia 77, 94, 95, 100–106 passim, 119, 120, 121, 124, 134, 137–138, 176
  and Lamaism 142
  and Manchus 143, **169 n. 13**,
  and monasteries 135–37
  and money lenders 141
Khamag Mongol 56, 82, 170 n. 3, 176
khamjilaga 120, 121–123, 143, 176
Khangai 52, 54, 73
khar-shavi 173 n. 10, 176. *See also shavi*
kharuul 47
khebtekul 86
Khentii 52–54, 82, 112
khermel 125
Khiad 112, **170 n. 2**
Khiagt **100–101**, 107, 168 n. 6
khishikten 86
Khitan (Kidan) 3, 61, 84, 151, 173 n. 1
Khökhöchü 112
Khonkhirad 82
khorchin 86
Khori-Tümed 82
khoroo 62, 149
khoshuu 44–47 *passim*, 55, 57–60, 69, 74, **96–97**, 98, 103, 117, 123–125, 134, 143–144, 169 n. 15, 176
  in administration system 94, 99
  in Manchu administration 102–103, **104–106**
  and restructuring 100

khot (khot-ail) **68–71**, 73, 169 n. 12, 176. *See also ail*
  and communication 70
  as demographic unit 70
  economic system of 69
  ethical relations of 70
  and family **71–74**
  leadership in 73
  number of families in 74
  and pastoral rights 74
  political significance 70
  unions of **70–71**
Khotul 84, 172 n. 5, 176
Khovd 31, 46, 55, 100–101, 106, 137, 144, 170 n. 6, **171 n. 13**
Khublai Khaan 87, 90, 132, 176
  and Buddhism 132
  and Chinese culture 5
khüree (migration group) 61, 62, 67, 72
Khüree 67, 100–102 *passim*, 113, 124, 138, 149
  and relay lines 168 n. 6
khürged, **110**
khurildai 80, **83–84**, 97, 176
khutagt 46, 59, 124, 137–142 *passim*, **172 n. 9**, 176
khuvilgaan 124, 137–142 *passim*, 176
Kidan. *See* Khitan
Köde'ü Aral 9, **166 n. 8**

labour 67, 71
  children and youth 61
  cooperations 67–69, 72
  men 66
  women 66
lama 143–144, 146, 149, 153, 176. *See also* Dalai Lama
Lamaism 10, 14, 131, 133. *See also* Buddhism; monasteries
  and Genghis Khaan 131

and Khublai Khaan 132
and Mongolian nomads 130–131
as state religion 134
lama-*shavi* 171 n. 10, 176. *See also* shavi
Lhasa 124, 172 ch. 5 n. 3
Liao. *See* Khitan
Lifanyuan 10, **99–100**, 104, 105, 121, 166 n. 9, 177
Lifanyuan zeli 6, 44, 103, 105, 120, 121, 125, 177
Ligden Khaan 135, 177
livestock 46, 138–140, 144
  breeding 30
  kinds of 36. *See also* camel; cattle; goat; horse; sheep
  ownership 34
  quantity of **39–41**
livestock keeping 31–32, 48, 51, 53, 60, 63–64, 72, 110–114 *passim* 117, 121
  and agriculture 29, 30, **76**
  and climate 30
  and feudalism 23, 48
  and handicrafts **78–79**
  and hunting 76
  and land use 20, 34, 41
  and landownership **43–44**, 48
  under Manchu **122–124**
  nomadic **25–26**, 29, 30, 33, 48, 51, 72, 147–148, 150, 154, 157–160 *passim*
  and right to pasture land 47, 48, 74–75
  and seasonal migration 53, 54, 57, 63, 73–74
  and social position 121–126 *passim*
livestock keeping economy 28, 29, 63, 68–71, 141. *See also* Khot-ail
  labour within 64–67

Manchu 3, 39
  administration system **43–44**, 57, 59–60, 68, 98, 99–106 *passim*, 108, 120, 124, 166 n. 9. *See also* Lifanyuan
  on agriculture 77
  and animal counts 39
  banner system 97, 104, 169 n. 10
  conquest 44
  emperors 43, 45
  and Lamaism 135, 138, 143, 144
  legislation 123, 149
  minitary-administrative system 104
  political system 106
  and position of nobility **118–119**, 123–124, 125
  and rights to pasture land **45–47**, 59–60
  and *taij* 121
Marco Polo 13, 133
Marxism 11
Marxist
  theory 11, 16, 21, 86, 89
  literature 17
meiren 116
Merget 56, 82, 170 n. 3
monasteries 44, 133, 135, 138. *See also* Buddhism; Lamaism
  and economy **138–140**, 143
  and livestock keeping 34
  and money-lending 141
  service to 140–141
  size of 138
  as social phenomenon **135–136**
  as spiritual-cultural centres 137
Mongol-Oirat Regulations 42, 68, 73, 95–97 *passim*, 148
  on pasture land 23
  on social structure 117–118, **169 n.13**
Münkhe Khaan 13, 90, 112, 132, **167 n. 13**, 177

myangan (*myangat*) 85, 86, 177

Naiman 56, 82, 170 n. 7
nutug **41–42**, 117, 167 n. 1, 177
  and monastic ownership 137
nökhör **110**

Ogadai Khaan 6, 84, 90, 111, 131, 166 n. 8, 177
  and Shamanism 156–157
Oirat 82, 93, 104, 169 n. 13, 177
olon vang 92
Ölziit-Tömör 90, 177
Öndör Gege'en 134, 137, 177
Ongud 82
örkh 69, 177
örtöö 45, 47, 177
otog 46, 59, 68, 69, **95–96**, 98, 99, 106, 111, 117, 121, 143, 169 n. 14, 170 n. 7, 177
ötög 47, 177
ötög-buuc 47, 75, 177
otor **63**, 66
ovoo 58, 60

pasture land 48. *See also nutug; otog*
  of Buddhist dignitaries 43, **46–47**, 59. 60
  of common livestock keepers 47
  disputes of 58, **60–61**
  and ecology 51, 148
  and economy 34, 41, 149
  of emperor **45–47**
  and *khot-ail* **74–75**
  and migration 57, 59, 63, 150
  ownership of 23, 42, 49, 137, 139, 143
  and relay stations **45**
  of religious heads **46**
  rights to use 42, 47, **48**, 59–60, 141

Qing dynasty. *See* Manchu
Qianlong 39, 120, 135, 138, 166 n. 8

patriarchal system 17, 22, 81, 87, 161
Peking 4, 8, 10, 90, 99, 104, 124. *See also* Dadu

rJe-bcun dam-pa 46, 59, 124, 142, 143, **171 n. 11**
Russia 2, 12, 16, 72, 77, 78, 156. *See also* Soviet Union
  Mongolian invasion 12
  Mongolian studies in 15, 18, 42, 54
  trade with Mongolia 99, 101

Sain Noyan Khan 103, 177
Sain Noyan Khan *Aimag* 39, 69, 100, 103, 105, 139
sang **138–140**, 177
Secen Khan *Aimag* 35, 39, 40, 95, 101–105 *passim*, 141, 140
  animal count in **40**
Shandu 132
shavi 39, 59, 96, 101, 106, 137, 143–144, **171 n. 10**, 177
  rights to pasture land 46, 59, 140
  and service to monasteries **141–142**
sheep 29, 31, 36–37, 40–41, 168 n. 6. *See also* livestock
  as payment 167 n. 4
Shilgincig 9, 166 n. 7
Song history 3
Soviet Union 12, 16–17. *See also* Russia
  Mongolian studies in 22, 54, 114–115
Sübedei 156
sul albat 124, 125

süld 80, **170 n. 2**
sum 105, 121, 122, 125, 177
  organisation of **105**
  duties 105

tabunang 111, 118, 120
taij 46, 105, 118–120 *passim*, 121, 177. *See also* Manchu
takhilga 80
Tartar (Tatar) 6, 56, 81, 82
thunder. *See* winter thunderstorm
Tibet 10, 99, 172 ch. 5 n. 5. *See also* Buddhism; Lamaism ;
Togan 133
Togoon-Tömör 91, 177
torgud 86
Torguud 105, 106
tribal federation **82–83**, 85–86, 97, 112, 116, 170 n. 7, 171 n. 8. *See also aimag; ey-e; khurildai; myangan*
tribal groups 56–57, 92, 149. *See also khüree*
  migration in 61, 153
  struggles between 62, 112, 114, 150
tribal organisation 17–20, 22, 27, 56, 67, **80–82**, 94, 110, 112, 149, 157
tribe. *See obog; urug; anda*
bTson-kha-pa 142
tug 80, 170 n. 2
Tug-Tömör 91
Tului 5, 157, 167 n. 13, 178
Tümed 133
tümed 94, 171 n. 8
tümen (*tümet*) 86, 178
Turk (Turkish) 56, 84
Turkish-speaking Nomadic tribes 56
Tüsheet Khan 77, 99, 102–103, 134, 139, 178

Tüsheet Khan *Aimag* 35, 39, 95, 101, 102–105 *passim*

Uigurs 8, 84
Uliastai 45, 46, 100, 101, 168 n. 6
unagan albat 115
Ütü dürü-iin kümün (persons of free standing) 109, **111**

vang 105, 178. *See also ching vang; jinvang; jung vang; olon vang*

winter thunderstorm 35, 152

Xiongnu 87, 150, 156, 178. *See also* Hun(s)

yak 36
Yelü Chucai 84, 156, 178
Yesunkhii 90
Yesun-Tömör 90, 91, 178
Yongle 134
Yongzheng 137
Yuan period 3–5, 37, 39, 62, 77–78, 85, **90–91**, 93, 95, 165 n. 2
Yuanshi 4, 5, 36, 90, 92,166 n. 8, 178
yurt 36, 37, 42, 46, 47, 60, 65, 68, 169 nn. 11, 12
  monasteries 135–136, 137, 140

zalan 105
Zanabajar 134
Zasagt Khan 139, 178
Zasagt Khan *Aimag* 35, 39, 55, 95, 100, 103, 104, 105, 138, 172 n. 9
zuut 85, 178

For Product Safety Concerns and Information please contact our EU
representative GPSR@taylorandfrancis.com
Taylor & Francis Verlag GmbH, Kaufingerstraße 24, 80331 München, Germany

www.ingramcontent.com/pod-product-compliance
Lightning Source LLC
Chambersburg PA
CBHW051643230426
43669CB00013B/2415